Artificial Intelligence in Multimodal Learning Process Analytics

Artificial Intelligence in Multimodal Learning Process Analytics

Theories, Methods and Applications

Andy Nguyen

Associate Professor, Learning and Educational Technology (LET) Research Lab, University of Oulu, Finland

Kshitij Sharma

Associate Professor, Norwegian University of Science and Technology, Norway

Ha Nguyen

Assistant Professor, Learning Sciences and Psychological Studies, University of North Carolina at Chapel Hill, USA

EE Edward Elgar PUBLISHING

Cheltenham, UK • Northampton, MA, USA

Published by

Edward Elgar Publishing Limited
The Lypiatts
15 Lansdown Road
Cheltenham
Glos GL50 2JA
UK

Edward Elgar Publishing, Inc.
William Pratt House
9 Dewey Court
Northampton
Massachusetts 01060
USA

Authorised representative in the EU for GPSR queries only: Easy Access System Europe – Mustamäe tee 50, 10621 Tallinn, Estonia, gpsr.requests@easproject.com

A catalogue record for this book is available from the British Library

Library of Congress Control Number: 2026931831

This book is available electronically in the Elgaronline
Sociology, Social Policy and Education subject collection
https://doi.org/10.4337/9781035353811

MIX
Paper | Supporting responsible forestry
FSC® C013604

ISBN 978 1 0353 5380 4 (cased)
ISBN 978 1 0353 5381 1 (eBook)
ISBN 978 1 0494 0425 7 (ePub)

Printed and bound by CPI Group (UK) Ltd, Croydon, CR0 4YY

Contents

List of figures

List of tables

Author biographies

Andy (Khánh Xuân) Nguyen is an Associate Professor in the Hybrid Intelligence: Human-AI Co-evolution and Learning in Multi-realities (HI) Profiling program and works at the Learning & Educational Technology Research Lab, Faculty of Education and Psychology at the University of Oulu, Finland. He holds the title of Docent (Adjunct Professor) in Applied Artificial Intelligence at the Faculty of Information Technology and Electrical Engineering at the same university. His research on human–AI collaboration in learning and ethical principles for AI in education has been recognized through top-cited and most-read articles in leading journals, including *Studies in Higher Education* and the *British Journal of Educational Technology*. He is currently a co-chair of the Advances in Teaching and Learning Technologies minitrack at *Hawaii International Conference on System Sciences*, an Associate Editor of *ICIS2024* "Digital Learning and IS Curricula" track, an Editorial Advisory Board Member of *Artificial Intelligence in Education* (Emerald), an Associate Editor of the journal of *Policy Futures in Education*, an Editorial Board Member of the *British Journal of Educational Technology*, and Associate Editor of the *Behaviour & Information Technology* journal.

Kshitij Sharma is an Associate Professor at the Department of Computer Science at the Norwegian University of Science and Technology. His background is in the area of Artificial Intelligence and Collaborative/Cooperative Learning. In particular, his doctoral work was in the area of using multimodal data (electroencephalograms [EEG], eye-tracking, facial expressions, audio, dialogs, blood pressure, skin conductance, heart rate) to explain the differences between and predict: expert and novice groups, good and poor students, functional and non-functional groups. The main context for the application of his research has been education.

His research interests are primarily in the area of Applied Machine Learning, Artificial Intelligence, and Human–Computer Interaction with a heavy emphasis on groups' behavior and physiological data, such as eye-tracking, EEG, and facial expressions (theoretical and practical methods in digital interaction). He seeks to understand relations between users' data (EEG, eye-tracking, system log data, users' actions) and the profile of the user (expertise, motivation, strategy, performance) based on empirical experimentation (controlled experiments) and mixed methods analysis (utilizing a multitude of digital technologies). The knowledge gained from these studies is then used to provide feedback to the group or adapt to the needs of the group in a proactive manner.

For this effort, in his studies, he has combined eye-tracking and users' actions to provide more comprehensive results through data science, statistics, and machine learning practices. After finishing his doctoral studies in 2015, he started working on developing methods based on Extreme Values Theory (EVT), a methodological space to compute features from abnormalities in data emerging out of collaborative work. EVT is well suited for big data time series. The results show an improvement over contemporary feature extraction methods in terms of their prediction capabilities. During the same period, he has expanded his application area beyond collaborative and educational technologies and has conducted studies in the context of e-commerce, information systems, and entertainment computing.

Ha Nguyen is an Assistant Professor in Learning Sciences and Psychological Studies at the University of North Carolina at Chapel Hill. She uses design and learning analytics methodologies to explore how technologies can support collaborative learning and instructional improvement in STEM education. She is also interested in how educators, students, and researchers can collaborate with emerging AI technologies for teaching and learning. Her work has been supported by the National Science Foundation and appeared in top publications for learning analytics, educational technology, and science education, such as *Computers & Education*, the *Journal of Research in Science Teaching*, and the *Journal of Learning Analytics.* She is currently an early-career Editorial Board Member of the *British Journal of Educational Technology*.

Preface

This book emerges from rapid advancements in Artificial Intelligence (AI), the growing importance of multimodal learning analytics, and ongoing transformations in educational research and practice. It addresses the critical need for systematic, theory-driven analysis of multimodal data to better understand learning processes. Educational environments increasingly generate diverse data streams, including visual, auditory, physiological, and digital traces, providing deeper insights into learning than traditional, single-modal approaches can capture from learners' observable activities and interactions. Multimodal Learning Process Analytics (MLPA) leverages sophisticated AI methods to integrate these multiple modalities, offering richer perspectives on cognitive, affective, social, and behavioral dimensions of learning.

The motivation for writing this book stems from the authors' direct experiences and observations of multiple research teams encountering significant challenges in effectively collecting, processing, and analyzing multimodal data related to learning processes. Despite growing enthusiasm, particularly among early career researchers, the complexities involved in managing diverse and extensive datasets often lead to confusion and methodological inconsistencies. Consequently, this book aims to offer clear guidance, theoretical frameworks, and practical strategies to facilitate rigorous and meaningful multimodal learning process analytics research, ultimately enabling researchers to capitalize fully on the potential of multimodal data in educational contexts.

Throughout the chapters, readers will find robust theoretical discussions intertwined with methodological innovations and real-world applications, aimed at illustrating how multimodal analytics can inform educational practice. Theoretical insights from cognitive load theory, self-regulated learning, socially shared regulation of learning, and achievement emotions provide critical lenses to guide analytics, ensuring alignment between theoretical constructs and data-driven interpretations. Methodologically, this book presents a comprehensive overview of classical machine learning methods, deep learning models, and the emergent power of generative AI. These advanced methodologies empower researchers and practitioners to extract meaningful patterns from complex multimodal datasets, enhancing the accuracy, interpretability, and utility of educational analytics. By embedding ethical considerations systematically into the research and development processes, this book emphasizes responsible innovation and inclusive practices.

This volume targets researchers, educators, policymakers, and technology developers committed to leveraging multimodal analytics to enrich educational outcomes. It serves as both a foundational text for emerging scholars entering the field and a detailed resource for established researchers seeking to advance their analytical capacities. Ultimately, this book aspires to foster interdisciplinary collaboration and dialog among learning scientists, data scientists, educational technologists, and ethicists. By sharing cutting-edge research and practical guidance, we hope to inspire continued innovation, ethical responsibility, and impactful applications of multimodal learning process analytics in education worldwide.

List of abbreviations

Abbreviation	Full term	Description/Context
AI	Artificial Intelligence	Broad field of computer science focusing on creating intelligent systems that perform tasks requiring human intelligence
AIED	Artificial Intelligence in Education	Research area examining AI applications for teaching and learning
ASR	Automatic Speech Recognition	Technology converting spoken language into text
CBT	Computer-Based Training	Instructional method using digital systems for learning
DBR	Design-Based Research	Research methodology for iterative design and analysis of educational interventions
DCGAN	Deep Convolutional Generative Adversarial Network	GAN architecture for image synthesis using convolutional layers
DNN	Deep Neural Network	Neural network with multiple hidden layers used for feature learning and prediction
ECG	Electrocardiogram	Measurement of heart electrical activity
EDA	Electrodermal Activity	Skin conductance measurement associated with arousal or stress
EDM	Educational Data Mining	Research area applying data mining methods to educational data

Abbreviation	Full term	Description/Context
EEG	Electroencephalogram	Brain activity measurement capturing electrical signals
GAN	Generative Adversarial Network	Generative model using adversarial training between generator and discriminator
Generative AI	Generative Artificial Intelligence	AI systems capable of generating text, images, audio, or simulations
GSR	Galvanic Skin Response	Change in skin conductance reflecting emotional arousal
HR	Heart Rate	Number of heartbeats per minute
HRV	Heart Rate Variability	Variation in time intervals between heartbeats
LA	Learning Analytics	Collection and analysis of data about learners to improve learning
LLM	Large Language Model	AI model trained on large corpora for understanding and generating natural language
LSTM	Long Short-Term Memory	Recurrent neural network architecture for sequence modeling
ML	Machine Learning	Subfield of AI focusing on algorithms that learn from data
MLLM	Multimodal Large Language Model	LLM capable of processing and generating across multiple data modalities
MLPA	Multimodal Learning Process Analytics	Subset of MMLA emphasizing temporally ordered multimodal data to model learning processes

Abbreviation	Full term	Description/Context
MMLA	Multimodal Learning Analytics	Field integrating multiple data streams (video, audio, biosensors, etc.) to study learning
NLP	Natural Language Processing	AI field focused on computer interaction with human language
PPG	Photoplethysmography	Optical technique to measure blood volume changes for heart rate analysis
RQ	Research Question	Guiding question for empirical study design
SRL	Self-Regulated Learning	Learners' proactive management of cognition, motivation, and behavior
SSRL	Socially Shared Regulation of Learning	Collective regulation of learning processes within collaborative groups
ST	Skin Temperature	Physiological measure indicating arousal or stress levels
TTS	Text-to-Speech	Technology converting text into synthetic spoken voice
VBD	Value-Based Design	Design approach emphasizing ethical and societal value integration
VSD	Value-Sensitive Design	Design framework incorporating human values into technological development
XR	Extended Reality	Encompasses augmented (AR), virtual (VR), and mixed (MR) reality technologies

PART I

Introduction to multimodal learning process analytics

1. Foundations of multimodal learning process analytics

WHAT IS MULTIMODAL LEARNING PROCESS ANALYTICS?

The emerging capacities of Artificial Intelligence (AI) in education have facilitated more thorough evaluations of learning processes and shed light on the evolution and effectiveness of these processes for learning. Traditionally, analyses of learning processes rely on assessment data, such as assignments and knowledge tests, combined with conventional research methods like think-aloud protocols, observations, and interviews. Such analyses are insufficient to capture the nuanced and dynamic nature of learning, which encompasses multifaceted behavioral, cognitive, metacognitive, social, and emotional processes (Abrahamson et al., 2023; Järvelä et al., 2019). Advancements in AI and learning analytics have introduced new methods and techniques for capturing and analyzing learning processes (Azevedo & Gašević, 2019; Cukurova et al., 2020; Nguyen et al., 2020).

Multimodal Learning Analytics (MMLA) has emerged as a means to capture multifaceted data about learning and learning processes by integrating multiple high-frequency data streams (e.g., video, audio, logs, biosensors) for analysis in different learning settings (Ochoa et al., 2022). Built on multimodal interaction analysis foundations, the concept was formally introduced by Blikstein (2013) at the Third International Conference on Learning Analytics and Knowledge (LAK 2013) and quickly gained traction. Early efforts, including the first MMLA workshop in 2012, established a community and demonstrated the potential of combining diverse data sources with machine learning to glean novel insights into complex learning behaviors (Worsley, 2018). These foundations bridged theory and empirical data, enabling observation of cognitive and social processes in authentic environments beyond what traditional clickstream analytics could achieve.

MMLA encompasses outcome-focused and process-focused approaches alike to understanding learning, enabling researchers and practitioners to capture and analyze a wide range of cognitive, behavioral, and emotional data.

Outcome-focused MMLA often leverages multimodal data to predict academic performance or engagement metrics, while process-focused MMLA emphasizes the unfolding dynamics of learning interactions and strategies over time (Blikstein & Worsley, 2016; Di Mitri et al., 2017). This dual orientation allows MMLA to serve evaluative and formative purposes alike, contributing to the optimization of instructional designs and adaptive feedback mechanisms. Moreover, MMLA has been applied across diverse educational contexts, including traditional classrooms (Nguyen, Järvelä, et al., 2023), large-scale online learning environments such as Massive Open Online Courses (MOOCs; Becerra et al., 2023), immersive simulations (Birt et al., 2019; Sharma & Giannakos, 2020), and emerging mixed reality settings (Nguyen et al., 2025). These applications illustrate the versatility of MMLA in capturing rich, context-sensitive indicators of learning that extend beyond what can be gleaned from single-modal or retrospective assessments. As a result, MMLA offers a robust methodological framework for advancing both research and practice in technology-enhanced learning.

Recent work (especially post-2020) emphasizes grounding MMLA in learning science theory (cognitive, emotional, and behavioral engagement), while technical methodologies have concurrently matured with enhancement of AI. Multimodal fusion and sequential modeling techniques now capture how learning unfolds over time, and AI deep neural networks help to classify or predict learning states from combined data streams. Cukurova et al. (2020) highlighted the promise of such approaches—showing that MMLA can model in-situ learning processes more holistically—along with significant methodological and ethical challenges (e.g., data privacy and bias). MMLA's ability to incorporate affective and contextual data yields richer insights than log data alone but also raises concerns regarding transparency, fairness, and "surveillance" that researchers must address.

MMLA makes latent cognitive and emotional processes visible in learning, providing evidence to inform feedback and adaptive support. For instance, multimodal cues (eye gaze, facial expression, tool use, etc.) are used to detect when learners are confused, disengaged, or employing effective strategies, linking observable behavior to learning constructs. Pushing the technical frontier, Whitehead and colleagues have also applied Generative AI to MMLA: a recent study used a multimodal large language model to automatically extract student posture features from classroom video (Whitehead et al., 2025). Such innovations exemplify the post-2020 trend of harnessing advanced AI to efficiently analyze complex multimodal data, ultimately combining robust theoretical frameworks with cutting-edge analytics to yield actionable insights into the cognitive, emotional, and behavioral dimensions of learning.

In this book, we examine the role of AI for multimodal learning process analytics (MLPA), a specific subfield or refinement of MMLA that explicitly centers on analyzing the dynamics of learning processes, including the temporal and often fine-grained interactions across cognitive, social, and emotional dimensions. While MMLA often focuses on outcome prediction and real-time feedback, MLPA narrows the focus to the detailed examination of learning processes as they unfold over time, aligning closely with theoretical constructs from learning sciences such as self-regulated learning, socially shared regulation, and metacognition. MLPA emphasizes the temporal sequencing of multimodal indicators to capture dynamic interactions across cognitive, social, and emotional dimensions, thereby offering theory-driven insights into how learners regulate their learning in complex environments. The distinction is not merely terminological but reflects differing research objectives: MMLA often supports broad learning analytics applications, whereas MLPA prioritizes theory-grounded analysis to inform the design of process-sensitive educational technologies and interventions. We define MLPA as the systematic collection, integration, and analysis of temporally ordered multimodal data to examine and model learning processes.

In other words, as a subset of MMLA, MLPA focuses on how learning unfolds over time, capturing transitions, sequences, and co-regulated episodes by leveraging data from diverse modalities such as speech, gesture, gaze, facial expression, physiological signals, digital traces, and interaction logs. The aim is to better understand learners' cognitive, emotional, behavioral, and social engagement in situ, and to inform theoretical development and adaptive support mechanisms alike. MLPA particularly aligns formative assessment, learning sciences frameworks, and adaptive learning systems, where understanding and responding to learner processes, rather than only outcomes, is critical. Furthermore, this approach aligns with theories of learning that emphasize the situative and embodied aspects of cognition, recognizing that learning is not only evident in written test scores or discussion posts, but also in smiles and frowns, silences and overlaps in conversation, body orientation, and other subtle cues.

MLPA evolves from key needs to explore and interpret complex learning processes. Constructs important to measuring learning such as motivation, engagement, stress, and emotions are challenging to capture in a way that is timely and unobtrusive. Leveraging physical sensors allows for capturing physiological and behavioral indicators that are often unobservable (Cukurova et al., 2020). This approach shares commonality with AI in Education (AIED), Education Data Mining (EDM), and affective computing research (Baker, 2019; D'Mello & Graesser, 2012). While these adjacent fields focus on automation to detect behaviors and provide interventions, MLPA shifts the focus from digital interactions to physical and physiological spaces (Sharma & Giannakos, 2020). Further, it aims to expand a human's bandwidth to (1) recognize multimodal learning indicators, and (2) use technologies to enhance teaching and learning (Cukurova, 2024). These expanded aims promote human–analytics collaboration by considering the interactions among human learners and teachers, multimodal data, analytics, and learning technologies (Giannakos & Cukurova, 2023).

As an example of studies leveraging MLPA, Malmberg et al. (2019) examined interactions and learning regulation in collaborative learning, using video recordings to contextualize self-regulated learning interactions, physiological data to measure arousal among group members, and facial expressions to detect emotions. They found evidence of regulated learning when the groups' simultaneous arousal was at a high level. Leveraging multiple modalities and examining their temporal relations allow researchers to form a more comprehensive understanding of learning than if they were to rely on a single modality. It helps to model dynamic complex cognitive, affective, and social factors that might not be possible to capture with traditional educational research methods like surveys, think-aloud protocols, or knowledge assessments (Järvelä, Nguyen, & Hadwin, 2023). MLPA informs the development of advanced educational technologies that can detect and provide real-time and adaptive feedback to address individual learners' needs.

Despite these promises, the collection, integration, and analysis of data from diverse channels and modalities require robust domain and technical expertise. As explained by Azevedo & Gašević (2019), data collection needs to determine the type and amount of data to accurately detect and examine the learning processes. During data processing, researchers need to temporally align multimodal data sources, transform the raw data into interpretable segments, and consider missing data. Data analyses involve additional challenges, such as determining the granularity of the data for inference, aligning theoretical assumptions with data modeling, and establishing evaluation criteria for data inferences. Additionally, researchers need to translate data analytics into interpretable insights. These insights inform not only the analysis validation by researchers but also generate learning and instructional insights for students and teachers (Sharma & Giannakos, 2020).

We address these challenges in this book in two main ways. First, we present systemic, AI-based approaches to capturing, processing, and analyzing learning processes. We outline examples leveraging machine learning, deep learning, multimodal quantitative ethnography, and Generative AI methods. Second, through detailed case studies in educational contexts, we illustrate how to translate theoretical learning constructs into measurable indicators using multimodal data. The book offers value for researchers and practitioners interested in examining learning processes through the capture and analysis of multimodal data. Readers will be equipped with insights from theoretical foundations and practical case studies alike in order to navigate the complexities of multimodal data in educational research and practice.

We draw from various fields such as learning sciences, computer sciences, AIED, and educational technology to inform the book chapters. The complex nature of learning processes demands insights from multiple disciplines for effective analysis and application to improve learning outcomes. For instance, the learning sciences provide essential theoretical foundations concerning how individuals learn, including cognitive, social, and emotional dimensions. Computer science and AIED research offers further technical infrastructure from machine learning and Natural Language Processing (NLP). Finally, educational technology presents practical tools and applications to implement these insights in real-world educational settings. By drawing from these areas, we ensure that the analysis of learning processes is grounded in solid theoretical frameworks and enriched with practical methodologies and technological advancements.

DEFINING KEY CONCEPTS

We define the key concepts that the book covers as follows:

Learning analytics: The "measurement, collection, analysis, and reporting of data about the learners and their contexts" (Siemens & Long, 2011, p. 34), to understand and improve learning and learning environments.

Learning process: Learning is a multifaceted process that results in changes in a person or how they perceive the world (Alexander et al., 2009). The learning process can encompass cognitive, motivational, and emotional aspects (Zimmerman & Schunk, 2011). This process is also social, as learning is not restricted to individual learners but involves interaction with others (Hadwin et al., 2017).

Modalities refer to the distinct channels, forms, or types of information, expression, or experience through which learning is conveyed, perceived, or measured. In MLPA, modalities correspond to the different data channels used to capture learning processes. These channels can be classified by the environments in which they originate, for example, digital, physical, and physiological spaces (Molenaar et al., 2023; Noroozi et al., 2020). Examples in digital space include clickstream data (e.g., log data, keystrokes, and mouse behaviors) (Henrie et al., 2018; Spikol et al., 2018) and learning artifacts (e.g., co-created solutions to an engineering challenge, computer programs, written artifacts) (Blikstein, 2013). In physical space, examples include body and eye movement (Taub & Azevedo, 2019; Whitehead et al., 2024), facial expression and movement (Dindar et al., 2020; Nguyen, Li, et al., 2023), and gestures (Ruiz et al., 2011). Physiological data can involve electroencephalogram (EEG) (Antonenko et al., 2010), skin arousal (electrodermal activity, EDA; galvanic skin response, GSR; and skin temperature, ST) (Dindar et al., 2022; Nguyen, Järvelä, et al., 2023), and heart activities (electrocardiogram,

ECG; photoplethysmography, PPG; heart rate and variability; HR and HRV) (Malmberg et al., 2019, 2021). These data channels can be combined with traditional analytics methods, including self-reports, questionnaires, analyses of audio and video recordings, and learning assessments (Dang et al., 2024; Dindar et al., 2019).

Another way to classify the data modalities focuses on the specific ways in which learners interact with the learning tasks: behavioral, physiological, and contextual (Azevedo & Gašević, 2019; Järvelä, Nguyen, & Hadwin, 2023). Behavioral data capture learning behavior and reasoning processes (e.g., clickstream data, eye movements during learning, mouse clicks). Physiological data refer to bodily responses during learning. Finally, contextual data describe the context of learning interactions—with the learning technologies, resources, environments (e.g., face-to-face or online), and human actors (e.g., collaborator, instructor, AI agent). Video and audio recordings of learning interactions, concurrent think-aloud during problem-solving of learning tasks, and chat logs are instances of contextual data.

Multimodal learning process analytics (MLPA): The systematic collection, integration, and analysis of temporally ordered multimodal data to examine and model learning processes. A focus of MLPA is the alignment of learning theories to inform data collection, integration, and analysis, and the use of insights from multimodal data to understand cognitive, emotional, behavioral, and social learning processes as they unfold.

OVERVIEW OF THIS BOOK

The following chapters encompass the theoretical, methodological, and practical aspects of AI and learning analytics. Part I of the book, "Introduction to multimodal learning process analytics," lays the foundation for understanding the field. **Chapter 2** outlines the theoretical frameworks that underpin MLPA, drawing on foundational theories from educational psychology, instructional design, and data science to inform the methods and interpretations used in this field. **Chapter 3** discusses ethical considerations in MLPA, including frameworks and principles, issues of data integration, privacy, consent, and the ethical use of predictive analytics in education. Beyond technical considerations, this chapter presents pedagogical, legal, and sociocultural considerations for integrating MLPA in education contexts.

In Part II, "AI-enhanced multimodal data collection and processing for capturing learning processes," we discuss the practical aspects of gathering and preparing multimodal data. **Chapter 4** presents various strategies and case studies for data collection. The discussion involves practical considerations for study design, such as participant sampling, task selection, and multimodal data setup. It also includes an illustrative vignette of how to collect multimodal process data in different settings (K-12 classrooms, higher education, and informal learning environments). **Chapter 5** focuses on the technical steps for data cleaning, integration, and transformation to prepare for data analysis, followed by illustrations from our recent work (Edwards et al., 2025; Nguyen et al., 2025).

We then present various AI approaches in Part III, "AI methods for analyzing multimodal data on learning processes," including classical machine learning (**Chapter 6**), deep learning (**Chapter 7**), and Generative AI with multimodal data (**Chapter 8**). We examine the applicability, strengths, and limitations of each method within educational research contexts. Additionally, we review the tools and technologies currently available for conducting MLPA. This includes a detailed look at software for data collection, analysis, and visualization, as well as discussions about how these tools can be integrated into educational practices and research.

The text concludes in Part IV, "Future directions and final remarks," by considering the future directions in multimodal learning process analytics, highlighting potential innovations in technology and methodology that could further transform educational research and practice. **Chapter 9** outlines the directions for future research in MLPA. Finally, **Chapter 10** concludes with final remarks, aiming to inspire future research and encourage the adoption of the methodologies among new researchers and practitioners.

CONTRIBUTIONS

This book aims to address the evolving needs of educational research and practice in the age of AI. The advancement of AI technology, particularly the emergence of Generative AI with its capabilities to produce human-like text, has introduced significant threats to academic integrity (Kishore et al., 2023; Nguyen et al., 2024). As these AI tools become more adept at mimicking human writing styles and generating complex responses, there is a growing concern about their potential misuse, such as in completing assignments or producing academic work under false pretenses. This situation challenges educators to reconsider how learning is evaluated. Learning assessments should accurately reflect individual students' knowledge and abilities, with an understanding of the learning processes and not just learning outcomes.

The measurement of learning processes is inherently complex, owing to the abstract nature of cognitive and emotional operations. Traditional methods have often fallen short in capturing the full spectrum of these processes (Järvelä, Malmberg, Haataja, et al., 2021). The emergence of multimodal data collection and analysis methods presents a promising frontier in educational research. MLPA leverages diverse data streams to form a more comprehensive understanding of learning dynamics (Azevedo & Gašević, 2019; Cukurova,

2024; Cukurova et al., 2020). However, the integration of data from diverse channels and modalities presents significant challenges. This book addresses the critical gap in systematic guidance for conducting MLPA. It offers integrated approaches to enhance the capture and analysis of multimodal data related to learning processes.

Effective multimodal data collection relies on the precise operationalization of learning constructs (Giannakos & Cukurova, 2023). This book provides a comprehensive guide to translating theoretical learning constructs into measurable indicators using multimodal data sources. It discusses the interplay between domain knowledge and technical skills required to design effective studies. The technical aspects of collecting and analyzing multimodal data are non-trivial and require detailed knowledge of various devices and software applications. This book offers a practical overview of the key technologies used in multimodal learning analytics, including data acquisition, synchronization, and analysis tools.

Looking forward, the book discusses potential innovations and continuing challenges in the domain of multimodal learning analytics for examining learning processes. It highlights areas for further research and development, particularly in terms of improving data integration techniques and enhancing the scalability of analysis methods. As researchers and practitioners grapple with the complexity and diversity of multimodal data sources, the necessity for more sophisticated integration methodologies becomes apparent. Moreover, the scalability of these analysis methods is another significant area highlighted for advancement. As the application of MLPA expands to broader educational contexts and larger datasets, the ability to scale these solutions efficiently becomes imperative. By addressing these focal points, the book aims to pave the way for transformative impacts in educational research and practice, facilitating a deeper, more actionable understanding of learning processes.

The book is also driven by the recognition that learning analytics is an increasingly critical area within educational research and practice. As educational institutions worldwide continue to integrate technology into their curricula, the generation of large volumes of educational data presents opportunities and challenges alike. This book aims to address these by providing advanced analytical methodologies that can interpret complex data to improve learning outcomes and operational efficiencies. This book emerges as a critical resource amid the growing infusion of digital technologies in educational settings, which has led to the generation of vast amounts of data. By providing advanced analytical methodologies, the text aims to interpret this complex data to enhance learning outcomes and operational efficiencies, addressing opportunities and challenges alike in modern educational environments.

2. Theoretical frameworks in multimodal learning process analytics

INTRODUCTION

In this chapter, we outline influential learning theories and how the theories guide multimodal learning process analytics (MLPA). We drew from recent reviews of educational theories in learning analytics (Wong et al., 2019) and multimodal learning analytics (Giannakos & Cukurova, 2023) to identify the papers utilizing MLPA and key theories underlying these papers. We conducted an additional literature search (using search terms like "multimodal learning analytics," "multimodal analytics + learning processes") to identify additional articles that illustrate the theories.

We organize the chapter along four main clusters: cognitive, metacognitive, affective, and social learning theories. The first cluster includes research focusing on the cognitive aspects of learning, such as knowledge acquisition and information processing. The metacognitive cluster attends to how learners actively plan, execute, monitor, and adjust their strategies to achieve learning goals. We review theories that explore how affective processes—combining motivational and emotional processes—might influence one's willingness to learn and their learning engagement. Finally, considering that learning is mediated by social interactions with others and tools (e.g., language, signs, technologies, and contextual elements), we discuss theories that address the social aspects of learning. In each cluster, we include example MLPA studies that illustrate the learning theory focus. We highlight the intersection of cognitive, metacognitive, affective, and social processes given that the boundaries between them are not distinct (Molenaar et al., 2023; S. Schneider et al., 2022).

THEORETICAL FOUNDATIONS OF CORE LEARNING PROCESSES

Cognitive

Theories focusing on the cognitive aspects of learning evaluate the mental models behind the processing and storing of information and beliefs (McInerney, 2005). **Information processing theories** view the human mind as a processor of information and learning through applying cognitive processes for knowledge acquisition (R. E. Mayer, 1996). They approach learning as first storing, representing, and organizing knowledge in memory using a meaningful structure and then retrieving knowledge in response to environmental cues. A constructivist interpretation of the information processing model considers the integration of incoming information or experience with existing knowledge (R. E. Mayer, 1992). This interpretation necessitates active learning processes to select relevant information, organize it, and then integrate it with what the learner already knows. **Schema,** a structured knowledge representation about a concept, event, or situation, plays a role in information processing, as it explains how existing knowledge and experiences may influence how learners make sense of and learn new information (Axelrod, 1973; Winne, 2013).

The **cognitive load theory** accounts for the fact that the capacity for information processing is limited at any given time (Sweller, 1994, 2020; Sweller et al., 1998). Learners process information from learning materials within the working memory before transferring it into long-term memory. While learning happens in long-term memory, working memory might have limited capacity. Consequently, the processed information can add to learners' cognitive load. The cognitive load theory highlights three factors that influence cognitive load: (1) the number of elements to be processed in the working memory (element interactivity); (2) existing knowledge in the specific learning domain; and (3) the extent to which learners need to build new mental models to process the new information (DeLeeuw & Mayer, 2008; S. Schneider et al., 2022). Learners face a high cognitive load when they encounter high element interactivity but have limited prior knowledge and have to build new mental models. Conversely, too little cognitive load might not sufficiently engage learners (Van Merrienboer & Sweller, 2005). Instruction can reduce extraneous cognitive load to reserve appropriate resources for learning (Sweller, 1994; Van Merrienboer et al., 2003).

MLPA studies have built on the information processing model and cognitive load theory. Multimodal analytics involving eye-tracking and physiological data, including electroencephalogram (EEG), electrodermal activity (EDA), and heart rate variability (HRV), allow for the collection and inferences of cognitive loads and mental efforts in nonintrusive ways (Du et al., 2023; Larmuseau et al., 2020; Mangaroska et al., 2022). For instance, Mangaroska et al. (2022) leveraged EEG data and eye-tracking data (e.g., to identify fixations) to measure multiple constructs informed by cognitive learning theories, including attention, memory load, and cognitive load. The captured multimodal data can also be corroborated with learners' self-reported data (Vanneste et al., 2021).

Beyond processing information in the mind, **embodied cognition theories** underscore the role of sensorimotor engagement, specifically bodily movements, as resources for conceptual learning (Abrahamson & Lindgren, 2014; Wilson, 2002). This view builds on Piaget (1971)'s cognitive theory that also highlights sensorimotor experiences as resources. The theories posit that learning occurs through the intersection of perception, epistemic actions (e.g., to gather information), pragmatic actions (e.g., to implement a plan or reaction), and spatial systems. Conceptual reasoning stems from physical interaction, and technological and physical artifacts serve as resources to extend one's epistemic capacity for learning (Abrahamson & Lindgren, 2014).

Building on embodied cognition perspectives, MLPA studies have leveraged computer vision and videos (Oviatt et al., 2021), motion detection devices (Junokas et al., 2018; Worsley et al., 2015), and touchscreen devices (Pardos et al., 2022). Studies have examined gestures (A. Andrade et al., 2017; Walkington et al., 2024) and postures (Kosmas et al., 2018; Whitehead et al., 2025). Researchers often focus on how embodiment facilitates learning in conceptually challenging domains such as mathematics (Abrahamson et al., 2023; Tancredi et al., 2022) and science (Schönborn et al., 2011), with consideration for how to support different student populations, including learners with special needs (Kosmas et al., 2018).

Metacognitive

Self-regulated learning (SRL) involves the active planning, executing, evaluating, and reflecting on learning goals and activities (Zimmerman, 2002). SRL engages various cognitive, metacognitive, motivational, and affective processes depending on the individuals, the learning tasks, and the contexts (Efklides, 2011; Greene & Azevedo, 2010). Winne and Hadwin (1998)'s COPES (Control, Operations, Products, Evaluations, and Standards) model of SRL included several cyclical metacognitive processes: evaluating the tasks and cognitive conditions, including motivations, beliefs, and knowledge, and then determining the appropriate operation (e.g., learning strategies). These operations lead to a product, such as a task definition, that can be evaluated against the individual's standards for a successful learning outcome. A potential mismatch between product and standards can prompt SRL and adjustment of conditions, operations, and standards. The fine-grained processes described by Winne and Hadwin (1998) called for analyses that can capture micro-level metacognitive processes (e.g., positive and negative judgment of learning, feeling of knowing) and macro-level processes (e.g., task difficulty and demands, planning, monitoring) (Greene et al., 2017).

Because SRL involves multiple cognitive, metacognitive, affective, and motivational processes (Azevedo, 2015), analyses can consider different approaches: unimodal (studying one process, such as metacognitive, with one data stream), vertical (triangulating different data streams to measure one process), horizontal (examining the relations between multiple processes with one data stream), and integrated (combining vertical and horizontal approaches) (Molenaar et al., 2023). Using a horizontal approach, MLPA researchers have examined log files to indicate monitoring behaviors and cognitive learning tactics (Fan et al., 2021). A vertical approach might leverage think-aloud protocols to understand macro-level and micro-level processes and corroborate the codes from the think-aloud data with clickstream data from learning management systems (Bernacki et al., 2024). As no data stream can reflect all SRL processes, researchers have demonstrated the potential of integrated approaches—using multiple data streams to measure different SRL processes (Azevedo & Gašević, 2019; Taub et al., 2020; Van Der Graaf et al., 2021).

Affective

The **control-value theory of achievement emotions** (CVTAE) (Pekrun, 2006) provides a framework to detect and examine the effects of emotions in learning achievement. The theory pertains to achievement emotions, including activity-related ones like boredom, frustration, and enjoyment, and emotions arising as an outcome of the achievement activity, such as joy, pride, anxiety, or hopelessness. These emotions are classified based on their valence (positive versus negative), activation (activating versus deactivating), and focus (future outcome versus past performance) (Pekrun & Perry, 2014). Cognitive antecedents, specifically perceived control (i.e., whether learners feel they have control over their success or failure) and value appraisals (i.e., how valuable learners perceive the tasks), activate different achievement emotions. For example, learners can experience enjoyment, if they view the activity as controllable and value it positively, but they might feel anxious, if they value the tasks but doubt their control. Perceived control encompasses causal attributions for past performance (e.g., determining who or what is responsible) and causal expectancies depending on the activity, outcome, and contextual conditions under which the task is undertaken (Pekrun et al., 2007). Value appraisals involve intrinsic values in the achievement activity (e.g., interest), as well as extrinsic values such as prizes or grades (Pekrun & Perry, 2014).

Multimodal analytics with advanced frameworks and tools allow for the exploration of learners' emotions during the learning process following CVTAE. Researchers have integrated CVTAE within MLPA, to detect emotions from facial recognition and eye-tracking data (Ahn & Harley, 2020; Ngo et al., 2024; Rajarathinam et al., 2024). The application of CVTAE in MLPA can be extended to collaborative learning contexts through the analysis of video data of group interactions. For instance, analyses of facial expressions and body language can provide insights into affective factors that impact collaboration quality (Nguyen, Li, et al., 2023). Rajarathinam et al. (2024) demonstrated the use of 360-degree video data and automated coding (using OpenFace) of facial action units, including brow lowering, eyelid tightening, and lip tightening. These facial action units could be integrated into models to detect affect and explore the interaction between affect and collaborative interactions.

Motivational frameworks, including **self-determination** and intrinsic motivation theories (Ryan & Deci, 2000), are also pertinent to frame learners' interest and perceived control over the learning activities and incentives. The self-determination theory (Ryan & Deci, 2000) describes intrinsic motivation as resulting from meeting the needs for autonomy (feeling in control of one's actions), competence (feeling effective and capable), and relatedness (feeling connected to others). Emerson et al.'s study (2020) provides an example of a MLPA study that investigated the relations between learners' real-time interest and performance. They illustrated the feasibility of combining gameplay data, facial expression, and eye-tracking data to predict student performance in game-based learning.

Researchers have also built on the construct of **flow** (Csikszentmihalyi, 1997), a mental state where individuals experience focus, enjoyment, and full involvement in the learning activities. Flow occurs when there is a balance between the degree of challenge of the task and the individual's skill level. Building on flow theory, Pastushenko et al. (2020) analyzed in-game user data logs and self-reported data to provide automatic identification of students' flow experience in gamified assessments. As another example, Di Mitri et al. (2017) collected heart rate, step count, and learners' self-reported data to predict learners' performance.

Social

Learning is not confined to individuals but evolves through social interactions (Kalina & Powell, 2009; Palincsar, 1998). Drawing from Piagetian and Vygotskian accounts, the social constructivist perspective underscores that (1) learning is a cultural process; and (2) interactions facilitate cognition and learning, and thus interpersonal analyses are relevant to understand learning

(Palincsar, 1998). **Proxemics** (Hall, 1966; Hall et al., 1968) provides a theoretical lens to understand communication and social interactions. Hall (1966) identified four zones of personal space, each with specific distances and social meanings: intimate, personal, social, and public. Proxemics is important in educational and collaboration settings. How teachers and students utilize physical space (e.g., positions within classroom space) can mediate learning interactions. Building on the lens of proxemics, MLPA researchers have utilized log data from a digital interface, body positions and gestures, and behaviors from wearable devices (e.g., movements, interactions, transitions between states) to predict learning progression and performance (Martinez-Maldonado et al., 2020; B. Schneider & Blikstein, 2015; Yan et al., 2023).

We highlight learning theories that cover the interplay of cognitive, motivational, affective, and social processes. **Socially shared regulation of learning (SSRL)** extends SRL models that emphasize individual agency in cognitive and metacognitive activities (e.g., Zimmerman, 2002) to consider learning regulation in collaborative contexts. In these contexts, learners regulate themselves (SRL), the sociocultural situations and people (co-regulated learning), and the group towards shared goals (SSRL) (Hadwin et al., 2017). SRL describes a learner's iterative and strategic planning, execution, reflection, and adaptation as they engage in the learning tasks (see Metacognitive section earlier in this chapter). Co-regulated learning is linked to interpersonal exchanges, where group members become aware of one another's learning goals and beliefs and transfer or offer regulatory support (e.g., reminding peers to check the time or revisit their goals). Finally, socially shared regulation of learning involves collective task monitoring, negotiation, performance, and adaptation towards joint goals and standards. Co-regulated learning and socially shared regulation of learning require joint efforts and interactions to coordinate affective, cognitive, and behavioral processes among group members (Dindar et al., 2022).

MLPA provides new opportunities to explore learning regulation and attend to affective and cognitive processes at the group level. Combining physiological (e.g., EDA), audio (e.g., speech alignment), and video data can reveal rich insights into group interactions when combined with contextual events for regulated learning (Lämsä et al., 2024; Li et al., 2024; Nguyen, Järvelä, et al., 2023). Physiological data provide insights into adaptive processes that underlie regulated learning (Dindar et al., 2022; B. Schneider et al., 2020). This data stream can be extended to collaborative learning contexts to examine physiological synchrony, defined as joint activations of affective and cognitive processes linked to socially shared regulated learning (Dindar et al., 2022; Nguyen, Järvelä, et al., 2023). For example, Nguyen, Järvelä, et al. (2023) used process mining—constructing a process model based on the sequences of events from physiological (EDA) and video data—to illustrate the sequential relationships between learners groups' shared arousal events and regulatory activities. Together, these studies illustrate the potential of leveraging multimodal data to analyze and support learning processes.

USING THEORIES TO INFORM MLPA

In reviewing studies that have applied multimodal learning analytics in education research, Giannakos and Cukurova (2023) highlighted that some studies only describe the theories without linking them to the research design. Additionally, only a few studies have synthesized different learning theories or used them as analytical tools, specifically using empirical evidence to refine theories. This somewhat limited use of theory hinders the depth of interpretation and the ability to build cumulative knowledge.

In this section, we provide a vignette from our work to illustrate possible framing of learning theories and MLPA. The vignette illustrates how learning theories can be used to inform research design (i.e., determining research questions and determining theory-aligned data streams).

Emotional synchrony through regulatory triggers in high school collaborative learning: In a controlled experimental study conducted by Nguyen, Li, et al. (2023), eight triads of high school students engaged in a collaborative learning task designed to provoke regulatory responses through systematically introduced triggers. Midway through the 30–40-minute task, the groups were exposed to one cognitive and up to three emotional regulatory triggers. The aim was to explore how such interventions could influence learners' emotional dynamics, particularly emotional synchrony, reflecting the sharedness in emotional states.

One group, working on a sustainability challenge, initially demonstrated scattered attention and inconsistent engagement, evident in their muted facial expressions and low verbal interaction. Upon introduction of the first emotional trigger—a manipulated narrative suggesting limited time and heightened importance, the group's interactional tone shifted. Facial expression recognition technologies, using EmoFAN for real-time emotional classification, detected increased expressions of surprise and concern. Cross-recurrence quantification analysis subsequently revealed heightened emotional synchrony, with aligned emotional trajectories emerging among the group members. This alignment was not evident after the cognitive trigger, indicating that emotional, rather than cognitive, disruptions were more effective in eliciting shared regulatory responses.

This study is a direct empirical application of the Trigger Regulation Framework proposed by Järvelä and Hadwin (2024), which defines triggers as events or signals that interrupt the flow of learning and invite regulatory responses. The observed increase in emotional synchrony after the emotional triggers provides evidence of affective alignment as a strategic regulatory response. By capturing these responses through multimodal data, including facial expression analysis, the study demonstrates how emotional and cognitive triggers can be operationalized as measurable signal events within SSRL cycles. This alignment validates the framework's central proposition: regulation is not constant but occurs when triggered by situational conditions that disrupt learning and demand strategic adaptation. Furthermore, the controlled design allows for distinctions between types of triggers, supporting the framework's emphasis on the need to detect and contextualize regulatory responses in relation to specific trigger classes, including emotional, cognitive, behavioral, motivational, or metacognitive triggers.

This vignette highlights how emotionally charged events, even if artificially introduced, can foster affective alignment among peers. The group's synchronized emotional reactions served as a pivot point, facilitating metacognitive negotiation and coordinated problem-solving strategies. It demonstrates the potential for artificial intelligence-supported detection of SSRL processes in situ and offers empirical grounding for the concept of regulatory triggers as mechanisms to activate and sustain collaborative regulation.

3. Ethical considerations for AI in multimodal learning process analytics

INTRODUCTION

Multimodal learning process analytics (MLPA) with artificial intelligence (AI) bring substantial ethical concerns, given the sensitivity of multimodal data such as facial expressions, audio recordings, and physiological measures. The implementation of MLPA entails risks concerning data security, algorithmic bias, fairness, and, in AI-integrated MLPA applications, the potential erosion of learner agency (Nguyen, Ngo, et al., 2023). Given the personal and granular nature of multimodal data, ethical frameworks must be embedded throughout the design and deployment of AI-enhanced MLPA research and the development of MLPA systems. Researchers and practitioners must balance technological potential with ethical responsibilities to safeguard learner rights and privacy.

Nguyen, Ngo, et al. (2023) synthesized international guidelines for AI in education, outlining essential ethical principles, including governance and stewardship, transparency and accountability, sustainability and proportionality, privacy and security, inclusiveness and fairness, and human-centered design. These principles serve as the conceptual foundation for examining ethical challenges specific to AI in MLPA across technical, pedagogical, legal, and sociocultural dimensions. Furthermore, this chapter is informed by prior work on ethical considerations in MMLA, including those identified by Alwahaby et al. (2022), which highlight the importance of addressing ethical implications alongside evidence of impact.

Ethical considerations are relevant across all levels of education, from early childhood to higher education and lifelong learning. Nevertheless, each context presents distinct challenges, for example, protecting minors and obtaining informed consent in K-12 settings, or ensuring equitable participation and preserving autonomy in postsecondary education. This chapter discusses the ethical principles related to MLPA and offers concrete recommendations for researchers, educators, and institutions committed to the responsible use of MLPA.

KEY ETHICAL CHALLENGES

Legal and Policy Dimension

Compliance with international and local laws is a baseline ethical requirement. MLPA researchers and practitioners must be familiar with the legal frameworks relevant to their context, be it the EU General Data Protection Regulation (GDPR) in Europe, state privacy laws in the US (like California's student privacy acts), or emerging AI-specific regulations. However, laws often lag behind technology. As of 2026, while there is movement (the EU AI Act, UNESCO recommendations, etc.), much of the world does not have AI-in-education-specific laws. Therefore, an ethical approach might mean going *beyond* compliance—adopting best practices, even if not legally mandated. For example, even if not required, an institution might conduct a Privacy Impact Assessment before launching a Multimodal Learning Analytics (MMLA) project to systematically evaluate risks and mitigations. Or it might adhere to ethical principles like those outlined by Nguyen, Ngo, et al. (2023) and ethical frameworks like DELICATE (Drachsler & Greller, 2016)—a checklist for trusted learning analytics with eight action points (Determination of purpose, Explanation to stakeholders, Legitimation of data use, Involvement of stakeholders, informed Consent, Anonymisation of data, Technical protection of privacy, and governance of External providers) to ensure a robust privacy and data protection strategy.

Issues of data ownership and voluntary consent emerge prominently, particularly given inherent power imbalances in educational settings. Ensuring genuine, informed consent involves transparent communication about data practices and providing meaningful options for opting out without penalties. Furthermore, institutions must clearly establish accountability and liability mechanisms for potential harms caused by AI systems, underscoring the importance of robust governance frameworks. Ethical practices demand clear and transparent communication to students and guardians about what data are collected, how they are utilized, and under what conditions they can be accessed or deleted.

Technical Dimension

The technical dimension of ethical considerations in MLPA is concerned with the design, implementation, deployment, and maintenance of systems and/or processes that capture, process, and interpret complex data streams. These include, but are not limited to: audio, video, eye-tracking, physiological signals, keystrokes, and interaction logs. When AI systems analyze such rich and sensitive data, their technical architecture must be developed with ethical safeguards to prevent misuse, misinterpretation, or harm to learners. The ethical risks in this dimension primarily involve data quality, algorithmic bias, model transparency, explainability, and system robustness, all of which directly impact the fairness, privacy, and trustworthiness of AI-powered MLPA (Nguyen, Ngo, et al., 2023; OECD, n.d.).

DATA QUALITY AND REPRESENTATIVENESS

The foundation of any AI model lies in the data used to train and evaluate it. In the context of MLPA, the integrity and representativeness of multimodal datasets are critical for producing valid and equitable insights. Multimodal datasets are often derived from controlled environments with specific populations, which can result in sampling biases that limit generalizability. For instance, models trained on data from university students in Western contexts might perform poorly or inaccurately interpret signals from learners in different cultural or educational settings (Blikstein & Worsley, 2016; Nguyen, Ngo, et al., 2023). This is particularly problematic when AI systems are used to provide adaptive feedback or generate inferences about cognitive or affective states.

To mitigate these risks, technical design must prioritize data diversity and quality assurance protocols during data collection, preprocessing, and annotation. Given the inherent variability in multimodal signals, developing standardized data collection procedures and ensuring consistent labeling across modalities are essential. Moreover, researchers must document the provenance and limitations of datasets using practices such as data sheets for datasets (Gebru et al., 2021) to enhance transparency and support ethical reuse.

ALGORITHMIC FAIRNESS AND BIAS MITIGATION

AI models can inadvertently encode and amplify social and demographic biases present in the training data. In MLPA, these biases might manifest in how attention, engagement, or emotion is inferred from facial expressions or voice features, which can vary across age, gender, ethnicity, and cultural background. For example, emotion recognition systems have been shown to exhibit lower accuracy for individuals with darker skin tones or non-Western facial features. This raises critical ethical concerns when such systems are used to assess or intervene in learners' processes.

Furthermore, AI models are susceptible to biases originating from training data, potentially disadvantaging certain student groups based on gender, ethnicity, cultural background, or disabilities (Holmes et al., 2021). If training datasets are not diverse, resulting systems might systematically disadvantage certain learner groups (Nguyen, Ngo, et al., 2023). Such biases risk reinforcing existing inequities in education, underscoring the importance of inclusive and representative datasets and robust bias-mitigation techniques (Alwahaby & Cukurova, 2024). Robust validation procedures, bias audits, and diverse data representation are necessary to ensure fairness and accuracy in multimodal analytics systems.

Addressing these issues requires the application of fairness-aware machine learning techniques, such as reweighting, adversarial debiasing, or outcome parity constraints. However, these technical interventions must be guided by contextual understanding. There is no universally "fair" algorithm, i.e., fairness must be aligned with educational goals and the expectations of stakeholders (Holstein et al., 2019). Therefore, MLPA researchers and technical developers of MLPA systems should engage in interdisciplinary collaboration with educators, ethicists, and learners to define fairness objectives and interpret model behavior within appropriate learning contexts.

TRANSPARENCY AND EXPLAINABILITY

Another central ethical concern in the technical dimension is the opaqueness of many AI models, particularly those based on deep learning architectures. These systems often operate as "black boxes," making it difficult for educators and learners to understand how decisions or predictions are made. In high-stakes educational environments, lack of explainability undermines trust and accountability, especially when models generate feedback, flag at-risk students, or trigger pedagogical interventions.

Algorithmic transparency refers to the clarity and openness of AI systems regarding how data are processed and interpreted. Given the complexity of multimodal data and the use of sophisticated machine learning algorithms, achieving transparency is particularly challenging yet essential for fostering trust and accountability among educators and learners (Nguyen, Ngo, et al., 2023).

To address this, explainable AI techniques must be integrated into the development of MLPA tools. These include model-agnostic methods such as LIME or SHAP that provide local explanations of predictions, as well as inherently interpretable models such as decision trees or rule-based systems where feasible. However, explanation alone is insufficient unless it is designed to be accessible and meaningful to intended users. For MLPA, this means that visualizations or textual explanations must be adapted to the pedagogical context and cognitive needs of educators and students. In practice, explainability should not only support model validation by developers but also foster informed agency among learners and teachers.

DATA PROTECTION AND SECURITY

Moreover, MMLA systems require stringent security protocols to safeguard sensitive data from breaches and unauthorized access, reflecting broader concerns about privacy and student safety (Drachsler & Greller, 2016). MLPA systems collect and process highly sensitive data streams, often in real time and over extended periods. Technical systems must ensure that data storage, transmission, and access are governed by robust security protocols. This includes encryption, secure authentication, anonymization or pseudonymization of personal identifiers, and compliance with data protection regulations such as the EU GDPR. The granularity of multimodal data increases the risk of re-identification even in anonymized datasets, particularly when multiple modalities are combined.

Furthermore, privacy-preserving machine learning techniques such as federated learning and differential privacy offer promising directions for mitigating these risks. Federated learning allows models to be trained locally on users' devices without transferring raw data to central servers, thereby reducing the potential for breaches. Differential privacy introduces statistical noise to outputs to prevent individual data from being reverse-engineered. However, implementing such techniques in educational contexts remains technically complex and often underdeveloped in current MLPA systems.

Additionally, the protection of educational data through robust cybersecurity measures, including encryption and secure storage protocols, is paramount to prevent breaches or unauthorized access (Nguyen, Ngo, et al., 2023). These safeguards are particularly critical, given the sensitive nature of multimodal data, which can reveal intimate details about learners' behaviors, emotions, and cognitive states. Ensuring data integrity and confidentiality is therefore not only a technical requirement but also a core ethical obligation in MLPA research and practice.

ACCURACY, ROBUSTNESS, AND RELIABILITY

Technical robustness, including accuracy and reliability, constitutes another critical ethical aspect (Nguyen, Ngo, et al., 2023). Multimodal systems are inherently vulnerable to missing or noisy data, which can lead to degraded performance or incorrect inferences (Lahat et al., 2015). For instance, occluded facial landmarks, poor audio quality, or sensor dropout can lead to spurious interpretations of learner behavior. This can have ethical consequences when learners are unfairly judged or classified based on flawed inputs.

Accuracy is a critical concern, as inaccuracies in AI-driven assessments can lead to inaccurate insights or misguided educational interventions, potentially stigmatizing students or affecting their learning outcomes negatively. Erroneous AI-driven inferences could lead educators to make incorrect decisions, negatively affecting student outcomes and undermining trust in educational systems. Hence, rigorous validation of AI tools, including thorough real-world evaluations, is essential to minimize potential harm and enhance effectiveness.

To enhance system robustness, technical design should include mechanisms for detecting and handling missing data, assessing confidence levels in predictions, and alerting users to uncertainty or limitations. Models should be tested across a range of real-world conditions and user demographics to ensure reliability beyond controlled environments. Additionally, continuous monitoring and performance auditing should be incorporated into system deployment to detect and respond to errors or drifts over time.

DOCUMENTATION, AUDITING, AND ACCOUNTABILITY

Ethical MLPA development also requires technical documentation and auditability. This involves maintaining detailed records of research design choices, data preprocessing pipelines, model training procedures, and validation metrics. The documentation should be structured to support third-party audits and internal reviews, ensuring that the system can be evaluated for ethical compliance, performance validity, and unintended consequences.

In practice, researchers conducting MLPA should maintain thorough documentation throughout all stages of the research process, including data collection, preprocessing, analysis, and system implementation. This documentation should clearly record technical and analytical decisions, such as data selection criteria, sensor configurations, preprocessing techniques, feature extraction methods, model parameters, and validation procedures. Transparent reporting not only facilitates reproducibility and peer evaluation but also supports ethical accountability, particularly when working with complex and sensitive multimodal data. Such practices align with open science principles and are essential for ensuring the reliability, credibility, and responsible use of MLPA. Furthermore, MLPA researchers can adopt tools such as model cards (Mitchell et al., 2019), which summarize key information about model purpose, intended use cases, evaluation benchmarks, and known limitations. This supports transparency and enables stakeholders, including teachers, learners, administrators, and researchers, to make informed decisions about how and when to use such systems.

Pedagogical Dimension

The introduction of AI analytics significantly affects pedagogical practices, raising concerns about teacher autonomy, learner agency, and educational integrity. The pedagogical dimension of ethical considerations in AI-enhanced MLPA concerns how the models interpret or even shape teaching and learning processes, influence learner development, and interact with pedagogical values and intentions. While MLPA offers powerful opportunities to generate insights into learning processes and inform instructional decision-making, its pedagogical use raises complex ethical questions. These include concerns about learner agency, formative versus summative use of analytics, interpretability for educational stakeholders, alignment with pedagogical goals, and the risk of over-reliance on behavioral proxies of learning. Ethical pedagogy in AI-powered MLPA must be grounded in principles that prioritize human development, instructional transparency, and meaningful participation.

RESPECTING LEARNER AGENCY AND AUTONOMY

Learner agency represents a significant concern, particularly regarding potential excessive monitoring or control. Constant AI-driven surveillance could lead students to alter their natural behaviors, thus negatively influencing their psychological comfort and ability to engage authentically in learning (Holmes et al., 2021). Pedagogically ethical practices involve ensuring that students clearly understand how their data are used and maintaining their rights to meaningful choices and self-regulated learning. The AI systems should be designed to foster students' autonomy, resilience, and intrinsic motivation rather than imposing excessively prescriptive instructional interventions (Nguyen, Ngo, et al., 2023; UNESCO, 2019).

One of the central pedagogical concerns in the applications of MLPA is the potential erosion of learner agency. As AI systems increasingly intervene in learning processes by providing real-time feedback, adapting content, or alerting instructors to "at-risk" behaviors, they might inadvertently promote passivity or dependence on automated support. When learners come to rely on systems to detect or regulate their emotions, engagement, or strategy use, they might miss opportunities to build essential self-regulated learning skills (Fan et al., 2025). Maintaining psychological safety in learning environments requires careful calibration of analytics systems, avoiding intrusive monitoring while promoting student agency and self-regulated learning.

To counteract the risk of over-reliance on automation, MLPA should be designed within a hybrid intelligence framework that fosters meaningful human–AI collaboration, where human and artificial agents alike contribute distinct strengths (Cukurova, 2024; Nguyen, 2025). Rather than replacing metacognitive processes, MLPA systems should be developed to augment learners' capacity for self-regulation through co-adaptive and learner-centered design. Learner-facing tools should encourage reflection, self-explanation, and agency by supporting sense-making rather than delivering definitive answers or system-led evaluations. When visualizations of learning traces are embedded in pedagogically grounded scaffolds, they can promote learners' critical engagement with their own behaviors and AI-generated insights alike. From a sociotechnical standpoint, ethical implementation involves not only technical robustness but also social responsibility—ensuring that learners remain active participants in interpreting their data and negotiating the role of AI in their learning trajectories.

ALIGNMENT WITH INSTRUCTIONAL INTENT AND CONTEXT FOR INTERPRETABILITY AND PEDAGOGICAL TRANSPARENCY

The interpretation of MLPA research and the design of MLPA-powered systems must align with the intended pedagogical approach and instructional design of the learning environment. Ethical tensions emerge when analytics tools are applied in contexts that do not match their assumptions or affordances. For instance, analytics designed to detect attention or cognitive load might be inappropriate in inquiry-based or open-ended tasks where exploration and ambiguity are encouraged. Similarly, systems that evaluate affective states or collaboration quality based on surface-level behavioral features might misinterpret productive struggle or off-task dialog as indicators of disengagement (D'Mello et al., 2017). Additionally, aligning AI analytics with core educational values is vital. Analytics should support, not undermine, holistic educational objectives, avoiding the reduction of complex learning processes to simplistic quantifiable metrics. Pedagogical ethics involves critical reflection on the actual value that AI analytics adds to the educational process.

Pedagogically aligned MLPA requires that system design is sensitive to the epistemic and instructional goals of the learning activity. This entails involving educators early in the design process to ensure that analytic indicators correspond meaningfully with valued learning behaviors and outcomes. Furthermore, teachers must be provided with professional development to critically interpret MLPA outputs and integrate them into their instructional strategies. Without such support, analytics risks being used as normative or punitive tools, contradicting pedagogical principles of inclusivity and learner-centeredness.

Interpretability is not only a technical issue but a pedagogical one. Teachers, students, and educational stakeholders must be able to understand what MLPA systems are measuring, how they interpret behavior, and what actions are recommended. Without interpretability, educators might misapply or over-trust analytics outputs, and learners could feel alienated or surveilled by opaque systems. This undermines the pedagogical value of data-informed instruction and risks reducing complex learning processes to simplistic indicators.

To promote interpretability, MLPA systems should provide pedagogically meaningful explanations. For teachers, this might involve presenting analytics in relation to pedagogical goals (e.g., collaboration quality, strategic help-seeking) and offering decision-support rather than prescriptive actions. For learners, analytics should be contextualized within learning objectives and offered in language that supports reflection. Transparency in analytics also means revealing the thresholds, assumptions, and possible errors behind system outputs, thereby promoting critical engagement and trust.

AVOIDING REDUCTIONISM IN LEARNING REPRESENTATIONS

A persistent ethical concern in the pedagogical dimension is the risk of reductionism. MLPA systems often rely on observable behaviors—eye gaze, speech turns, facial expressions—as proxies for latent constructs such as motivation, emotion, or cognitive engagement. While such inferences can be informative, they are inherently limited and context-dependent. Over-reliance on behavioral proxies might obscure deeper, less visible dimensions of learning, such as identity development, epistemic beliefs, or cultural ways of knowing (Knight & Shum, 2017).

Ethically responsible pedagogy requires that educators and system designers acknowledge the limits of inference and avoid overgeneralizing from analytic data. Rather than using MLPA to "detect" learning, systems should be positioned as tools for *co-constructing* understanding—prompting questions, supporting interpretation, and enriching dialog among learners and teachers. Mixed-method approaches that combine quantitative analytics with qualitative inquiry can help to preserve pedagogical richness and resist the flattening of learning into machine-readable signals.

PROMOTING EQUITY AND INCLUSION IN PEDAGOGICAL DESIGN

The pedagogical use of MLPA must be guided by a commitment to equity and inclusion. Analytics systems can unintentionally marginalize learners whose behaviors or expressions do not conform to dominant norms—whether owing to neurodiversity, cultural background, language use, or educational history. Pedagogical ethics demand that MLPA be designed and implemented in ways that are responsive to diverse learner needs and do not impose deficit models of performance.

Inclusive pedagogy involves questioning whose behaviors are considered normative, whose data are represented in training sets, and whose learning goals are prioritized in system design. It also means ensuring that learners are not merely subjects of analytics but active participants in shaping how their learning is understood and supported. Participatory approaches, such as learner co-design or dialogic use of learning data, can help to democratize MLPA and align it with values of justice and empowerment.

Sociocultural Dimension

The sociocultural dimension highlights broader implications concerning equity, inclusivity, cultural sensitivity, and community trust. The use of AI analytics in education could unintentionally exacerbate existing inequalities, particularly where technological resources or expertise are unevenly distributed across schools or communities (Holmes et al., 2021). Ethical practices necessitate addressing these digital divides through inclusive policymaking and equitable resource allocation to ensure fair access to advanced learning technologies for all students (Nguyen, Ngo, et al., 2023). The sociocultural dimension of ethical considerations in AI-powered MLPA highlights how social norms, cultural values, power structures, and histories of inequality shape and are shaped by the development and deployment of AI in education. Unlike technical, pedagogical, or legal perspectives that primarily focus on system design, instructional alignment, or regulatory compliance, the sociocultural lens emphasizes questions of identity, equity, inclusion, and justice. It calls attention to who is represented in MLPA systems, whose norms and behaviors are embedded in their algorithms, and whose interests are served or marginalized by their use in educational contexts.

CULTURAL VALIDITY OF MULTIMODAL INDICATORS

A central sociocultural issue in AI-enhanced MLPA relates to the cultural validity of the indicators used to infer learning processes. Cultural sensitivity emerges as a crucial concern, recognizing that educational AI applications must respect diverse cultural norms and values. Systems designed without cultural responsiveness might misinterpret behaviors, leading to biased educational outcomes or alienating learners whose cultural expressions differ from normative assumptions embedded within algorithms (Nguyen, Ngo, et al., 2023). Ethical AI-enhanced MLPA design thus requires multicultural and multilingual considerations, ensuring that systems are adaptable to diverse educational settings and inclusive of varied learner populations.

MLPA systems are not neutral tools. They operate within broader social contexts and inevitably reflect prevailing assumptions about what counts as "normal," "productive," or "successful" learning. When these assumptions go unexamined, MLPA risks reinforcing systemic inequities by privileging dominant cultural norms while rendering invisible or pathologizing the experiences of learners from minoritized or underrepresented groups.

Many AI models rely on behavioral cues, such as gaze patterns, facial expressions, speech rhythms, or physical posture, as proxies for cognitive or affective states. However, the expression of engagement, motivation, or confusion is deeply shaped by cultural norms, socialization practices, and communicative conventions. For instance, sustained eye contact can be interpreted as attentiveness in some cultures but as disrespect or discomfort in others. Similarly, silence in collaborative tasks might reflect disengagement in some contexts but be a sign of respectful listening or internal processing in others. When AI-enhanced MLPA models are trained on homogenous datasets that do not capture this diversity, they might systematically misinterpret or penalize learners whose behaviors deviate from the assumed norm.

Addressing this requires a fundamental shift from assuming universality to recognizing cultural situatedness. Developers and researchers must ensure that MLPA models are validated across culturally diverse populations and that multimodal indicators are interpreted within appropriate sociocultural frames. Participatory design approaches that involve learners and educators from diverse backgrounds can help to surface culturally specific practices and avoid deficit-oriented interpretations of non-normative behavior.

REPRESENTATION AND DATASET BIAS

Bias in MLPA is not only a technical issue but also a sociocultural one, rooted in historical patterns of inclusion and exclusion. The datasets used to train AI models often underrepresent learners from certain linguistic, cultural, or socioeconomic backgrounds. This lack of representation can lead to systemic inaccuracies or exclusions when the models are deployed at scale. For example, voice recognition systems might perform poorly for speakers with non-dominant accents or dialects, while facial analysis tools can struggle to interpret emotional expressions of learners with darker skin tones or from non-Western cultures. These issues can result in disproportionate misclassifications, reduced access to support, or inappropriate feedback for minoritized learners.

Ethically responsible MLPA development must prioritize inclusive data practices. This includes actively collecting diverse datasets, reporting demographic coverage, and analyzing model performance across subgroups. It also requires asking critical questions about the purpose and impact of the analytics: Whose data are being used? Who benefits from the insights? Who is at risk of harm?

LANGUAGE, IDENTITY, AND EQUITY

Language plays a powerful role in shaping access and inclusion in MLPA systems. Many AI tools are developed with assumptions rooted in dominant languages—particularly English—leading to limitations in recognizing or responding to learners who use other languages or dialects. This can result in inaccurate transcriptions, flawed sentiment analysis, or irrelevant feedback, disproportionately affecting multilingual and non-native speakers.

Moreover, language is closely tied to identity, and how learners express themselves in collaborative or reflective tasks might reflect their cultural positioning and epistemic values. For instance, some learners might prefer collective over individual responses or prioritize harmony over critique in group discussions. MLPA systems that rely on standardized interaction norms might fail to capture these nuances, leading to misinterpretations or inequitable evaluations.

To support linguistic equity, MLPA researchers and developers must engage with sociolinguistic expertise, design multilingual-compatible systems, and resist the imposition of monolingual norms. Educational institutions should also consider how MLPA can be used to support, rather than constrain, diverse linguistic repertoires and cultural ways of knowing.

INTERSECTIONALITY AND VULNERABILITY

Ethical analysis in the sociocultural dimension must also attend to intersectionality—the way in which multiple identities and forms of marginalization intersect to shape learners' experiences with technology. For example, a low-income, neurodivergent student of color might face compounded risks of misrecognition, exclusion, or harm from MLPA systems that are not designed with their experiences in mind.

Such intersectional vulnerabilities require targeted attention during both development and deployment. Risk assessments should go beyond general demographic categories and consider how overlapping structural inequalities might amplify the potential for adverse impact. Ethical guidelines for MLPA must explicitly address these compounded forms of bias and incorporate strategies to mitigate disproportionate harm.

This also implies that equity cannot be treated as a one-size-fits-all objective. MLPA research and interpretation must offer flexibility and customization to accommodate diverse learner needs, preferences, and contexts, rather than forcing conformity to a narrow model of "ideal" learning behavior.

CONTEXTUAL SENSITIVITY AND IMPLEMENTATION JUSTICE

The effectiveness and ethicality of MLPA depend not only on the tool itself but on how and where it is implemented. Educational contexts vary widely in terms of resources, pedagogical norms, digital literacy, and sociopolitical dynamics. A system that works well in a well-funded urban university may be inappropriate or even harmful in a rural, under-resourced school.

Implementation justice requires that MLPA adoption be accompanied by contextual inquiry and adaptation. This includes assessing the readiness of the learning environment, the cultural expectations of learners and educators, and the infrastructural constraints. Moreover, institutions must consider the broader implications of MLPA for existing inequalities: Will it exacerbate gaps between well-resourced and marginalized schools? Will it create new forms of stratification or surveillance?

Socioculturally aware policy frameworks should guide MLPA implementation to ensure that benefits are distributed equitably and that risks are not disproportionately borne by already disadvantaged groups.

Community trust and stakeholder engagement further underpin sociocultural ethical practices. The adoption of AI-driven analytics should involve transparent dialog and active participation from educators, students, families, and community members, fostering shared understanding, trust, and acceptance. Community engagement not only ensures alignment with local educational values but also enhances the sustainability and meaningful integration of AI technologies within education (Nguyen, Ngo, et al., 2023; UNESCO, 2021).

PART II

AI-enhanced multimodal data collection and processing for capturing learning processes

4. Collecting multimodal data to capture learning processes

INTRODUCTION

The real learning process is multifaceted and dynamic, so researchers must collect multiple data streams to build a more holistic picture of learning. Multimodal learning process analytics (MLPA) incorporates diverse data sources, from digital interaction logs to video, audio, and sensor readings, to capture the rich tapestry of cognitive, emotional, and behavioral processes involved in learning. Relying on only one data modality (for example, only clickstream logs) provides a partial and potentially misleading view of learning.

A key motivation for multimodal data collection is to capture learning processes that are otherwise hidden or hard to infer from a single modality. Self-regulated learning (SRL) is one prominent example. SRL refers to learners' active management of their cognition, motivation, and emotion during learning (Järvelä et al., 2021; Sharma & Giannakos, 2020). These regulatory processes (planning, monitoring, strategy use, reflecting) often leave subtle traces (e.g., shifts in gaze, changes in facial expression, physiological arousal) (Järvelä & Hadwin, 2024) that can be missed if one relies solely on test scores or click logs. As SRL theory explains, successful learning involves coordinating cognitive, metacognitive, motivational, and emotional components. Researchers have begun using multimodal data (such as eye movements, concurrent think-aloud speech, interface logs, facial expressions, and physiological signals) to investigate the triggers and temporal dynamics of SRL and relate them to learning outcomes. For example, by capturing these parallel streams, we can begin to decode when learners are struggling, how they employ strategies, or when they lose motivation—all from data collected as the learning unfolds.

This chapter provides a comprehensive how-to guide for designing and implementing multimodal data collection to study learning processes. It spans multiple educational contexts—from K-12 classrooms and higher education settings to informal learning environments—to illustrate general principles and practical techniques. We begin by overviewing the types of learning processes that AI-enhanced MLPA can help to capture. Next, we describe common data modalities (e.g., clickstream logs, speech audio, facial video, physiological signals, eye-tracking gaze points, etc.) and what each can reveal about learning. We then discuss instrumentation—the sensors, devices, and software platforms needed to collect these data—and considerations for synchronizing and integrating multiple data streams into a unified timeline for analysis. Practical considerations for study design are addressed, including participant sampling, task selection to elicit target processes, setting constraints (lab vs classroom vs in the wild), and ensuring data quality (calibration and noise reduction). Finally, we present two illustrative vignettes of multimodal data collection in action across different learning contexts. Throughout, the goal is to provide clear, actionable guidance for researchers (especially early-career scholars) aiming to leverage multimodal methods to capture and analyze learning processes. By the end of this chapter, readers should appreciate not only why multimodal data are valuable for MLPA, but also how to design and implement a multimodal data collection protocol in practice.

LEARNING PROCESSES CAPTURED THROUGH MULTIMODAL DATA

One of the first steps in designing a multimodal study is to clarify which learning processes or constructs you aim to capture. Different modalities lend themselves to observing different aspects of learning. Recent literature on multimodal learning analytics often refers to these as learning indicators or dimensions that multimodal data can inform. In general, multimodal data can tap into several broad categories of learning processes and states: behavioral, cognitive, metacognitive, affective/emotional, motivational, and social.

- **Behavioral processes** involve observable actions and interactions that learners make within learning environments. These include digital interactions such as navigation choices, quiz attempts, and resource accesses, typically captured through event logs or clickstream data (Kizilcec et al., 2013). Physical behaviors like posture, hand gestures, note-taking, or manipulation of learning tools also form part of this category (e.g., Whitehead et al., 2025). Behavioral data alone primarily indicates what learners did; however, multimodal integration with other data types provides insight into underlying cognitive or emotional states. For instance, researchers have used clickstream data from online courses to measure student engagement (Kizilcec et al., 2013), and video recordings in face-to-face classrooms have been analyzed to infer students' attention levels (Whitehead et al., 2024). When combined with facial expression data, behavioral traces such as sudden pauses in interaction patterns can signal confusion or a breakdown in understanding.

- **Cognitive processes** refer to the mental activities underlying learning and problem-solving, including attention, memory, reasoning, and strategy use. Although cognition is not directly observable, multimodal data can offer valuable proxies. Eye-tracking data, for example, provides insight into attention and cognitive strategies by showing where learners focus, for how long, and their scanning patterns (C. W. Mayer et al., 2023). Patterns such as fixations and saccades have been linked to cognitive processes such as information comparison and progress monitoring (Taub & Azevedo, 2016). Additionally, think-aloud protocols in which learners verbalize their cognitive processes can reveal reasoning steps, confusion, and metacognitive judgments. Detailed interaction logs, including response times and sequential behaviors, have been analyzed to identify distinct cognitive strategies during educational gaming activities (Taub et al., 2021). Combining eye movements with clickstream data can provide enhanced predictive power in modeling cognitive processing compared to single-modality analyses. Thus, modalities like eye gaze, verbal utterances, and action logs collectively offer powerful lenses into learners' cognitive states.
- **Metacognitive processes** involve learners' awareness and regulation of their learning activities, including planning, monitoring, and self-reflection. Multimodal analytics can capture these subtle processes through methods such as think-aloud protocols where explicit verbalizations reveal students' internal monitoring and regulatory decisions (Järvelä, Malmberg, Haataja, et al., 2021; Järvelä, Malmberg, Sobocinski, et al., 2021). Integration of verbal data with eye-tracking can further confirm whether learners' gaze behaviors match their articulated strategies, such as revisiting content to improve understanding. Interviews or prompted self-reports, despite being less continuous, provide complementary metacognitive insights when synchronized with sensor-based data. Researchers often triangulate these modalities, combining gaze and log data for cognitive insights, facial expressions for emotion, and interviews for metacognition, to validate and enrich interpretations of learner behaviors. Consequently, capturing metacognition through multimodal means usually involves inferring internal regulatory processes from observable external behaviors.
- **Affective and emotional processes** are central to learning experiences, encompassing states such as interest, confusion, frustration, boredom, and excitement. Facial expression analysis using video-based computer vision technologies has successfully detected affective states like confusion or delight during learning activities (Nguyen, Hong, et al., 2022; Nguyen, Li, et al., 2023; Taub et al., 2021). Similarly, speech analysis not only captures content but also vocal characteristics, such as prosody, pitch, and

hesitation, which reflect emotional states such as engagement or boredom. Physiological signals offer more implicit and continuous measures, including heart rate and electrodermal activity (EDA), commonly linked to stress, excitement, and cognitive load (Lane & D'Mello, 2019). For example, wrist-worn EDA sensors have identified spikes corresponding to high frustration or mental effort during challenging tasks. Multimodal combinations of facial expressions and physiological sensors can thus create a more nuanced picture of learners' emotional trajectories, including subtle internal stress not immediately visible externally but crucial in studies of learning processes where managing emotions is key.

- **Motivation and engagement** are closely related to affect but specifically concern learners' drive, sustained attention, and active participation. Engagement has been studied extensively through multimodal approaches, as engaged learners display characteristic behavioral patterns (consistent interactions, minimal idle time), specific postures (leaning forward, nodding), and physiological responses indicative of moderate arousal (Emerson et al., 2020). Video-based tracking devices like the Microsoft Kinect have been utilized effectively to monitor posture dynamics and attention as proxies for engagement (Li et al., 2024; Raca & Dillenbourg, 2013). Similarly, museum-based studies analyzing body movements, facial expressions, and interaction logs have demonstrated improved predictive accuracy of visitor engagement by integrating multiple modalities compared to single data sources alone (Emerson et al., 2020). Thus, multimodal analytics highlights how different signals such as posture, facial affect, and speech tone collectively inform more robust assessments of learner motivation and engagement.
- Furthermore, **collaborative and social processes** emphasize the interactions within group learning scenarios, encompassing verbal dialog, gestures, participation dynamics, and shared emotional climates. Multimodal approaches are essential here, as social interactions inherently span multiple communication channels (Järvelä, Malmberg, Haataja, et al., 2021). Audio recordings of group dialogs, when paired with video-based gaze tracking and facial expression analysis, allow researchers to examine participation patterns, emotional synchronization, and group dynamics in depth (Lubold & Pon-Barry, 2014). In collaborative classroom settings, researchers have used multimodal sensors such as overhead cameras, lapel microphones, and physiological monitors to explore coordination and synchronization among students (e.g., Dindar et al., 2022). These approaches reveal important insights, such as identifying dominant versus passive participants based on speaking times and nonverbal cues like eye contact and gesture frequency. Thus, capturing collaborative learning processes often

necessitates multimodal data collection, providing comprehensive views into complex interactions, including socially shared regulation of learning.

By thoughtfully aligning specific data types and modalities to the processes of interest (e.g., eye movements for attention, speech for reasoning, posture for engagement, biosignals for stress), researchers design studies that shine light on the normally invisible aspects of learning. The next sections will delve into the practical side of how to gather these rich data, followed by guidance on designing a study that successfully captures the complexity described here.

CHALLENGES AND SOLUTIONS IN CAPTURING COMMON DATA MODALITIES FOR MLPA

Audio and Speech Data Collection

Audio data, particularly recordings of student speech, constitute a valuable modality in MLPA, offering insight into learners' verbalized thoughts, self-explanations, questions, and peer interactions. In educational research, audio recordings are commonly used to document think-aloud protocols, capture small-group discussions, analyze student presentations, and detect paralinguistic signals such as tone, rhythm, and pacing (Blikstein, 2013). Collecting high-quality audio is challenging, but this modality provides rich qualitative and quantitative data that are central to understanding learning processes.

The selection of appropriate audio instrumentation is crucial for ensuring data quality. When the objective is to transcribe student speech accurately, for instance, for content analysis or automatic speech recognition—close-talk microphones (e.g., headset or lapel microphones) are preferred to reduce environmental noise (Blikstein & Worsley, 2016). Directional microphones positioned near the learner's mouth enhance signal clarity, making them ideal for individual settings. In contrast, if the aim is to capture broader speech characteristics (e.g., volume, pitch) rather than verbal content, environmental microphones placed centrally in the room might be adequate. In group learning environments, researchers often employ multiple microphones or microphone arrays to distinguish between speakers or to localize voices using beamforming techniques (Ochoa & Worsley, 2016). However, overlapping speech and ambient noise remain common issues that can impair manual and automated transcription efforts alike.

To mitigate such challenges, it is recommended to test the acoustic environment in advance and adopt noise-reduction strategies, such as using microphone arrays or multiple low-cost microphones configured for spatial filtering. Regardless of equipment, the general principle is to position microphones as close as possible to the speakers of interest and to reduce ambient interference. For example, in a human–AI tutoring scenario, an audio log might capture a student saying, "Hmm, I don't get this," immediately before submitting an incorrect answer. When synchronized with system logs and facial expression data indicating confusion, the audio provides strong evidence of a breakdown in understanding. However, the effectiveness of such analysis depends heavily on audio quality. Noisy recordings or simultaneous speakers can complicate signal processing. To address these issues, researchers can use speaker diarization techniques or separate channels for each speaker, when feasible.

Despite the technical difficulties, audio remains a widely adopted and informative modality in MLPA. Its ability to capture both the content and delivery of learner speech—combined with appropriate analytic methods—offers significant potential for understanding and supporting learning. Best practices such as careful microphone placement, environmental calibration, and multimodal synchronization (e.g., aligning audio with video or interaction logs) can significantly enhance the interpretability and utility of audio data in MLPA.

Video Data Collection

Video data collection constitutes a foundational modality in MLPA, owing to its ability to capture a rich array of verbal and non-verbal learning behaviors in situ. Unlike digital trace data or physiological signals, video offers contextualized visual records of learners' facial expressions, body posture, gestures, spatial movements, and interactions with peers or materials. These data streams provide essential inputs for analyzing cognitive, emotional, and social aspects of learning, particularly in face-to-face or embodied learning environments (Molenaar et al., 2023).

Different Camera Technologies

Beyond conventional Red, Green and Blue (RGB) video cameras, MLPA researchers have incorporated specialized hardware such as depth-sensing cameras (e.g., Microsoft Kinect or Intel RealSense) to collect three-dimensional movement data without requiring wearable markers. These devices can detect skeletal pose estimations and offer accurate tracking of limb movements, body orientation, and proximity between learners (Li et al., 2024; Raca & Dillenbourg, 2013). The use of depth cameras is particularly effective in capturing gross motor behavior, such as standing, walking, hand-raising, or shifts in body orientation during instruction.

The selection of camera technologies depends on the targeted data to be captured. For video of faces and bodies, this could be as simple as a USB webcam, a digital camcorder, or specialized cameras (e.g., a 360-degree camera for capturing an entire classroom). Many studies use HD webcams for individual faces (which are affordable and easy to interface with a computer). For group settings, camcorders on tripods might capture different angles. Depth cameras provide both video and depth information, which can be useful for tracking body positions in 3D and even recognizing gestures.

Wearable and mobile camera systems are also used in more dynamic or informal learning contexts, such as museums, makerspaces, or outdoor learning. Wearable eye-tracking glasses, for example, include scene cameras that provide first-person video footage of what the learner is attending to. These data are particularly valuable for capturing learner interactions with physical artifacts, environmental features, or companions. In such cases, researchers must carefully calibrate the field of view and account for participant movement and environmental variability.

Multi-camera and Synchronized Systems

Advanced MLPA studies often require synchronized multi-camera systems to enable temporal and spatial alignment of captured behaviors. Systems might involve fixed tripods, wall-mounted cameras, or mobile camera units, depending on the flexibility required. Synchronization is achieved through time-stamping, often using external synchronization tools or built-in clock systems on recording software. In collaborative settings, it is common to use at least two camera angles: one capturing a frontal view of participants' facial expressions, and another offering a wide perspective of group dynamics (e.g., Edwards et al., 2024).

Camera Placement

The design of video data collection in MLPA is highly context-dependent. In individual learning scenarios, such as computer-based tasks or remote learning environments, single webcams positioned on laptops or desktops are often sufficient to capture facial expressions and gaze direction. These setups are commonly used in studies involving intelligent tutoring systems or online learning platforms where learners interact primarily with digital content (Taub et al., 2021).

In classroom or group learning settings, multiple cameras are typically employed to ensure coverage of all learners and relevant interactions (e.g., Edwards et al., 2024). Wide-angle cameras can be positioned at the back or sides of the room to capture whole-group dynamics, while additional fixed-focus cameras can be directed at individual learners or small groups to capture close-up details of posture and gesture. Some setups include ceiling-mounted cameras to provide an unobstructed overhead view, which is particularly useful for observing movement patterns and group formations.

The choice of camera placement must account for potential occlusion, field of view, and lighting conditions. Cameras should be positioned to minimize visual obstruction (e.g., one student blocking the view of another) and maximize coverage of relevant zones, such as workspaces or shared materials. Angled placements can help to capture facial expressions and hand gestures when students are seated. Elevated positions are often chosen to provide visibility into tabletop activities and minimize distractions caused by the presence of equipment.

Practical and Logistical Planning

The quality of video data depends not only on camera technology but also on environmental conditions. Lighting is a critical factor: low light, glare, or backlighting can degrade image quality and interfere with subsequent processing, such as facial detection or body tracking. Where possible, researchers should use evenly distributed ambient lighting and avoid placing cameras directly opposite light sources. Portable lighting equipment might be required in dimly lit classrooms or when recording during evening hours. The acoustic environment, although not directly visual, can influence decisions about video data collection, particularly when combined with audio. In dual-modality setups, camera placement should also support concurrent audio capture, either via built-in microphones or external recorders. Video cameras should be positioned to avoid capturing extraneous motion from unrelated activities or bystanders, particularly in open or shared learning spaces.

The duration and intensity of video recordings often lead to the generation of large volumes of high-resolution data, necessitating robust planning for storage, processing, and data management. Cameras must be tested in advance to ensure sufficient battery life, storage capacity, and recording fidelity across multiple hours of data collection. Researchers often use external hard drives, SD card backups, or direct-to-server streaming where local infrastructure permits.

To protect data integrity, video files are commonly stored in lossless or high-quality compressed formats (e.g., MP4, H.264 codec) and systematically labeled with metadata, including timestamps, session IDs, participant identifiers (pseudonymized), and camera location or angle. Secure handling and encrypted storage are essential, especially as video data contain identifiable facial features and are classified as sensitive under most ethical guidelines and data protection regulations.

Physiological Signals (Biosensors)

Physiological data refers to measurements of the body's biological responses, which often reflect subconscious reactions to stimuli, stress levels, emotional arousal, or cognitive workload. In the context of learning, common physiological modalities include heart activity (heart rate, heart rate variability), electrodermal activity (skin conductance, also known as galvanic skin response), brain activity (EEG, fNIRS), respiration rate, and even pupil dilation (which can also be measured via eye trackers). These signals can provide evidence of internal states such as anxiety, cognitive load, engagement, or fatigue that might not be evident from outward behavior.

Below are some common physiological sensors and what they measure:

- **Heart rate (HR) and heart rate variability (HRV)**: Typically measured with either chest-strap heart monitors (like those used by athletes, which detect electrical signals of heartbeats) or with wristbands using photoplethysmography (PPG)—the latter shine light to detect blood volume changes. HR is the beats per minute, while HRV refers to the variation in intervals between beats. Elevated heart rate can indicate physical activity or stress/excitement. HRV is often considered an index of stress and cognitive load; low HRV (more uniform beat intervals) tends to correlate with stress or high cognitive effort. In learning tasks, if we see a student's heart rate climb not due to physical movement, it might signal a reaction to a challenging problem or a moment of realization (some studies have found HR spikes at moments of insight). HRV has been used to detect mental workload (Paas et al., 2003), e.g., Paas et al. (2005) showed more difficult tasks lowered HRV as the learner concentrated intensely.
- **Electrodermal activity (EDA)**: Measured via sensors typically on the fingers or palm or a wrist wearable (like the Empatica E4 wristband). EDA reflects changes in skin conductance arising from sweat gland activity, which is controlled by the sympathetic nervous system (the arousal system). When a person is emotionally aroused or stressed (whether positively excited or negatively frustrated), EDA tends to increase (more sweat, higher conductance). EDA is a relatively slow signal—it has a gradual rise and fall over a few seconds in response to stimuli. In learning research, EDA is often interpreted as an indicator of engagement or stress. For example, a spike in EDA might occur when a student is presented with a difficult question or when they receive feedback on an answer. Lane and D'Mello (2019) in their review highlight many intelligent tutoring system studies where EDA was used to detect student frustration or engagement. One case: if a tutoring system sees sustained flat low EDA, it might infer boredom,

whereas frequent spikes might indicate either engagement or frustration, requiring disambiguation from other cues like facial expressions (smiling vs frowning).

- **Electroencephalography (EEG)**: Involves a set of electrodes placed on the scalp to measure electrical activity of the brain. EEG can provide insights into attentional focus (e.g., certain frequencies like the theta band increase during high cognitive load, whereas alpha band might indicate relaxation or disengagement). Some researchers have used more user-friendly EEG headbands (with a few dry electrodes) in classroom studies to get a rough measure of attention levels. For example, research has shown changes in frontal theta power when students struggle with a concept, which can correlate with confusion or effort. However, EEG in uncontrolled environments can be noisy and is more intrusive, so it is less common in typical classroom MLPA studies (more in lab studies). There are also functional Near-Infrared Spectroscopy (fNIRS) devices that measure blood oxygenation in the prefrontal cortex as an indicator of mental effort, although these are still relatively niche for education studies due to cost and setup.
- **Respiration and others**: Breathing rate and depth can be measured with chest bands. Faster, shallower breathing might indicate stress or anxiety, while slow breathing might indicate calm concentration or possibly mind wandering (if someone is dozing off, breathing becomes very slow and steady). Some multimodal studies include respiration to complement heart and EDA for a fuller picture of autonomic activation. Additionally, devices like smartwatches might offer composite indicators (e.g., "stress score") combining heart and movement data. Pupil dilation, measurable via eye-tracking, is also a physiological indicator: pupils tend to dilate with increased cognitive load or emotional arousal. Researchers have used pupil size as a measure of interest or difficulty faced in real time.

Physiological signals are not very specific on their own—they tell us that something is happening (increased arousal, increased heart rate), but not why. This is why physiology in MLPA is almost always used in conjunction with other modalities or context. If we see an EDA spike, we look at the same timestamp in the log (maybe the student hit a snag or moved to a new topic) and in video (maybe the student suddenly sat up or exclaimed something). Context can disambiguate whether a spike was "good" arousal (excitement from solving a challenge) or "bad" arousal (frustration from being stuck). Similarly, heart rate changes could be due to emotional stress or simply adjusting posture (which can transiently change heart rate). Thus, physiological data shines in triangulation.

Physiological data are also useful for time-series modeling of engagement. For instance, researchers can segment a learning session into high vs low engagement periods based on continuous EDA signals. This can then be compared with other data—"Were there fewer eye fixations on the material during low-engagement (low EDA) periods? Did the student fidget more?"—thus linking physiology with behavior.

Physiological sensors are typically wearable. A common setup might involve the student wearing a wristband that logs EDA, skin temperature, and motion, plus perhaps a clip or chest strap for heart rate. These need to be started and stopped in sync with the session. Calibration for physiology is usually about establishing baseline: e.g., measure a resting period to know the student's baseline heart rate and EDA, so that increases can be interpreted properly. Movement can introduce physiological confounds in these signals (if a student runs upstairs, their heart rate and EDA spikes due to physical exertion rather than learning-related processes). In a sedentary learning task, movement is less, but even shifting posture can cause EDA spikes, owing to skin pressure changes, etc. One solution is to also record accelerometer data from the wearable to later filter out segments of high movement (to avoid misinterpreting motion-induced changes as emotional). Data syncing is vital; physiological devices often have their own clocks and sampling rates (EDA might sample at e.g., 4 Hz, heart rate at every heartbeat). We discuss synchronization later, but note that aligning these physiological data streams with events like "user submitted answer at 10:32:05" is necessary to draw connections.

Despite these caveats, physiological sensors greatly enrich analysis, because they capture the intensity of learner states continuously. They are also usually unobtrusive—a lightweight wristband or chest strap is easy to wear, and after a few minutes learners forget about it, so it does not disrupt natural behavior. The cost of many biosensors has also come down (some research-grade wristbands are only a few hundred dollars, and even smartwatches can provide basic heart/EDA data). The potential of physiology in MLPA is growing with better algorithms to interpret signals and with integration into real-time systems (e.g., a system that could detect "stress is rising, maybe offer a hint"). We will not delve into real-time adaptation, as this chapter focuses on data collection, but being aware of physiology's role is useful for future-oriented designs.

Eye-tracking

Eye-tracking is a specialized modality that captures where a learner is looking (their gaze point) and how their eyes move. It provides a moment-by-moment index of visual attention and information intake. In learning tasks that involve reading, observing diagrams, interacting with a screen, or even watching a teacher, eye-tracking data are incredibly informative about the focus and sequence of cognitive processing. Two main types of eye trackers are used: screen-based eye trackers (remote trackers that sit below or above a computer monitor and track the user's eyes as they look at the screen) and eye-tracking glasses (wearable devices that look like glasses and track the wearer's gaze in real-world environments).

An eye tracker typically outputs the coordinates of gaze on a display or in the environment, along with timestamps. From raw gaze data, we derive metrics like fixations (moments when the eye is relatively still and focused on a specific area, usually indicating attention to that area) and saccades (quick jumps of the eye from one point to another). By mapping fixations to areas of interest (AOIs) on the learning material, we can tell what content the learner paid attention to, in what order, and for how long. For example, in a digital textbook, AOIs might be paragraphs or figures; eye-tracking can show if a student skipped a figure or re-read a particular paragraph several times (possibly indicating confusion or interest). Eye movements have been described as the "windows to the mind," because they often reflect underlying cognitive processes: e.g., if a student frequently looks back and forth between a diagram and a question, they are likely integrating information (a good sign of active reasoning), whereas if their gaze wanders to irrelevant areas, they might be distracted or unsure where to focus

In a computer-based learning scenario, a screen-based eye tracker (like a Tobii device) is commonly used. These are often placed just below the monitor and use infrared to detect the pupil and corneal reflection, calculating gaze position with an accuracy of ~0.5 degrees of visual angle. Calibration is required for each user (they look at a few dots on screen to calibrate). Once calibrated, you can record gaze points at, say, 60 Hz or 120 Hz. The output might be a gaze stream like: at time 12.400s, gaze at (x=300, y=150) on the screen, etc. These can then be mapped to interface elements or content regions.

For real-world or paper-based tasks, eye-tracking glasses are employed. These have inward-facing cameras to track the eye and an outward-facing camera to capture the scene. They can compute gaze in world coordinates (like a dot overlaid on the scene video showing where the person is looking). This is useful for, say, observing a student in a lab setting (you can see if they are looking at the experiment setup, at a lab manual, or at a peer) or in a classroom (whom are they looking at—the teacher, the board, or out the window?). One drawback of mobile eye-trackers is that analyzing data is more complex; often you have to manually map gaze to objects in the scene video unless you have some computer vision to identify objects.

STRATEGIES FOR MULTIMODAL DATA COLLECTION

Setting and Environment

Laboratory vs in field: A lab setting (quiet room with controlled lighting, only researcher and participant) is ideal for minimizing noise in data (literal noise for audio, and "noise" in terms of extraneous activity for video and physiology). It also allows using more equipment with ease (you can set up cameras without worry about others, etc.). However, lab settings might alter participant behavior (they might try harder, because they know they are observed one-on-one, or they might be nervous with all the gear). In-field settings (i.e., in vivo/ in the wild, like an actual classroom or a museum floor or at the learner's home computer) provide realism but introduce variability—e.g., other people talking which interferes with audio, unpredictable movements, difficulties in synchronizing if everyone starts at slightly different times, etc. One approach is a controlled field experiment: bring equipment to the real setting but still have a controlled task. For instance, in a classroom, you might pull a few students aside to a setup at the back during an independent work period.

Consider how the presence of equipment might affect the environment. Will cameras obstruct anyone's view or be distracting? Sometimes one can use smaller form-factor devices or camouflage them. For example, some studies put cameras in corners or use ones with lights off, so that they are less noticeable. Eye trackers often have lights (for infrared), some have "low-profile mode" to dim those. Work with teachers (if in a classroom) to integrate the setup in a non-disruptive way (maybe set up during a break, so it is not noticed, etc.). You must always be clear that recording is happening (it is unethical to hide it from participants), but you can avoid making it a big focus ("the camera is just to record so we do not miss anything you do, please ignore it and do your task").

Calibration and setup time: Build time into your session for calibrations (eye tracker calibration could be ~5 minutes, getting someone to wear sensors properly maybe 5–10 minutes). If running multiple participants serially, schedule gaps for resetting devices (charging or transferring data). If in a classroom and calibrating many participants individually, have a plan to do it efficiently (maybe calibrate one by one while others work on something).

Data quality in environment: Environmental factors can affect data quality:

- **Lighting**: Low light can cause grainy video (harder for face analysis), and some eye trackers struggle in extreme lighting (especially sunlight glare). The ideal is even, moderate lighting. If in a classroom with windows, maybe pick a time of day or position to avoid direct sunlight on the eye tracker.

- **Noise**: If audio analysis is key, try to reduce background noise (close doors/windows, pick a quiet corner, or use directional mics). In group settings, you will inevitably have overlapping talk; using multiple mics can help to separate later (or you can accept it and do more qualitative analysis).
- **Network and power**: Ensure all devices have power (batteries charged or plugs and extension cords available). If using wireless (Bluetooth sensors, Wi-Fi cameras), check that connections are stable in that environment (some schools have congested Wi-Fi, etc.). In some cases, wired connections are preferred to reduce the risk of data loss caused by wireless dropouts.
- **Space**: If doing movement capture, you need enough space for Kinect's field of view or camera coverage. Mark those areas and, if necessary, tell participants: "stay within this area so we can capture you on camera" (but phrase it naturally: "so everything you do on the table is in view").

Ensuring Data Quality

Ensuring data quality in MLPA involves multiple strategies across the data lifecycle. Prior to data collection, sensor calibration, environmental setup, and pilot testing help to minimize errors. During collection, real-time monitoring and synchronization across modalities ensure temporal alignment and completeness. Post-collection, data validation techniques—such as signal filtering, noise reduction, and cross-modal consistency checks—enhance reliability. Documenting anomalies and establishing clear protocols for data cleaning further support transparency and reproducibility. Below are some essential strategies for ensuring data quality in MLPA research.

- **Pilot testing**: This cannot be stressed enough—do a pilot with all modalities running. Ideally, pilot with someone similar to your participants (a fellow student perhaps) who is doing a similar task. This will reveal issues such as: sensor slipping off, calibration failing for some users (maybe they wear glasses that interfere with eye tracker—you must then plan to ask participants to remove reading glasses if possible or adjust calibration), audio not picking up because someone spoke too softly, etc. It also helps you to gauge how much data will be generated and how to handle it.
- **Planning for synchronization and combining modalities properly:** A practical point is how to *meaningfully* integrate different data types during analysis. A novice mistake would be drowning in data without a plan. It is advisable to formulate a coding scheme or analysis plan for each modality

beforehand. For example, you might decide: from video we will code instances of off-task behavior, from audio we will transcribe and code help-seeking utterances, from logs we will mark success/failure on each problem, from physiology we will extract peaks as indicators of high stress events. This plan helps to target what to look for and reduces bias (you will not go fishing arbitrarily in data as much). It also ensures you collect what's needed—e.g., if you plan to analyze facial emotion, confirm that the camera angle and resolution you have is sufficient for that analysis.

- **Calibration procedures**: For eye trackers, perform calibration carefully and validate it (most software shows an accuracy measure or allows a validation pass). If validation shows poor accuracy (>1 degree off), recalibrate. For physiology, ensure that sensors have good contact (for EDA, the strap should be snug on the skin; for chest HR, moisten the electrode area slightly for good conduction). For digital pens, ensure that they sync to the paper properly (some require pairing or that the pen is turned on). For any camera, ensure that focus is set (some webcams have auto-focus, which is usually fine, but if not, manually focus to the typical position of participants). If using multiple cameras, ensure timestamps (some camcorders have time-of-day; if you rely on that, set them all to correct time).
- **Monitoring during data collection**: If possible, monitor live signals to catch problems. For example, many eye trackers have a live gaze plot—if you see it freeze or go erratic, you know that tracking was lost (maybe the participant moved too far or a marker fell off). If feasible, pause and fix it (depending on study design—sometimes you cannot pause a class in action, but in a lab you could). Similarly, check that microphones are recording (some recorders have level meters that you can glance at to ensure that it is picking up sound). This kind of real-time monitoring might be done by an assistant while you run the session.
- **Redundancy**: It is good to have some redundant measures in case one fails. For instance, if the high-end eye tracker fails to record, having a screen recording and webcam video means that you can do a rough manual gaze analysis, or at least means you did not lose everything. Or if a wearable's data are too noisy, perhaps the facial video can still give affect info. In a classroom, having two cameras from different angles ensures that if one is blocked at a particular moment, the other might still capture. Redundancy can save a study from being ruined by one sensor glitch.
- **Data management**: Multimodal studies produce lots of files, including video files (which are large), audio, logs, etc. Having a systematic naming convention and storage plan is crucial. For example, create a folder for each participant or for each session, name files with participantID_modality_timestamp. Keep a *log sheet* (on paper or electronically) during collection where you note any incidents (e.g., "P5: Eye tracker lost tracking in

middle for ~1 min, recalibrated at 10:45"). These notes will help later when analyzing data quality or explaining anomalies.

- Also, ensure that you have backup storage (do not rely on one laptop's drive—transfer to an external or cloud for backup regularly). Large video files might need compression or at least careful handling; ensure memory cards are swapped out in timely fashion if using cameras. One trick: record lower resolution or frame rate, if ultra-high quality is not needed—e.g., 720p video might suffice for face analysis instead of 1080p, which halves file size.
- **Dealing with missing data**: Inevitably, you might have segments of missing or bad data: eye tracker might be off when student looked away from the screen, or audio might be inaudible during a loud, unexpected noise. Plan analysis methods that are robust to these interferences (such as not requiring continuous data from all modalities at every millisecond). You might decide to focus analysis on moments where you have at least two modalities confirming something and ignore times where one modality failed. Some advanced techniques can interpolate or predict missing modality data from others, but that is complex. At minimum, document how much data was lost, and if it is random or systematic (e.g., if the tallest students had more missing eye data because they sat further from the tracker, note that).
- **Participant behavior and comfort**: One challenge is that participants might behave unnaturally initially because of sensors. They might be excessively conscious of being watched or wired up, leading to less spontaneous behavior (the "observer effect"). Strategies to mitigate: give them a few minutes to acclimate (perhaps have a warm-up task or casual conversation while they are already wearing the gear, so that they get used to it). Emphasize that the equipment is there to record signals, not to "judge" them, and that there are no right/wrong behaviors. Sometimes humor helps—"You look like a cyborg with all this on, but do not worry, we're collecting science data, not turning you into a robot!". Ensure physical comfort: tape wires, if necessary, so they do not dangle; fit device straps so they are not too tight or too loose, etc. If a participant is *very* uncomfortable or nervous, that itself will reflect in physiological data (which might confound what you are measuring). You might then consider dropping that participant's data or at least account for it. Building rapport with participants and having them trust the process will improve natural behavior.
- **Context and metadata**: Collect background data that might help to interpret results. For example, ask participants after the session how they felt or whether anything was uncomfortable or distracting. If someone reports "I was very nervous because I had never done this before," this could explain high physiological arousal unrelated to the learning task. Also note any

external events: "A loud car horn outside at 10:40 startled participant", as such events may produce spikes across multiple sensors that are not related to learning processes but to environmental disturbances. Keeping an observation log or recording the broader context on video can assist during analysis in identifying and filtering out such interference.

CASE STUDIES ON EFFECTIVE MULTIMODAL DATA COLLECTION FOR MLPA

In examining effective strategies for multimodal data collection within the context of MLPA, this section presents two illustrative case studies that integrate diverse data modalities and reflect on the practical and methodological lessons drawn from each. The first case focuses on capturing data related to socially shared regulation of learning (SSRL) with the objective of evaluating and informing the design of support mechanisms provided by a metacognitive artificial intelligence (MAI). This was operationalized through a Wizard of Oz (WOz) prototyping approach, enabling the simulation of AI-driven support while collecting rich process data on collaborative regulation. The second case centers on the collection of data related to human–AI interaction and learning within a mixed reality environment, where students engaged with an embodied Generative AI agent. This case illustrates how MLPA can be applied to understand the dynamics of learning in immersive contexts that blend physical and digital modalities, highlighting technical challenges and design implications for future human–AI collaborative learning systems.

Capturing Socially Shared Regulation of Learning (SSRL) with Metacognitive Artificial Intelligence (MAI)

In the first case study, we examine the work of Edwards et al. (2024), which investigated how MAI agents can be designed and evaluated to support SSRL in collaborative learning contexts. The study offers a critical example of how early-stage prototyping and multimodal data collection can inform both the technical development and pedagogical integration of AI systems within learning environments.

Research context

The researchers adopted the echeloned Design Science Research (eDSR) methodology, which facilitates iterative design, implementation, and evaluation of educational technology interventions by explicitly integrating theory-driven problem formulation with empirical validation. This structured approach allowed the team to link theoretical constructs of SSRL with technical instantiations of MAI prompts and to assess their efficacy through situated interactions among learners. To simulate the AI-driven interactions without the need for fully autonomous systems at this stage, the team employed a WOz prototyping technique. This involved a human operator covertly controlling the AI agent's responses during live collaborative learning sessions, thereby enabling the researchers to prototype a wide range of AI interventions while maintaining ecological validity in the interaction dynamics. Such a method is especially effective for exploring the design space of MAI functionalities prior to system automation.

Multimodal data collection

To capture the complex dynamics of these interactions, the study employed a rich multimodal data collection strategy that integrated behavioral, physiological, and contextual data. Audio recordings and text logs captured the verbal and written exchanges between learners and the MAI agent. Audio recordings documented spoken interactions among learners and the influences by AI agent (operated via WOz), while text logs from the collaborative platform provided a record of written prompts and learner responses. This multimodal dataset enabled fine-grained analysis of how learners responded to various types of metacognitive prompts, how regulation episodes unfolded across time, and how group-level coordination emerged. In parallel, physiological signals were recorded using Shimmer sensors, including data on electrodermal activity and heart rate variability, providing insights into learners' affective and arousal states during regulation episodes. These physiological measures were instrumental in identifying stress responses and fluctuations in engagement that are not directly observable through interaction data alone.

Additionally, the researchers utilized depth video captured by a Microsoft Kinect camera to document learners' body posture, spatial orientation, and gestural behaviors during collaborative tasks. This layer of data enabled the identification of nonverbal cues related to coordination and engagement, such as mutual gaze, physical alignment, and gesture synchrony—all of which are relevant to the enactment of SSRL in face-to-face interactions. The Kinect-based depth recordings complemented the audio-textual data by providing temporal markers and behavioral indicators for moments of shared planning, monitoring, or breakdown in regulation.

Figure 4.1 illustrates a prototype setup designed for the multimodal data collection of the study. The central area of the setup consists of a group table surrounded by participants, with an iPad placed at the center representing the MAI agent interface, controlled covertly by a human operator (the "wizard"). Surrounding this interaction space is an array of recording and sensing equipment.

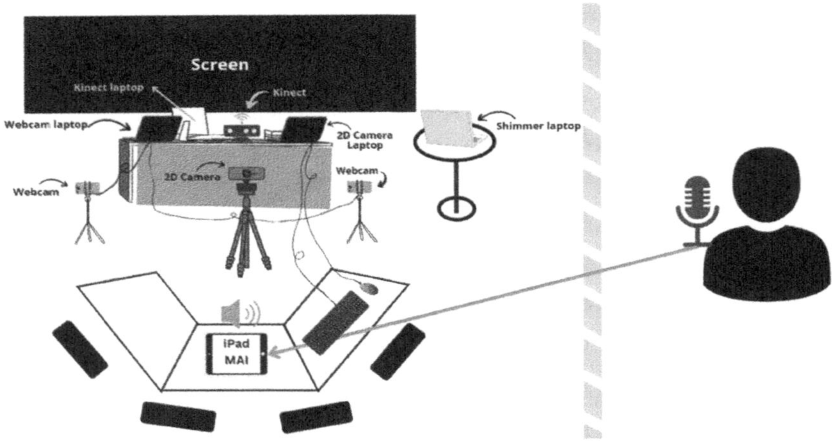

Source: Author's own, previously published at https://doi.org/10.1111/bjet.13534

Figure 4.1 Data collection prototype

- **Two webcams** placed on tripods capture front-facing video of participants in close-up, capturing facial expressions, gestures, and interpersonal interactions.
- **2D camera** mounted centrally and connected to a dedicated laptop records high-resolution video of the group's shared space, offering a holistic view of embodied interaction.
- **Kinect camera**, paired with a corresponding laptop, captures depth data including posture, movement, and spatial orientation of participants throughout the session.
- **Shimmer sensor system**, interfaced with its own laptop, records physiological signals, such as electrodermal activity and heart rate variability. These biosignals provide indicators of cognitive workload, arousal, and stress that are crucial for interpreting the affective dimension of SSRL.
- A large **screen** behind the operator desk is used to display digital task content or learning stimuli to the group.

This multimodal data infrastructure is purposefully arranged to ensure optimal coverage of the collaborative learning processes from behavioral, verbal, and affective dimensions.

Orchestrating such a multimodal setup demands extensive pre-session planning and careful spatial arrangement. Each recording and sensing device must be positioned to avoid interference while maximizing the quality and coverage of the data collected. The placement of the Kinect sensor requires unobstructed sightlines to track depth accurately, while the Shimmer sensors need to be comfortably and securely worn by participants to ensure reliable physiological recordings.

Equally important is the synchronization of all devices. Given the diversity of modalities (audio, videos, physiological, and digital interaction logs), it is essential to implement timestamp alignment protocols or use a master synchronization signal to ensure that data streams can be merged for post-hoc analysis. Misalignment across data sources could lead to invalid inferences about the relationship between behavioral and affective states and the corresponding AI intervention.

A multimodal setup of this complexity cannot function effectively without a well-defined operational protocol. The high volume and heterogeneity of data sources require tightly coordinated procedures to ensure data quality, synchronization, and reproducibility. A comprehensive operational script serves as the backbone of the data collection process, detailing every step from device calibration to post-session data handling. It ensures that technical and human elements of the session proceed in a standardized and efficient manner across repeated trials. Without such a protocol, there is a high risk of data loss, corruption, or inconsistencies that could compromise the validity of the study. The script must clearly define the sequence of actions, roles, and responsibilities of all personnel involved, and contingency measures for technical or procedural failures. It should be developed iteratively, refined through pilot testing, and shared with all involved team members ahead of time.

Capturing Active Learning with an Embodied Generative AI Agent

This second case study presents a multimodal data collection protocol developed to evaluate Kai, an embodied Generative AI agent embedded in a mixed reality (MR) environment (Dang et al., 2025, Nguyen, Gul, et al., 2025). Designed to promote active and self-regulated learning, the study focused on how learners engaged with Kai during a guided exploration of ethical considerations in AI use. The setup exemplifies a high-fidelity experimental infrastructure for capturing individual learner interaction in immersive, AI-mediated learning environments.

Research design and context

The study, grounded in the Human–AI Shared Regulation of Learning framework (Järvelä et al., 2023), applied an echeloned Design Science Research (eDSR) methodology (Tuunanen et al., 2024) to evaluate the implementation of Kai in a controlled laboratory setting. Kai was built using Unity and the InWorld API (incorporating GPT-3), allowing for real-time verbal and non-verbal interaction with participants through the Meta Quest 3 headset. The study involved 26 higher education students (22 master's and four doctoral), who each completed individual 30-minute MR learning sessions with Kai.

Multimodal data collection design

To support the comprehensive evaluation of learner experience and active learning processes, data was collected from four key sources:

1. **Pre- and post-questionnaires**: These instruments assessed learners' prior experience with Generative AI and XR technologies (Nguyen, Gul, et al., 2025), their perceptions of Kai as a conversational partner (Doyle et al., 2025), cognitive load (Andersen & Makransky, 2021), and engagement and interest (Jennett et al., 2008). Changes in learners' perceptions before and after interaction were used to assess Kai's perceived anthropomorphism and educational utility.
2. **Headset-based first-person video and audio**: The Quest 3 headset provided continuous capture of learners' in-environment perspective, including their verbal interactions with Kai and visual attention within the MR space. This first-person recording was critical for linking learners' dialog with their physical orientation, gestures, and gaze behavior.
3. **2D camera recordings from two angles**: External TP-LINK Tapo C225 cameras captured third-person video from two fixed positions to document full-body movements and embodied engagement from multiple angles. This provided essential data on learners' physical interaction with MR elements (e.g., pointing at flashcards, navigating video panels), supporting behavioral analyses aligned with embodied cognition frameworks.
4. **External wireless microphone audio**: A high-fidelity wireless lapel microphone was attached to each participant to capture clean, continuous audio, ensuring transcription accuracy and enabling voice analytics. This audio source was synchronized with both first- and third-person video data for integrated multimodal analyses.

This multimodal instrumentation enabled a detailed, time-synchronized dataset capturing how learners navigated the MR space, interacted with Kai, and responded physically and cognitively throughout the learning process.

The MR experiment was situated in a fixed area within a lab equipped with controlled lighting and minimal distractions. Prior to entering the MR environment, participants received orientation and donned wearable equipment under facilitator supervision. The pre-defined physical boundary of the Quest

3 headset ensured that learners remained within the camera frame and safety zone.

The data collection protocol followed a tightly scripted sequence:

- **Pre-task phase**: Participants completed pre-questionnaires and were equipped with the Quest headset and microphone.
- **Familiarization**: A five-minute acclimatization period introduced learners to gesture controls, the MR interface, and Kai's presence.
- **Interaction phase**: Participants engaged in a 20-minute structured dialog with Kai, guided by the agent's multimodal prompts on ethical AI topics.
- **Post-task phase**: A five-minute oral task allowed participants to summarize or reflect on their learning, followed by post-questionnaire completion.

Throughout, facilitators followed an operational checklist to manage device startup, signal monitoring, data verification, and contingency procedures in the event of technical failure.

This case illustrates how embodied Generative AI agents in MR can facilitate immersive and reflective learning experiences, especially when supported by robust multimodal data collection. The integration of headset-based and external recordings enabled the triangulation of learner perceptions with observable behaviors. Moreover, the tight coupling of instructional design and data architecture ensured that the evaluation aligned with both pedagogical goals and technical constraints.

Importantly, the study emphasizes the necessity of a carefully orchestrated data collection script, incorporating real-time device coordination, session monitoring, and participant safety protocols. Given the complexity of the hardware involved and the cognitive sensitivity of immersive environments, structured operational routines are essential for ensuring the validity and replicability of findings in MR-enhanced educational research. This prototype establishes a replicable model for future studies examining active and self-regulated learning processes in AI-augmented MR contexts and contributes methodologically to the expanding field of hybrid intelligence in higher education.

5. Preprocessing multimodal learning process data

INTRODUCTION

These rich data sources for artificial intelligence (AI)-enhanced multimodal learning process analytics (MLPA) promise a more holistic understanding of learning processes, but they also introduce significant complexity in preprocessing and analysis. Before any meaningful analysis or application of AI in MLPA can occur, researchers must carefully preprocess and integrate these heterogeneous data. Preprocessing is the critical foundation: it involves cleaning raw data, synchronizing and aligning different streams, transforming data into useful features, and validating the prepared dataset. This chapter provides a comprehensive overview of how to handle and preprocess multimodal data in learning contexts. We discuss common challenges and outline techniques for data cleaning, integration (fusion and alignment), and transformation. We also detail how to prepare multimodal datasets for analysis through segmentation, annotation, and validation workflows. Throughout, we ground the discussion in scholarly literature and illustrate key points with use cases from two recent studies: (1) an embodied Generative AI agent in a mixed reality learning environment (Nguyen et al., 2025); and (2) a human–AI collaborative system to support socially shared regulation (Edwards et al., 2024). The goal is to equip researchers and practitioners with a solid understanding of preprocessing strategies in order to harness AI effectively for multimodal learning analytics.

HANDLING AND PREPROCESSING CHALLENGES OF MULTIMODAL DATA

Preprocessing multimodal data is inherently more challenging than dealing with single-source data. Multimodal learning process data typically includes a combination of modalities such as video (capturing visual behaviors), audio (spoken utterances or paralinguistic cues), textual logs or transcripts, physiological signals (e.g., heart rate, electroencephalogram [EEG], eye-tracking), and interaction logs (clickstream data from online platforms). Each modality comes with its own format, scale, and noise characteristics. Before delving into specific techniques, it is important to understand the key challenges that arise when handling such data. Recent literature in multimodal machine learning and learning analytics consistently highlights several fundamental issues that preprocessing must address

Heterogeneity of Data Sources

Different modalities have distinct data types, structures, and statistical properties, making it non-trivial to combine them in a meaningful way. For example, a video stream consists of images at a certain frame rate, audio might be a continuous waveform or transcript text, and clickstream logs are discrete event records. These data differ in dimensionality (e.g., high-dimensional image pixels vs a single scalar from a sensor), in scale (e.g., numerical vs categorical), and in semantic meaning. Aligning and integrating such heterogeneous data into a unified representation is a non-trivial task requiring careful preprocessing. This gap between modalities, sometimes called the *modality gap,* means that the same concept or event can be expressed very differently in each modality, complicating direct comparison or fusion.

Temporal Misalignment

Multimodal data often comes from devices or sources that are not perfectly synchronized in time. Modalities might have different sampling rates or timing granularity (e.g., video at 30 frames per second, keystroke events timestamped to milliseconds, survey responses with no time dimension). Moreover, relevant events in each modality might not occur simultaneously; for instance, a spike in a physiological signal could lag behind an external stimulus, or a student's gaze (video) might shift a moment before they click a button (log). Such temporal misalignment can impede meaningful cross-modal analysis. A key preprocessing challenge is to synchronize data streams, correcting for any clock offsets or delays, so that data from different sources referring to the same moment or event are properly aligned in time. This often requires adding or adjusting timestamps, resampling signals to a common timeline, or using alignment algorithms to match patterns across streams. Domain knowledge is often needed to decide how to handle differing time scales and to ensure alignment is semantically valid.

Missing Data and Incomplete Modalities

It is common to encounter missing values or even entirely missing modalities in multimodal learning datasets. Various factors can lead to incomplete data: hardware malfunctions or sensor dropouts, participants opting out of certain recordings (e.g., disabling a camera for privacy), human error in data collection, or environmental conditions causing data loss. For example, an eye-tracker might lose track of the pupil when a student looks away, or an audio recording might fail for one session. Missing data pose serious issues for analysis, as many algorithms expect complete cases. Preprocessing must thus detect missing data and decide on strategies to handle them. Common approaches include imputation of missing values (using methods like interpolation for time-series gaps, or statistical imputation for questionnaires) and designing the analysis to be robust to missing modalities. In some cases, entire modalities might be dropped from analysis if data quality is too low; in other cases, advanced techniques allow models to learn with incomplete inputs (e.g., training models that can ignore or down-weight missing modality inputs). Regardless, identifying the extent and pattern of missingness is an important first step in preprocessing.

Noise and Unreliable Signals

Real-world multimodal data are inevitably noisy. Noise can come in many forms: sensor measurements might include random fluctuations and artifacts (e.g., muscle noise in EEG signals, or background noise in audio recordings); video frames might be blurry or occluded; log data might include spurious events or irrelevant actions. Without cleaning, noise can mislead analysis and model training by introducing false correlations or masking true patterns. Preprocessing must therefore include noise reduction and filtering steps. For time-series physiological data, this might involve smoothing filters or artifact removal techniques (for instance, applying a band-pass filter to heart rate data to remove high-frequency noise, or using independent component analysis to remove eye-blink artifacts from EEG) (e.g., Dindar et al., 2022). For audio, noise cancellation or filtering can improve speech clarity. For video, one might remove frames with too much motion blur or use computer vision techniques to stabilize images. For clickstream logs, noise reduction could involve removing obviously erroneous records or out-of-scope actions. Outlier detection is also crucial: extreme values or events that are likely errors should be identified and handled (either removed or corrected if possible).

Data Volume and Complexity

Another challenge (closely related to heterogeneity and noise) is the sheer volume and complexity of multimodal data. A single learning session can produce hours of video, thousands of log events, and gigabytes of sensor data. The high frequency and high dimensionality of these data mean that preprocessing can be computationally intensive and requires efficient methods to reduce data to manageable forms. Techniques such as sampling or down-scaling might be employed (e.g., to reduce video resolution or frame rate if ultra-high fidelity is not needed, or to summarize log events into counts per interval). There is often a trade-off between retaining rich detail and achieving feasible data sizes for analysis.

These challenges are widely recognized in the field. As Cukurova et al. (2020) note, while multimodal learning analytics holds great promise, it also "poses significant methodological, practical and ethical challenges." Methodologically, the lack of standardized approaches to handle the above issues means that each study must carefully craft its own preprocessing pipeline (often guided by the specific research questions and data at hand). Technically, integrating diverse data streams and dealing with noise/missingness require advanced skills in signal processing and data engineering, which can be a barrier for many educational research teams. In practical terms, if preprocessing is not done rigorously, the subsequent analyses (whether statistical models or machine learning algorithms) can be fed unreliable data and thus produce misleading results. In the remainder of this chapter, we discuss techniques to tackle these challenges, moving from initial data cleaning to integration/fusion of modalities, transformation into features, and final preparation steps. Addressing these challenges systematically ensures that the multimodal data are in a state where AI and analytics methods can be applied effectively to gain insights into learning processes.

TECHNIQUES FOR DATA CLEANING, INTEGRATION, AND TRANSFORMATION

Once the challenges are understood, researchers can deploy a range of techniques to preprocess multimodal data. Preprocessing typically involves three broad phases: data cleaning (including noise reduction and basic formatting), data integration (synchronizing and fusing multiple modalities into a coherent dataset), and data transformation (feature engineering, scaling, and dimensionality reduction to prepare for analysis). These phases often overlap and iterate: for instance, one might clean each modality separately, then integrate them and discover further issues (requiring additional cleaning or adjustments), and finally transform the integrated data into features. In this section, we outline key techniques in each category, with attention to how they apply to common modalities in learning analytics, such as physiological signals, video, audio, and clickstream logs. We also highlight strategies for multimodal fusion and alignment, as well as processes for engineering useful representations from raw data.

Data Cleaning and Noise Reduction

Data cleaning is the first line of defense against the errors and noise discussed earlier. *Cleaning* involves detecting and correcting errors in the data, filtering out unwanted portions, and standardizing formats across data sources. The specific cleaning steps depend on the modality:

- **Physiological signals:** These include data like heart rate, galvanic skin response (GSR), EEG, or other wearable sensor readings of learners. Such signals are prone to noise from various sources (electrical interference, sensor misplacement, motion artifacts). Cleaning techniques commonly include applying filters (low-pass, high-pass, or band-pass filters to remove frequency noise outside the range of interest), smoothing via moving averages or more sophisticated methods (e.g., Kalman filtering), and artifact removal. For example, in EEG processing, independent component analysis can isolate and remove components associated with eye blinks or muscle activity. Missing data in physiological time-series (owing to momentary signal loss) might be interpolated using linear or spline interpolation, or if larger segments are missing, one might mark those segments as invalid. It is also important to calibrate sensors, if necessary (e.g., zeroing a baseline or normalizing readings to a personal baseline measured at the start). Outlier detection is key: extreme spikes or drops in a physiological signal that are physiologically implausible (or not relevant to the experiment) should be identified. Sometimes a domain-driven rule can be applied (e.g., discard heart rate values above a certain maximum if they likely indicate device error).
- **Video data:** Raw video recordings of learning sessions can contain segments that are not useful (before/after the session, or if the participant temporarily left the frame). Cleaning video often involves trimming to the relevant timeframe and possibly editing out segments where nothing is happening (if, for instance, the data needs to be clipped to segments of interest). A critical cleaning step is ensuring the video's timestamps are in sync with other data (this will be explained further in the next section on synchronizing and combining data). If multiple cameras are used (e.g., one capturing the whole classroom and another focusing on a student's face), their footage must be time-aligned and possibly merged (e.g., via picture-in-picture or by coding events from each). Video quality issues such as poor lighting can sometimes be mitigated by preprocessing (e.g., histogram equalization to improve contrast, or stabilization if the camera moved). However, many video "cleaning" operations blend into feature extraction (such as extracting pose or facial expressions); at the cleaning

stage, the goal is mainly to ensure that the video is watchable, synchronized, and segments unrelated to analysis are removed. If using automated computer vision later, one might also consider cropping or resizing frames to focus on the area of interest (for instance, cropping to just the learner's upper body if only posture and gestures matter, removing irrelevant background, etc.).

- **Audio data:** Audio (e.g., recordings of students' speech or classroom discussion) often requires denoising. Using filtering or advanced noise reduction algorithms (such as spectral subtraction or using a pre-trained denoising model) can help to reduce background noises (air conditioning hum, shuffling papers). If the audio contains multiple speakers, voice activity detection can be applied to segment speech vs silence and possibly to separate speakers. In learning settings, if multiple microphones are used (e.g., a lapel mic on teacher and another ambient mic), their recordings must be combined or at least aligned in time. Audio is also typically converted into a uniform format for analysis: e.g., downsampling to a common sample rate (like 16 kHz) and converting to mono channel if stereo is not needed. Transcription (converting audio to text) is a crucial step if the content of speech is to be analyzed; while transcription is more of a feature extraction task, it is often considered part of preprocessing for audio. Automatic Speech Recognition tools (e.g., Google Speech API, CMU Sphinx) can produce transcripts, but these transcripts might need cleaning too, removing transcription errors, adding punctuation, and tagging who is speaking, if possible. As Ochoa et al. (2022) notes, one can use services such as Google's Speech-to-Text services to extract verbal content from audio, but it is important to understand the limitations of such algorithms and correct obvious mistakes or inaudible segments. Overall, cleaning audio ensures that subsequent text or acoustic analyses are based on clear, synchronized sound data.
- **Clickstream and log data:** This modality includes any digital interaction logs—clicks on a learning platform, keystrokes, navigation events, or even more specialized logs (e.g., eye-tracker gaze coordinates could be considered here if not treated as a continuous signal). Cleaning log data involves standardizing timestamps (ensuring a consistent time zone and format across all logs), removing duplicate or irrelevant events, and possibly translating raw logs into a more semantic form. For instance, if the raw data are a sequence of page URLs a student visited, one might map those to meaningful labels (e.g., "opened video module" or "attempted quiz question"). Often, log data contains IDs or codes that need to be mapped to readable forms (like mapping a problem ID to a problem topic). Erroneous entries (e.g., a negative time or an event that is known to be a software bug) should be filtered out. Additionally, if the log data are extremely fine-grained

(e.g., every mouse movement), the cleaning stage might aggregate or sample them to a higher level (e.g., only record significant events) in order to reduce noise. Sparsity is also a consideration; logs can have long periods of no activity if a student is idle; one must decide whether to represent those as explicit "no event" gaps or simply have irregular timestamps.

During cleaning, researchers often create a data log or diary to record what was done (e.g., "Removed 2 outlier segments from heart rate signal for Participant 5 due to signal dropout" or "Filtered audio above 8 kHz to reduce noise"). This documentation is important for transparency and for replicability of the analysis. By the end of the cleaning phase, each modality's data should be as *reliable* and *consistent* as possible, free from obvious errors, trimmed to relevant segments, and ready to be combined. The cleaning phase sets the stage for integration, where the separate modalities will be brought together.

Data Integration: Synchronization and Fusion Strategies

Data integration is the process of combining multiple modalities into a unified dataset that can be analyzed holistically. This includes temporal synchronization of data streams and various fusion strategies to merge information. In multimodal learning analytics, integration is critical, because we often want to understand how different signals relate to each other (e.g., how a spike in electrodermal activity coincides with a difficult problem in an online quiz, or how a gesture in video corresponds to spoken words). Integration can be challenging, but several techniques and conceptual strategies can guide this process.

Temporal alignment and synchronization: As discussed, a prerequisite for integration is aligning modalities in time. The simplest strategy is to use timestamps. Ideally, all data sources share a common clock or reference time (for example, using coordinated universal time or the system clock of the computer running the experiment). In practice, one device might start recording a few seconds before another, or clocks might drift. A common method to synchronize is to use a sync event—for instance, a clap at the start of a session that is visible in the video, audible in the audio, and perhaps triggers an entry in the log. This known event can then be used to line up the timelines (e.g., shift the time axis of one modality so that the clap occurs at time 00:00 in all). When a clear sync event is not available, researchers might rely on finding distinctive patterns: e.g., match the moment a specific word is spoken (audio) with when a student's mouth moves (video) or when a slide change event is logged. Tools and algorithms exist for alignment, such as dynamic time warping for aligning time-series that might be stretched relative to each other, or correlation methods to align signals based on maximal correlation. According to Baltrušaitis et al. (2019), input-level alignment in preprocessing aims to mitigate temporal misalignment caused by differing sampling intervals and missing data across modalities, ensuring data are properly synchronized before fusion. This often requires domain knowledge; for example, knowing that a given sensor's reading is expected to react with a delay of a few seconds to an event can inform how alignment is performed.

After synchronization, data from multiple sources can be fused. There are several fusion strategies commonly referenced in multimodal machine learning:

Early fusion (Feature-level fusion): In early fusion, data from different modalities are combined *before* higher-level modeling occurs. Practically, this means concatenating feature vectors from each modality into one large feature vector, or otherwise merging raw data streams into a single stream. For example, if we have a feature for each second of a learning session describing facial expression (from video) and another feature describing keystroke frequency (from logs) for that same second, early fusion would combine these into a joint feature set for that second. Early fusion allows the model/analysis to consider cross-modal interactions right from the beginning. The advantage is that it can capture complex relationships (e.g., a certain combination of tone of voice *and* gesture might indicate confusion). However, early fusion can lead to very high-dimensional data and requires that modalities are well aligned (since we assume features at the same time/index correspond). It can also be problematic if one modality has much more data than another (one might overwhelm the combined representation).

Late fusion (decision-level fusion): In late fusion, each modality is first analyzed separately (e.g., separate models or statistical analyses), and the results (or decisions) are then combined. For example, one might have one classifier analyzing speech to detect frustration, and another analyzing posture from video to detect engagement; late fusion could then combine the outputs (like probabilities of frustration and engagement) to make a final judgment (e.g., an algorithm that averages or multiplies these probabilities, or uses a rule like "flag the student as struggling, if both frustration and low engagement are detected"). Another example of late fusion (decision-level fusion) is provided by Nguyen, Järvelä et al. (2022), where multimodal streams such as video-based behavioral indicators and physiological signals are first processed independently to derive modality-specific features, and the resulting indicators are subsequently integrated during the analytical stage to examine patterns of socially shared regulation rather than combining raw multimodal features at the model input stage. Late fusion has the benefit of letting each modality "speak for itself" with specialized processing, and it sidesteps some alignment issues (as each analysis can happen on its own timeline, and only the outputs need alignment, perhaps by interpolating output signals). The downside is that it might miss subtler cross-modal cues that only make sense when data are considered together at a fine grain. Nonetheless, in many educational applications, late fusion is useful—for instance, combining survey results with sensor data at the level of final scores or interpretations, rather than trying to merge raw survey text with raw sensor signals.

Hybrid or intermediate fusion: There are also approaches in between early and late fusion. One can perform partial fusion at intermediate stages—for example, extract features from each modality separately (such as computing a set of statistical features from a physiological signal and performing speech transcript analysis for textual features) and then fuse those feature sets into a joint model. Another intermediate approach is to use attention mechanisms or gating mechanisms in a model to let modalities influence each other during the modeling process. In deep learning contexts, one might have separate networks for each modality that then merge in later layers (late fusion in network terms) or share some layers (early fusion of representation). The appropriate level of fusion often depends on the data and task. As Li and Tang (2025) summarize, "early fusion involves merging data from different modalities at the feature extraction stage, allowing interactions to be captured early, whereas late fusion combines outputs of individual models at the decision level; hybrid fusion combines aspects of both."

In educational research, beyond these technical fusion strategies, semantic integration is crucial. Semantic integration means ensuring that the meaning of data from different modalities is aligned. For instance, if a student says "*I don't get this*" (audio/text modality) and at the same time their mouse cursor is hovering over a "Help" button (interaction modality), these two observations together indicate a high likelihood of confusion. To integrate semantically, one might code both modalities in terms of events or constructs (e.g., label the utterance as an "expression of confusion" and the hover as a "help-seeking action") and then examine their co-occurrence. This often requires an ontology or coding scheme that spans modalities, so that, say, a head nod in video can be equated or related to a verbal "yes." Achieving this kind of alignment might involve human expertise (annotation, which we cover in the previous section on "Techniques for Data Cleaning, Integration, and Transformation") or algorithmic linking (e.g., using keyword spotting to align with certain gestures).

Integration also encompasses data merging into a single table or database for analysis. Once data are time-aligned and possibly fused, one common practice is to segment the data into analysis units (e.g., for each student for each task, or for each one-second window as a row) and then include features from all modalities in that unit. This requires deciding on a resolution (time window or event unit) that will be the basis for analysis. Integration thus sets up the multimodal feature set that will feed into statistical tests or machine learning models.

It is worth noting that developing optimal fusion algorithms remains an active area of research. In MMLA, finding the right way to combine signals to detect meaningful learning behaviors is often experimental. Ochoa et al. (2022) points out that the construction of multimodal fusion algorithms is still an open challenge in learning analytics and is often guided by the specific analytic goals. A recommended approach is to use theory or human-coded observations to inform fusion: for example, first define (or observe) the target behavior using human judgment, then identify which combination of low-level signals might predict it.

Data Transformation: Feature Engineering, Normalization, and Reduction

After cleaning and integrating multimodal data, the next step is transforming the data into forms suitable for analysis. Data transformation includes creating features from raw data, scaling or normalizing features, and reducing dimensionality if necessary. Transformation is essential, because raw multimodal data can be unwieldy—for instance, a ten-minute video at 30 frames per second has 18,000 frames, which is too many raw inputs for most analyses. Instead, one might extract a few meaningful features for each time window (e.g., average movement or number of gestures per minute). The choice of transformations is guided by theory (what features might indicate the learning processes we care about?) and by practical considerations (what features can be extracted reliably? How can we make features from different modalities comparable?).

Feature engineering

This is the process of deriving higher-level metrics or indicators from raw data. In multimodal contexts, feature engineering is often done separately for each modality before combination, although some features can be cross-modal. Here are examples across modalities:

- From video, one can extract features such as body pose (angles of joints), facial expressions (smile frequency, gaze direction), motion energy (how much movement in each time segment), or proximity (if multiple people, how close they are). Many studies use computer vision algorithms or deep learning models to get these features. For instance, a pose estimation algorithm can turn video frames into a time-series of coordinates for arms and head; from that, features such as "hands raised or not" or "average posture openness" can be computed. Eye gaze direction can indicate attention; for example, a feature could be the percentage of time a student looked at the tutor or screen. Voice pitch can be extracted from audio as a feature indicating intonation or affect, and speech rate (words per minute) can indicate cognitive load or stress. These are examples of features that reduce raw signals into interpretable measures.

- From audio (speech), aside from transcribing words (textual features), paralinguistic features like pitch, volume (loudness), speaking rate, and pauses can be informative. One might compute the average pitch of a student's voice in each segment as a feature, or the fraction of time they were speaking vs silent (participation level). If transcripts are available, text analysis features include the number of words, vocabulary diversity, presence of certain keywords (e.g., "confused", "understand"), or even latent semantic analysis scores comparing the student's utterances to expert explanations. These textual features are essentially transformations of the raw dialog into quantitative measures.
- From physiological signals, typical features could be average values over a window, maximum and minimum values, frequency-domain features (such as power in certain frequency bands for EEG), or established biomarkers (for example, for heart rate or GSR, features such as peak frequency of skin conductance responses, or heart rate variability metrics). Often these signals are summarized into statistical features for each event or interval such as the mean heart rate during a task, or a binary feature showing whether the heart rate exceeded a threshold during a critical moment. Some studies also derive derivative measures such as the slope or change in a signal (e.g., increasing heart rate trend) as features.
- From clickstream/log data, features usually involve counts or frequencies: number of clicks, time spent on each page, number of times a student switched between resources, etc. Sequence features can also be extracted, such as the order of actions (although representing sequences as features might require techniques such as n-gram frequency or Markov models). In collaborative settings, logs might include chat messages or collaborative tool usage—features might then include how many messages a student sent, or network metrics such as how central they were in the communication network.

Crucially, feature engineering should be guided by the constructs of interest. If the goal is to detect engagement, one might design features such as frequency of on-task gaze (from video), volume of participation (from audio or logs), and physiological activation (from sensors). If the goal is to measure cognitive load, features might include pupil dilation (from eye-tracking video), pause length in speech, and self-report ratings. Ochoa et al. (2022) emphasize that low-level unimodal traces (features) often need to be combined into higher-level traces that correspond more directly to the constructs. For example, a single feature like eye gaze direction might not fully indicate joint attention, but combining multiple gaze features from different people can yield a better measure of a group's joint visual attention. Similarly, combining features of turn-taking and speech content can lead to detecting complex events such as idea uptake in conversation. These higher-level derived variables often involve both feature engineering and fusion together.

Normalization and scaling

Once features are extracted, it is important to normalize them to make them comparable and to avoid bias in analyses. Different modalities and features might have vastly different value ranges (e.g., a feature counting clicks could range in the tens, whereas a feature measuring time in seconds could be in the thousands). Common normalization techniques include min-max scaling (scaling values of each feature to a 0–1 range) and z-score standardization (subtracting the mean and dividing by the standard deviation for each feature). In an educational context, one might normalize per participant (especially for physiological measures, as absolute levels can vary greatly between individuals—e.g., one student's "high" heart rate might be another's "low"). By normalizing, we account for individual differences and focus on relative changes or patterns. For example, instead of raw skin conductance, one could use a normalized increase from that student's baseline. Normalization is also critical when combining features: if one feature is not normalized and has a large scale, it could dominate distance metrics or learning algorithm behavior, overshadowing other features.

Another aspect of normalization is making categorical or textual data into numeric form if necessary. For instance, if log data includes categorical labels (such as resource type = video/quiz/forum), one might one-hot encode these categories into binary features. If transcripts have been encoded with certain codes (say, dialog acts or regulatory strategies), those can be turned into feature counts (e.g., how many times a student showed a certain strategy).

Dimensionality reduction

With many modalities and features, the feature space can become very large. High-dimensional data can be problematic for both statistical analysis (risk of overfitting and multicollinearity) and for visualization or interpretation. Dimensionality reduction techniques aim to distill the feature set to the most important factors. A classic technique is Principal Component Analysis (PCA), which can reduce correlated features into a smaller set of uncorrelated components that explain most variance. For example, if one extracts 50 features from various sensors, PCA might reveal that much of the variance falls along a few dimensions (perhaps corresponding to overall arousal vs engagement, etc.). By projecting data into these principal components, one can work with fewer variables. Another approach is feature selection, which can be manual (choose features based on theory or data quality) or algorithmic (using methods such as stepwise selection or regularization techniques that shrink less important feature weights to zero). In machine learning contexts, embedded methods such as decision trees or LASSO regression can help to identify which features are most useful for predicting the outcome.

A more advanced technique is using representation learning—for instance, training an autoencoder (a type of neural network) on the multimodal data to learn a compressed representation. Such learned representations might capture complex combinations of the original features and can sometimes be more effective than manually engineered features. In recent AI applications, there is interest in learning a common embedding space where data from different modalities are mapped (through neural networks) into a shared vector space. This can be viewed as a form of dimensionality reduction combined with fusion: e.g., mapping text and video features into a joint 128-dimensional space where related text and video are close to each other. While powerful, these techniques typically require a lot of data and careful tuning, so simpler methods such as PCA or selecting a moderate number of features are more common in smaller-scale learning analytics studies.

Throughout the transformation phase, it is important to keep track of what each transformed feature represents. This is where a codebook or metadata for features is useful—documenting, for example, that *Feature1 = average speech volume during task*, *Feature2 = proportion of time looking at screen*, etc. This not only aids interpretation later but also helps to ensure that the transformation steps are transparent and reproducible.

By the end of this phase, the raw multimodal data has been converted into a structured dataset: typically a table of examples (which could be students, student-task instances, or time windows) by features, with all features numeric and on comparable scales. This dataset is ready for analysis—be it inferential statistical tests, training a machine learning model, or other analytic techniques. Before jumping into analysis, however, researchers should consider additional steps to ensure the data's integrity and usefulness for answering the research questions. This includes segmenting data into meaningful units, annotating ground truth or categories if necessary, and validating that the preprocessing did not introduce biases or errors. We address these considerations in the next section on preparing data for analysis.

PREPARING MULTIMODAL DATA FOR ANALYSIS

After cleaning, integrating, and transforming multimodal data, a few additional steps help to ensure that the data are ready for effective analysis or model training. These steps include segmentation (dividing data into meaningful episodes or units of analysis), annotation (labeling data with ground truth or categories, often for supervised learning or qualitative analysis), and validation workflows (checking that the preprocessed data are sound and that any derived measures are reliable). Preparing data for analysis also involves organizing the data (e.g., splitting into training and test sets if doing predictive modeling, or setting up comparisons if doing an experiment) and often performing some initial exploratory analysis to verify that the data behaves as expected. In this section, we outline how segmentation, annotation, and validation apply in multimodal learning analytics projects. We also illustrate these steps with two use case studies from recent research, highlighting how they dealt with multimodal data preparation in practice.

Segmentation and Annotation of Multimodal Data

Segmentation and annotation are foundational steps in MLPA, enabling the structuring of continuous data streams into meaningful units for analysis. Segmentation involves identifying temporal or event-based boundaries within modalities such as audio, video, or sensor data, while annotation assigns labels or codes based on predefined schemes or emergent patterns. These processes require careful alignment across modalities to preserve temporal coherence and ensure analytical validity. Whether manual, semi-automated, or automated, segmentation and annotation must be guided by clear theoretical and pedagogical objectives to support reliable interpretation of learning processes.

Segmentation

Segmentation refers to dividing a continuous stream of multimodal data into discrete units that make sense for the analysis. The appropriate segments depend on the context: common segmentation schemes in educational settings include by task or activity, by time windows, or by events of interest. For example, if an experiment consists of distinct phases (introduction, learning phase, assessment phase), the data might be segmented accordingly, so that each phase can be analyzed separately. Alternatively, one might segment by a fixed time interval (e.g., analyze data in one-minute slices throughout a lesson to see how engagement fluctuates). Another approach is event-based segmentation, where segments are defined by the occurrence of a certain event—for instance, the moment a student asks a question could define a segment around that question (such as 30 seconds before and after the question) to analyze what happened in response.

In multimodal data, segmentation must often be applied simultaneously across all modalities. If we decide to segment by time (say, five-minute intervals), we need to cut the video, audio, logs, etc. at those same boundaries. If segmenting by events, we should mark the timestamp of that event and then collect data from all modalities around that timestamp. Many multimodal analytics systems use timestamp markers in a master timeline to demarcate segments (for instance, using specialized software where one can annotate the video timeline with segment labels, which can then be applied to all synchronized data). When segments are not pre-defined by the study design, algorithms can assist: change-point detection algorithms can sometimes automatically find boundaries where the statistical properties of data change (e.g., a sudden change in speech rate or interaction pattern might signal a new phase in the activity).

Annotation

Annotation in this context means labeling the data with additional information that is not directly measured by sensors or logs. In learning analytics, annotation is often done by human coders who watch the video or read transcripts and identify occurrences of specific behaviors or constructs (such as "student confusion," "collaborative planning episode," or "off-task behavior"). These annotations provide *ground truth* for certain analysis—especially if training an AI model to automatically detect those behaviors or simply to count how often certain events occurred. Annotation is also critical for qualitative and mixed-methods analysis, where researchers might correlate those coded behaviors with sensor data patterns.

A typical annotation workflow might involve creating a coding scheme (categories of interest), training coders to reliably identify those categories in the multimodal data, and then using software tools (such as ELAN, NVivo, or ChronoViz) to tag the data. For instance, coders might go through a video and mark segments where a student exhibits self-regulated learning behaviors, or tag lines in a transcript that show socially shared regulation among group members. Each tag could then be associated with a time segment, which enables alignment with other modalities—e.g., linking an "off-task" tag with physiological data at that same moment to see if there is a drop in arousal.

One important consideration is inter-rater reliability when human annotation is used. Multiple coders should annotate some overlapping segments, and metrics such as Cohen's kappa are computed to ensure that the coding is consistent and reliable. This addresses the subjectivity in human labeling. In later analysis, these human-coded labels might serve as the target variable (e.g., to train a classifier that predicts "confused vs not confused" from sensor data) or simply as a means to filter data (analyzing sensor patterns only during segments labeled as "high engagement").

Sometimes annotation can be automated or semi-automated. For example, if we have a rule that whenever a student's score drops, we label it as a "struggle event", then this could be an automatic annotation based on log data. Or sentiment analysis on student discourse could automatically label utterances as positive/negative sentiment. These approaches can supplement human annotation, but they themselves often require validation.

Combining segmentation and annotation

These two often go hand-in-hand. One might segment the data into episodes and then annotate each episode with a label (e.g., each five-minute segment of a collaborative session is rated for "degree of collaboration"). Conversely, one might annotate fine-grained events and then define segments around them. In both cases, the goal is to enrich the raw data with meaningful units and labels that align with research questions.

For example, in a classroom study one could segment each lesson by pedagogical stages (lecture, group work, individual practice) and annotate instances of student questions or teacher feedback. Then one could compare physiological or engagement metrics across those segments or aligned with those annotations. In a lab study, one might segment by each problem a student solved and annotate whether they solved it correctly or not; this allows the multimodal data to be tied to performance outcomes on each problem.

It is important to ensure that segments are comparable in length or context if they will be aggregated. If segments vary widely in length, some normalization (such as features per minute) might be needed when comparing them. Similarly, annotation categories should be well defined and ideally mutually exclusive (unless using a multi-label scheme). Sometimes hierarchical annotation is used (e.g., labeling broad phases and also specific events within phases).

As a final note, segmentation and annotation not only prepare data for analysis—they *are* often part of the analysis. Particularly in exploratory phases, researchers use segmentation and coding to discover patterns, which then informs more automated analysis later. In all cases, these steps serve to link the low-level data traces to higher-level interpretations of learning processes.

Validation and Quality Assurance in Preprocessing

The culmination of preprocessing is ensuring that the data are valid, consistent, and suitable for the intended analyses. *Validation* in this context has multiple facets:

- **Validation of integration and alignment**: We need to confirm that our synchronization and fusion steps were successful. This might involve spot-checking the data: for example, pick a moment in the session and verify that at time T, the video, audio, and log data all reflect the same event (say, the student answered a question—the video shows them writing, the audio has them saying "Done", and the log records a submission). If any misalignment is found, adjustments are needed. Visualization is a powerful tool here: researchers often create timeline plots where events from different modalities are plotted together. For instance, one could overlay a student's heart rate curve with markers of when they clicked "hint" in the software. If those markers appear shifted relative to known points of high heart rate, it might signal a timing mis-sync. By verifying alignment on a few examples (especially at the start and end of sessions to catch any drift), one gains confidence that all data streams are properly locked in step.
- **Validation of data consistency and integrity**: After cleaning, one should confirm that no obvious data corruption occurred. For example, check basic statistics of each feature to see if they are in plausible ranges (no negative times, no sensor values beyond physical limits, etc.). If certain values were imputed, verify that they do not create anomalies (such as a perfectly constant heart rate for five minutes might indicate an imputation fill that could distort variance). Consistency checks also include ensuring that every participant or every session has data for each modality (unless intentionally missing and accounted for). If some participants have missing modalities, a decision should be made and documented (e.g., "Participant 12's EEG data was discarded due to noise, but other data kept"—thus any analysis on EEG will exclude P12).
- **Triangulation and cross-validation of signals**: In multimodal data, an interesting form of validation is cross-checking one modality against another. For example, if the data suggest that a student had high engagement according to a sensor, do we see corroborating evidence in another modality (such as attentive behavior on video)? While this is not always feasible to do in every instance, doing a small qualitative pass—looking at a few cases in detail—can validate that the quantitative features extracted truly represent what we think. This is akin to establishing *construct validity* of features. For instance, if we created a feature "frustration level (high/low) from speech tone," we could validate it by listening to a sample of audio to see if the times labeled as "high frustration" by our algorithm do indeed sound frustrated. Such sanity checks help avoid situations where a feature is miscomputed. For example, a speech analysis system might incorrectly interpret microphone noise as "frustration." Researchers sometimes involve domain experts or participants themselves to verify whether the signals reflect reality, for example by asking participants to confirm

whether the interpretations match their experiences (a process often called member checking) or by comparing sensor-based measures with self-reports).

- **Reliability of derived measures**: If the preprocessing yielded some key measures (e.g., a computed score for each student's level of collaboration based on multiple indicators), checking the reliability of those measures is crucial. This could involve statistical reliability (if it is an index combining multiple items, check internal consistency) or test-retest reliability (do we get similar values in segments that should be similar?). Ochoa et al. (2022) note that because multimodal detection of behaviors has more uncertainty, *the reliability of automatic detection should be assessed similarly to inter-rater reliability for human coding*. In practice, if an automated algorithm identifies ten instances of "mind wandering" in the data, one might take a subset and have human coders verify how many of those are true mind wandering. If the "precision" is low, the measure might not be trustworthy without further refinement. Thus, validation can also mean *comparing automated measurements to human-annotated ground truth*. For example, if posture and gaze were used to classify engagement, one could validate the classifier's output against engagement ratings from observers or from student self-reports.
- **Statistical validation (if applicable)**: If the next step is statistical hypothesis testing, the data might be validated by checking assumptions (normality, homogeneity, etc.). For instance, if we plan to run an ANOVA on engagement levels across conditions, we might check that our engagement metric roughly follows a normal distribution or apply a transformation if it does not. Or if building a regression model, we check for multicollinearity among features (perhaps using variance inflation factor)—if two features are extremely correlated, one might be dropped or combined. These steps ensure that the analysis results will be valid and interpretable.
- **Ethical and privacy check**: Although not always discussed as part of preprocessing, in education and learning analytics it is important to validate that data handling complied with privacy and ethical standards. For example, ensuring that any personally identifiable information is removed or coded (such as replacing student names with IDs), and that video frames or audio that are not allowed (owing to consent issues) are excluded. Before releasing or sharing a processed dataset, one must confirm that all necessary anonymization has been done in the preprocessing phase.
- Finally, a **documentation** step underpins validation: keeping detailed notes of all preprocessing decisions, parameters used for filtering, alignment adjustments made, and any data excluded. This documentation is invaluable for reproducing the study and for others to understand the

prepared dataset. Some projects produce a data preprocessing report or appendix describing these steps in detail.

With the data segmented, annotated, validated, and fully prepared, it is now ready to be analyzed to address research questions—whether through AI models (e.g., training a model to predict learning outcomes from multimodal features) or through human interpretation (e.g., identifying patterns of behavior in synchronized data visualizations). The next part of this chapter presents two case studies that exemplify many of the concepts discussed so far, illustrating how actual researchers dealt with multimodal data preprocessing in educational AI contexts.

CASE STUDIES FOR AI IN PREPROCESSING MULTIMODAL LEARNING PROCESS DATA FOR MLPA

Case Study: Human-AI Collaboration in Preprocessing Multimodal Data for Socially Shared Regulation of Learning

In their 2023 study, Järvelä, Nguyen, and Hadwin explored the integration of human and artificial intelligence (AI) to enhance socially shared regulation of learning (SSRL) in collaborative settings. The researchers introduced the Human–AI Shared Regulation in Learning (HASRL) model, which leverages multimodal data to identify and respond to regulatory triggers during group learning activities.

Data collection and preprocessing

The study involved collecting a range of multimodal data streams, including:

- **Video recordings** to capture facial expressions and body language.
- **Audio recordings** to analyze speech patterns and verbal interactions.
- **Physiological measures**, such as electrodermal activity (EDA), to monitor emotional arousal.
- **Log data** from digital learning platforms to track user interactions.

Preprocessing these diverse data types required synchronizing temporal data, cleaning noise from physiological signals, and segmenting video and audio recordings into analyzable units. The researchers employed AI techniques to automate parts of this preprocessing, such as using machine learning algorithms to detect patterns indicative of regulatory triggers.

The study also illustrates how human–AI collaboration can be applied to the transcription and segmentation of verbal data, where AI tools support the initial processing while human researchers refine and validate the outputs for analysis (as demonstrated in Figure 5.1).

Implementation and outcomes

By applying the HASRL model, the study demonstrated how AI could assist in identifying moments when learners might benefit from regulatory support. For instance, sudden changes in EDA combined with specific verbal cues could signal a need for intervention. The AI system could then prompt learners with tailored feedback or strategies to enhance their collaborative regulation processes.

Implications for practice

This case study highlights the potential of combining human insight with AI capabilities to preprocess and analyze multimodal learning data effectively. Such collaboration enables the timely identification of regulatory needs within learning groups, allowing for interventions that support and enhance SSRL. The approach highlights the importance of interdisciplinary efforts in developing tools that can adapt to the complex dynamics of collaborative learning environments.

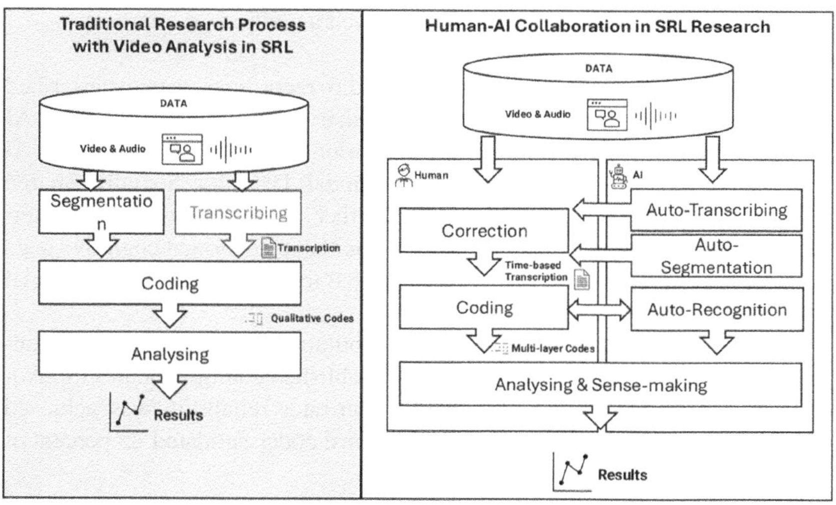

Source: Järvelä, Nguyen, and Hadwin, 2023.

Figure 5.1 Example of human–AI collaboration process in SSRL research

Use Case: Examining the Cognitive and Socioemotional Interactions of Human-AI Collaborative Learning in Mixed Reality

This case study draws on Belle Dang et al. (2025)'s empirical investigation of cognitive and socioemotional interactions between learners and an embodied Generative AI agent, KAI, in a mixed reality (MR) learning environment. The study demonstrates an advanced preprocessing workflow to analyze multimodal data collected from immersive human-AI collaborative learning scenarios.

Data collection and environment

Data were collected from 26 higher education students engaged in structured dialog tasks with an embodied Generative AI agent using Meta Quest 3's passthrough MR mode. The environment integrated digital and physical space, enabling spatially anchored interactions and naturalistic communication using gestures and speech (Nguyen et al., 2025). Multimodal data sources included: (1) first- and third-person video recordings; (2) audio from wireless microphones; (3) system interaction logs; and (4) learner questionnaires on Generative AI partner perception.

Preprocessing pipeline

The preprocessing of multimodal data followed a multi-stage approach:

- **Transcription and segmentation:** Audio recordings were transcribed and segmented into meaningful discourse units through a human–AI collaboration approach (similar to the prior Case Study *on* "Human-AI Collaboration in Preprocessing Multimodal Data for Socially Shared Regulation of Learning"). Each unit, either a complete or partial utterance, was manually coded using a scheme that categorized cognitive (e.g., reasoning, questioning) and socioemotional (e.g., personal feelings, social pleasantries) dimensions of interaction.
- **Coding (labelling) and validation:** Quantitative content analysis was conducted on 1,317 discourse units using established coding schemes (Shukor et al., 2014; Kauffeld et al., 2018). Inter-rater reliability was achieved through multiple coding rounds, and a third coder validated 25 percent of the dataset to ensure consistency.
- **Sequence alignment and clustering:** Learner–Generative AI interaction sequences were modeled using the optimal matching algorithm and clustered via Ward's method. This step identified recurring interactional patterns across sessions.

Then the preprocessed data were analyzed using Ordered Network Analysis (ONA), which allowed the researchers to visualize the temporal flow and structural patterns of cognitive and socioemotional interactions, highlighting how different types of exchanges co-occur and unfold over time within the learner–Generative AI dialog.

Insights and contribution

This case exemplifies how rich multimodal datasets in MR environments can be systematically preprocessed and analyzed to reveal nuanced human–AI collaboration patterns. It demonstrates the utility of combining manual annotation, sequence modeling, and network visualization to unpack complex interaction dynamics. The preprocessing enabled the identification of two distinct interaction types, AI-Supported Exploratory Questioning and Learner-Initiated Inquiry, each with unique implications for socioemotional and cognitive engagement.

PART III

AI methods for analyzing multimodal data on learning processes

6. Classical machine learning modeling

INTRODUCTION TO MACHINE LEARNING

Machine learning (ML) plays a central role in Multimodal Learning Analytics (MMLA) and especially in multimodal learning process analytics (MLPA), where it enables systems to automatically analyze, interpret, and make sense of complex data from multiple sources in educational settings. In this chapter, we will present how one can build and evaluate basic ML pipelines for multimodal data. We will also present three different case studies from different multimodal contexts to showcase the methods.

ML models can automatically discover patterns in complex, multimodal datasets—something that humans would struggle to do at scale. For example, classical ML algorithms, such as support vector machines, decision trees, and random forests, have been used to classify learners' engagement levels based on features extracted from eye-tracking, keystroke, and physiological data (e.g., Huang et al., 2020; Ifenthaler & Widanapathirana, 2014). Such efforts reduce the need for manual annotation and feature engineering, uncover subtle or non-obvious relationships between multimodal signals and learning outcomes, and enable data-driven understanding of the learning process that complements theoretical models, such as self-regulated and co-regulated learning (Cukurova, 2024; Järvelä, Nguyen, & Hadwin, 2023; Järvelä, Nguyen, & Molenaar, 2023).

ML provides the methods to combine diverse data types into a unified model that understands how different signals interact (Baltrušaitis et al., 2019). There are three different fusion types that we can explore (as explained in more detail in Chapter 5), including: early fusion: merge raw features (e.g., concatenate text embeddings and audio features); late fusion: make separate predictions from each modality, then combine them; and hybrid fusion: combine intermediate representations, often using attention mechanisms (this is something we will talk about in Chapter 7). In recent works, research has fused different data modalities for prediction, for example, by combining raw signals from video, audio, and physiological data to predict self-regulated learning behaviors (Nguyen et al., 2021; Nguyen, Järvelä, et al., 2022). Such efforts are important, because learning is complex and cannot be captured by a single modality

(Azevedo & Gašević, 2019). Furthermore, fused models lead to richer and more accurate interpretations of learner behavior by capturing complementary information across modalities (D'Mello et al., 2022).

ML models can be deployed in real-time environments to monitor and respond to learner behavior as it happens. Such feedback provides timely interventions that help learners to stay on track (Pardo et al., 2019) and enable adaptive learning systems that adjust pace, difficulty, or content based on the learner's state (Khosravi et al., 2022). In recent MMLA developments, there have been several contributions in this area. For example, Worsley and Blikstein (2018) used sensor data to identify patterns of physical interaction with learning materials in maker-based environments, enabling adaptive prompts during construction tasks.

ML models can also be used to predict future outcomes, such as task-based performance, learning gains, or dynamic learning processes (e.g., attention, cognitive load, frustration, boredom, confusion). Such predictive modeling enables the development of proactive feedback tools that respond before performance drops. For example, Moreno-Marcos et al. (2020) analyzed various data streams to predict learners' performance in Massive Open Online Courses (MOOCs), including previous grades, forum activity, exercise-related variables, clickstream data, course duration, assignment types, data collection procedures, and exam question formats. They found that exercise-related variables were the most effective predictors, while forum activity variables were less useful. Clickstream data served as acceptable predictors when exercise data was unavailable but did not enhance prediction accuracy when exercise data was present.

ML models can further extract key trends and behavioral patterns, as well as generate visualizations from raw multimodal data, turning it into actionable insights for teachers. For example, a dashboard might display: which students frequently show confusion during instruction, which topics are associated with increased frustration, and correlations between physiological signals and test performance. These insights can be drawn from webcam feeds, audio logs, and interaction data. Such dashboards are known to help teachers to personalize their instruction, promote reflective teaching based on real-time evidence, and support early identification of students needing targeted interventions (Ramaswami et al., 2023).

Based on the aforementioned benefits of using ML to analyze the multimodal data, we can support the claim that ML is a useful tool to be used in the current MLPA landscape. In this chapter, we will focus on classical ML approaches to predict/forecast the learning outcomes/processes. In the next chapter, we will focus on the deep learning methods to do the same. The remainder of the chapter is organized as follows. The next section provides the details of feature engineering, model development, evaluation metrics, and how to present and discuss results. The final section provides three case studies from individual debugging, adaptive assessment, and collaborative debugging. In all three case studies we will show prediction of one performance variable and forecasting of one learning process captured by one of the multimodal data sources.

BUILDING AND EVALUATING PREDICTIVE MACHINE LEARNING MODELS FOR MULTIMODAL LEARNING PROCESS ANALYTICS

Feature Engineering

A feature is an individual measurable property or characteristic of a phenomenon being observed. In ML, features are the inputs that models use to learn patterns and make predictions. Feature engineering involves: selecting relevant variables (features) from the raw data; transforming data into useful formats (e.g., scaling, encoding); creating new features that better represent the underlying patterns; and reducing noise and redundancy. It can be manual (domain-expert designed) or automated (using tools such as FeatureTools or deep learning embeddings). Feature engineering is important for several reasons. For example, one of the most direct benefits of feature engineering is the enhancement of model performance. Raw data often lack the structure and clarity that algorithms need to identify patterns. By extracting or creating features that highlight the most relevant information (e.g., time-on-task, frequency of interaction, sentiment score), models can learn more effectively. Well-engineered features can lead to higher accuracy, precision, and recall, particularly in complex domains like education. Algorithms such as gradient descent benefit from normalized and scaled features, which help models to converge more quickly. This makes training not only faster but also more stable. Feature engineering can reduce the dimensionality of the data by eliminating irrelevant or redundant information, further improving computational efficiency. In many domains, especially those involving human behavior, such as education or healthcare, transparency and explainability are critical. Manually engineered features such as "number of incorrect answers before seeking help" or "average delay between quiz attempts" provide insights that are easy to understand and explain to stakeholders. This interpretability can build trust and support data-driven decision-making. This type of interpretability becomes more important in education than in any other field because the feedback, which might be generated from the outcomes of the ML pipelines, must be actionable. Otherwise, such feedback is useless for the learners and/or teachers. Real-world data are often messy, with missing values or noise. Feature engineering allows for data cleaning and imputation strategies that enhance robustness. It can smooth out irregularities, filter noise, and derive proxy variables when direct measurement is not available. Finally, in settings such as multimodal learning analytics, data come from multiple sources (e.g., gaze, video, audio, text). Feature engineering is crucial to unify these inputs into a coherent representation that a ML model can understand and use effectively. Each of these multimodal data sources requires a different type of preprocessing and feature engineering steps. The following Tables 6.1 and 6.2 summarize the features/measurements that can be computed from the different data sources.

Table 6.1 Example interpretation of EEG measurement

EEG measurement	Interpretation
Lower Alpha wave power (8–9 Hz)	Relaxed, but not drowsy
Upper Alpha wave power (10–12 Hz)	Normal, relaxed yet focused
Lower Beta wave power (13–17 Hz)	Normal, relaxed yet focused
Upper Beta wave power (18–30 Hz)	Active thinking, alertness
Gamma wave power (more than 30 Hz)	Higher mental activity
Theta wave power (4–7 Hz)	Idling, inefficiency, related to ADHD
Fractal dimensions	Long-term memory
Bursts in Alpha wave	Performance
Alpha magnitude	Workload
Decreasing Alpha and Theta band power	Cognitive load
Phase coupling of Theta and Gamma	Short-term memory
Alpha band power	Attention
Wavelet coefficients of gamma band	Emotional intensity
Theta band power	Memory load
Increasing Theta and decreasing Alpha	Increasing performance
Gamma-band activity	Short-term memory load
Decreasing Theta and increasing Alpha	Working memory

Table 6.2 Example interpretation of eye-tracking measurement

Eye-tracking measurement	Interpretation
AOI hit AOI = Areas of interest that are defined by the researcher.	How much attention is paid to the different parts of the visual field, such as faces, screen, Lego kit, robot, keyboard
AOI transition	Attention shift proportions
AOI revisit on the screen	Failure of memory Need for confirmation
Local or global saccades (threshold on the saccade length)	Focal or ambient cognitive processing Focal = short saccades and long fixations Ambient = long saccades and short fixations
Short fixations on a specific part	Anticipation of finding information
Number of saccades per unit time	Decreasing task difficulty Increasing mental workload Increasing arousal
Number of blinks per second	Time on task, mental workload, fatigue
Blink duration	Drowsiness, mental workload
Number of fixations per second	Decreasing search efficiency Expertise based on the task (e.g., high for pilots low for chess and tennis players) Difficulty in interpretation
Fixation duration	Attention
Skewness of fixation duration histogram	Cognitive processing
Pupil diameter	Increased emotions, anticipation, mental workload Decreased drowsiness, fatigue
Saccadic velocity	High cognitive load, task difficulty, memory load
Scanpath velocity = number of forward saccades/number of backward saccades	Amount of information processing
Saccade duration	Task difficulty Decrease in information processing
Saccade velocity	Low arousal and sleepiness
Saccade velocity skewness	Anticipation
Cross-recurrence (probability of looking at the same place at the same time)	Increases during dialog episodes Also increases during certain dialog types and verbal and deictic references Correlates with collaboration quality and outcome

Eye-tracking measurement	**Interpretation**

Scanpath shape similarity
• Overall shape
  • Same shape but different scale
  • Similar subparts
	Collaborative outcome

Gaze similarity	Similar to cross recurrence but temporal measurement
Mean and standard deviation (SD), pupil diameter, number of long fixations, saccade length.	Cognitive load

Table 6.3 presents example interpretations of wristband sensor measures.

We can compute the action units (AUs) from the faces of the students:

Table 6.3 Example interpretation of wristband measures

Wristband measures	**Interpretation or predicted variable**
EDA peak height EDA peak rate EDA slope	Cognitive load
BVP power spectrum low/high ratio BVP amplitude # EDA responses detected EDA mean EDA rising time TEMP slope	Stress
TEMP (mean, SD, kurtosis, skewness) EDA peaks HR variability (mean, SD, kurtosis, skewness)	Emotional stress
EDA change detection measures	Acute stress cycle (normal, aroused, stressed, relaxed)
HR recovery rate changes (duration and counts)	Chronic stress

Note: Wristband measures are mostly used in prediction, so we lack the measures that are directly interpreted: HR = heart rate; EDA = electrodermal activation; BVP = blood volume pressure; TEMP = skin temperature.

Once we have these AUs, then we can compute the different emotions as the combination of these AUs, for example. Here is the list for how these are mapped to the numbers:

Happiness: AU6, AU10

Sadness: AU1, AU4, AU15

Surprise: AU1, AU2, AU5, AU26

Fear: AU1, AU2, AU4, AU5, AU7, AU20, AU26

Anger: AU4, AU5, AU7, AU23

Disgust: AU9, AU15

Contempt: AU12, AU14

Second, *emotional profile* (entropy of AUs, stability of emotions, emotional similarity between the peers) of the students could be computed and Figure 6.1 illustrates examples of facial regions, including the eyes, mouth, and lower face, displaying different emotional expressions.

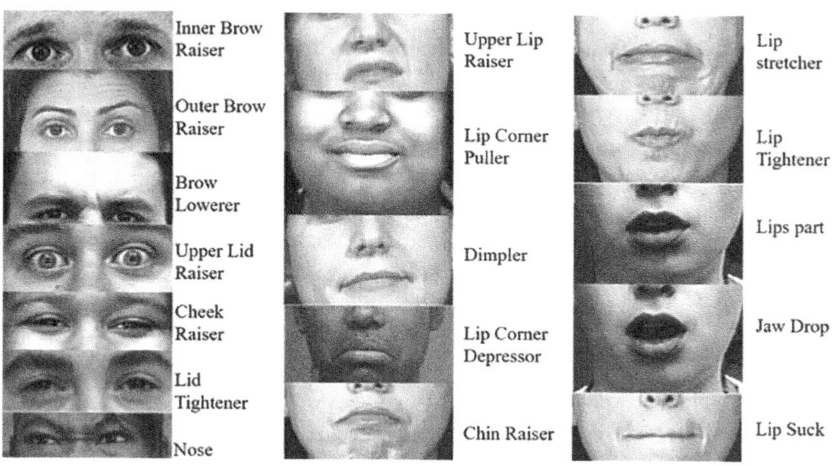

Figure 6.1 *Examples of facial regions (eyes, mouth, and lower face) displaying different emotional expressions*

Model Development

In this section, we will critique, compare, and contrast some of the most common classical ML algorithms. For the purpose of this chapter, we will restrict ourselves to supervised ML algorithms because in many cases we know the classes/categories for the learning outcomes or, in terms of forecasting, we know the ground truth from the data itself.

Logistic regressions (binary classification, used to predict for example, performance from facial data)

Logistic regression is a supervised learning algorithm used for classification tasks, especially binary classification (e.g., pass/fail, engaged/disengaged). Unlike linear regression, which predicts continuous values, logistic regression predicts probabilities and maps them to two or more categories using a sigmoid function. For binary outcomes:

$$P(Y = 1|X) = \frac{1}{1 + e^{-(\beta_0 + \beta_1 X_1 + \beta_2 X_2 \_ .... + + \beta_n X_n)}}$$

Y is the predicted class (e.g., high or low performance), X_1 ,...,X_n are input features (e.g., cognitive load, login frequency, quiz scores), βi are learned coefficients.

There are certain advantages of using logistic models. Coefficients will inform us about how each feature affects the outcome, which is useful for educators and decision-makers. These models require little computational power, making them ideal for early prototypes or real-time analytics. Logistic regressions work for simple yes/no predictions and can be extended to multiple categories. They provide probabilities, allowing for risk-based interventions (e.g., students with 80 percent chance of failing the given task based on their multimodal data). Finally, they perform well when a linear relationship exists between inputs and log-odds of the outcome. However, there are certain drawbacks as well. For example, logistic regressions assume a linear relationship between features and log-odds, which might not hold in complex learning behaviors. They cannot capture non-linear patterns or interactions as effectively as tree-based models or neural networks. These models require careful preprocessing (e.g., scaling, handling multicollinearity) and might struggle when class distributions are skewed (e.g., very few students who fail the task). Finally, logistic regressions do not natively handle image, audio, or sequential features and require separate processing and flattening. It is important that we evaluate the ML task carefully before using this algorithm. The typical cases when the logistic regression can be used are: when we need a simple, explainable model; the data are structured and labelled; the prediction task is binary and datasets are small; or we want a baseline for benchmarking. However, we should avoid it when we have to use complex models or we have many classes or imbalanced data.

Support Vector Machines (SVM, high dimensional classification)

A Support Vector Machine (SVM) is a supervised ML algorithm used for classification and regression tasks. SVMs work by finding the best boundary (hyperplane) that separates data points of different classes with the maximum margin. At its core, a SVM finds the optimal hyperplane that separates two classes of data with the maximum margin. There are two separate cases with SVMs. The first one is the linear case, where we have the dataset:

$$\{(x_1, y_1), (x_2, y_2), \ldots, (x_n, y_n),\}$$

Where $x_i \in R^d$ is a feature vector (e.g., gaze time, mouse clicks, emotion scores), and $y_i \in \{-1, +1\}$ is the class label (e.g., disengaged = -1, engaged = +1). The goal is to find a hyperplane defined as:

$$w \cdot x + b = 0$$

Where w is the weight vector and b is the bias. We want to maximize the margin, i.e., the distance between the hyperplane and the closest data points from each class (called support vectors). This leads to the optimization problem:

Minimize $\frac{1}{2}\left\|w^2\right\|$, subject to:

$$y_i\left(w.x_i + b\right) \geq 1 \forall i$$

However, when the data are not linearly separable (common in education datasets), SVMs use a kernel function $K(x_i, x_j)$ to map data into a higher-dimensional space. Instead of computing w·x, we compute:

$$K\left(x_i, x_j\right) = \phi\left(x_i\right).\phi\left(x_j\right)$$

The most popular kernels are as follows:

Linear kernel: $K\left(x, x'\right) = x^T x'$

Polynomial kernel: $K\left(x, x'\right) = \left(x^T x' + c\right)^d$

RBF (Gaussian): $K\left(x, x'\right) = \exp\left(-\gamma \left\|x - x'\right\|^2\right)$

There are certain clear advantages of using SVMs in educational domains. SVMs work well when the number of features is large (e.g., multimodal data). They are also relatively robust to overfitting, particularly when appropriate kernel functions are used to model complex, non-linear relationships and regularization parameters are applied to control model complexity. SVMs can handle complex boundaries using non-linear kernels like RBF or polynomial kernels. They provide good performance without massive data, which, e.g., deep learning would require. Finally, they are designed to maximize the separation between classes. However, there are some disadvantages as well. For example, when complex kernels are used, the models become less explainable. Training time also increases as the dataset size and complexity grow. SVMs are inherently designed for binary classification, meaning they distinguish between two classes; therefore, multiclass problems, where the model must classify instances into more than two categories, require techniques such as one-versus-all or one-versus-one training.

Decision trees/random forests (interpretable models, ensemble learning)
A decision tree is a supervised ML algorithm used for classification and regression tasks. It models decisions and their possible consequences as a tree-like structure of nodes consisting of: a root node: the first feature split (e.g., "Time on Task > 15 min?"); decision nodes: Internal nodes that test features (e.g., "Quiz Score > 70?"); and leaves: final predictions or outcomes (e.g., "Likely to Pass," "Needs Help"). Educational datasets often involve complex, non-linear relationships and require explainable decisions. Decision trees are well suited for predicting student success/failure, classifying engagement levels, and recommending personalized interventions. The biggest advantage of decision trees is their interpretability, as they are easy to visualize and understand. They can handle mixed data types by working with numerical and categorical data alike. There is also no requirement of feature scaling (e.g., normalization or standardization). Decision trees can capture non-linear relationships and learn complex rules from feature interactions. However, there are also certain disadvantages. For example, they are prone to overfitting, as they can model noise in small or biased datasets. Furthermore they are often unstable, as small data changes can lead to very different trees. Single trees can be less accurate than ensemble methods, and this is why we recommend using a random forest.

A random forest is an ensemble ML algorithm that builds multiple decision trees and combines their results to make a more accurate and stable prediction. It works for both classification (e.g., student passed/failed) and regression (e.g., predicting final grade) tasks. The key characteristics of random forests include the following: bagging (bootstrap aggregating): each tree is trained on a random subset of the data; random feature selection: each split considers only a random subset of features; voting/averaging: final prediction is made by majority vote (classification) or average (regression). Random forests reduce overfitting common in single decision trees, making them reliable for predicting outcomes like task-based performance. They can seamlessly work with diverse inputs like log data, text scores, and gaze duration. These can also help educators to understand which factors (e.g., attendance, emotion, interaction) most affect outcomes. However, although better than deep learning, it is harder to explain decisions than a single decision tree or logistic regression—a challenge when explaining decisions to educators or stakeholders. Random forests can be computationally expensive at prediction time, especially in real-time adaptive learning systems. These are not good to handle time series data, unless there has been a feature engineering phase before. Random forests strike an excellent balance between performance and usability, especially in educational settings where data are complex, incomplete, and rich in behavior. While not always the most interpretable or fastest, they remain a powerful and reliable baseline for educational data mining and learning analytics.

Gradient boosted trees (XGBoost)

XGBoost is a highly efficient and flexible implementation of gradient boosting, designed for speed and performance. Below, we provide a detailed mathematical explanation of the key components of XGBoost.

Objective function: The objective function in XGBoost consists of two parts: the loss function (which measures how well the model is performing) and the regularization term (which controls the complexity of the model):

$$\mathcal{L}(\phi) = \Sigma_{i=1}^{n} L\left(y_i, \hat{y}_i\right) + \Sigma_{k=1}^{K} \Omega\left(f_k\right)$$

L is the loss function (e.g., mean squared error for regression, logistic loss for classification). $\Omega(f_k)$ is the regularization term for tree k.

Regularization term: The regularization term Ω controls the complexity of the model to avoid overfitting. For a tree f_k, the regularization term is defined as:

$$\Omega\left(f_k\right) = \gamma T + \frac{1}{2} \lambda \Sigma_{j=1}^{T} w_j^2$$

y is the parameter that penalizes the number of leaves *T* in the tree.

λ is the parameter that penalizes the *L*2 norm of the leaf weights w_j.

Additive training: XGBoost builds trees in an additive manner. For the tth tree, the prediction is updated as follows:

$$\hat{y}_i^{(t)} = \hat{y}_i^{(t-1)} + f_t\left(x_i\right)$$

Loss function and Taylor expansion: To optimize the objective function, XGBoost uses a second-order Taylor expansion of the loss function. This expansion approximates the loss function around the current predictions.

Let ŷ_i^((t-1)) be the prediction at the $(t-1)$th iteration, then the loss can be approximated as:

$$\mathcal{L}^{(t)} \approx \sum_{i=1}^{n}\left[l\left(y_i,\hat{y}_i^{(t-1)}\right)+g_i f_t\left(x_i\right)+\frac{1}{2}h_i f_t\left(x_i\right)^2\right]+\Omega\left(f_t\right)$$

Where g is the first order derivative (gradient) and h is the second order derivative (Hessian):

$$g_i=\frac{\partial l\left(y_i,\hat{y}_i^{(t-1)}\right)}{\partial \hat{y}_i^{(t-1)}}$$

$$h_i=\frac{\partial^2 l\left(y_i,\hat{y}_i^{(t-1)}\right)}{\partial \hat{y}_i^{(t-1)^2}}$$

Tree structure: XGBoost constructs the decision tree by selecting the split that maximizes the gain. The gain is calculated as the reduction in the loss function, which involves the gradients and Hessians. For a split that divides the data into left and right branches, the gain is:

$$\text{Gain}=\frac{1}{2}\left[\frac{G_L^2}{H_L+\lambda}+\frac{G_R^2}{H_R+\lambda}-\frac{\left(G_L+G_R\right)^2}{H_L+H_R+\lambda}\right]-\gamma$$

Where *GL* and *GR* are the sums of gradients for the left and right branches, *HL* and *HR* are the sums of Hessians for the left and right branches.

Pruning: XGBoost performs pruning after the tree is constructed. It removes nodes that do not provide a positive gain. This is controlled by the γ parameter in the regularization term.

Shrinkage and feature sampling: After each step, the model's contribution is scaled by a factor η (learning rate):

$$\hat{y}_i^{(t)}=\hat{y}_i^{(t-1)}+\eta f_t\left(x_i\right)$$

Similar to random forests, XGBoost can use column (feature) subsampling to prevent overfitting and reduce computation.

Approximate tree learning: For efficiency, XGBoost can use an approximate algorithm for finding the best split. It uses quantile sketches to maintain weighted quantiles of feature distributions, which allows for efficient split finding.

There are certain advantages of XGBoost. It consistently performs well on a wide range of problems. It is often the go-to model in ML competitions (e.g., Kaggle) because of its ability to capture complex relationships. Unlike basic gradient boosting, XGBoost includes L1 (Lasso) and L2 (Ridge) regularization in its objective function. This helps to reduce overfitting, which is especially important in small educational datasets. XGBoost can learn the best way to handle missing values during training, which is very useful for real-world educational data where student logs might be incomplete, or some sensor might have momentary failure. It implements parallelized training (tree building) and supports out-of-core computation for large datasets (e.g., involving electroencephalograms [EEG] and eye-tracking that are high-frequency sensor data). However, there are some disadvantages of XGBoost. For example, the training times can be high with large datasets. Furthermore, there are many hyperparameters that need to be tuned, because poor tuning can lead to underfitting or overfitting. XGBoost can also be memory-intensive, especially with deep trees and large datasets.

Gradient boosted trees (LightGBM)

LightGBM is a gradient boosting framework that builds models in a sequential manner using decision trees. At each step, it fits a new tree to the gradient of the loss function with respect to the current model's predictions. There are two facts that make LightGBM unique: histogram-based splitting and leaf-wise (best-first) tree growth. With LightGBM, we aim to minimize the loss function:

$$\mathcal{L} = \sum_{i=1}^{n} l\left(y_i, \hat{y}_i\right) + \Omega\left(f\right)$$

Where $l(y_i, \hat{y}_i)$ is loss function (e.g., MSE for regression, log-loss for classification), $\hat{y}_i$ is the prediction for the ith sample, and $\Omega(f)$ is the regularization term. Furthermore, at iteration t, we add a new function $f_t(x)$ to improve prediction:

$$\hat{y}_i^{(t)} = \hat{y}_i^{(t-1)} + f_t\left(x_i\right)$$

We want to find $f_t(x)$ that minimizes the loss:

$$\mathcal{L}^{(t)} = \sum_{i=1}^{n} \left[l\left(y_i, \hat{y}_i^{(t-1)} \right) + g_i f_t\left(x_i\right) + \frac{1}{2} h_i f_t\left(x_i\right)^2 \right] + \Omega\left(f_t\right)$$

Where g and h are the first and second order gradients, respectively:

$$g_i = \frac{\partial l\left(y_i, \hat{y}_i\right)}{\partial \hat{y}_i}$$

$$h_i = \frac{\partial^2 l\left(y_i, \hat{y}_i\right)}{\partial \hat{y}_i^2}$$

LightGBM discretizes continuous values into k bins, reducing complexity from $O(n \log n)$ to $O(n)$ and saving memory. Let x be a continuous feature. LightGBM buckets values into fixed-width bins:

$$Bin_j = \{x_i | lower_j \leq x_j < upper_j\}$$

Instead of scanning all values to find split points, LightGBM scans the histograms.

Instead of growing trees level by level (like XGBoost), LightGBM grows them leaf by leaf. It chooses the leaf with the maximum loss reduction at each step. This often leads to deeper trees and better performance. The split gain is computed as:

$$\text{Gain} = \frac{1}{2}\left[\frac{G_L^2}{H_L + \lambda} + \frac{G_R^2}{H_R + \lambda} - \frac{\left(G_L + G_R\right)^2}{H_L + H_R + \lambda}\right] - \gamma$$

Where GL, GR are the sum of gradients for left and right splits, HL, HR are the sum of Hessians (second-order) for each split, λ is the $L2$ regularization term, and γ is the complexity penalty (min_split_gain).

There are certain advantages of LightGBM. It uses histogram-based learning and leaf-wise growth to train much more rapidly than traditional gradient boosting methods. This is useful for large datasets. Leaf-wise growth allows it to reduce loss more aggressively than level-wise methods (e.g., XGBoost). It bins continuous features into discrete values, reducing memory consumption. LightGBM automatically learns optimal ways to handle missing data during training. As with all the algorithms. there are some disadvantages of LightGBM. Leaf-wise tree growth can create deep trees that overfit if they are not controlled via hyperparameters. The performance of LightGBM depends greatly on tuning parameters such as the learning rate or the number of leaves, etc. The complex ensemble structure of LightGBM makes it harder to explain predictions than, say, decision trees or logistic regression.

If you are required to choose between XGBoost and LightGBM, then the following scenarios can guide your choice.

1. Smaller dataset, interpretable results needed, then the best option is the XGBoost (better regularization, stable trees).
2. Large-scale studies, then the best option is the LightGBM (faster, efficient on large input).
3. If there are mixed data types, then the best option is LightGBM (native categorical support).
4. If re-training is the requirement from the experiment settings, then the best option is LightGBM (shorter training time).

k-Nearest Neighbors (k-NN, instance-based learning)
k-Nearest Neighbors (k-NN) is a supervised learning algorithm used for classification and regression. It is a non-parametric, instance-based method, which means that it stores all the training data to make a prediction, it looks at the "K" closest training examples (neighbors) based on a distance metric (e.g., Euclidean). The predicted output is determined by the majority vote (for classification) or average value (for regression) of the neighbors. k-NN is quick and easy to explain to educators and researchers. New examples can be added without retraining, and there is no requirement of large datasets for training. However, one must calculate distances to all training points, and k-NN is sensitive to noise, so it can provide poor results if unimportant data are not filtered. Finally, k-NN simply memorizes data and does not generalize well.

Evaluation Metrics

Below are the evaluation metrics that can be used to evaluate and compare different algorithms.

Classification metrics
Table 6.4 provides an overview of key classification metrics, outlining their definitions and specific benefits for MLPA.

Regression metrics
Table 6.5 presents the regression metrics applied in this study, including their definitions and relevance for evaluating continuous outcome predictions in MLPA.

Table 6.4 Classification metrics

Metric	Description	Use/Benefit in MLPA
Accuracy	Percentage of correct predictions	Overall model correctness (e.g., engagement detection)
Precision	Percentage of predicted positives that are correct	Used when false positives are costly (e.g., wrongly flagging students as struggling)
Recall (sensitivity)	Percentage of actually positive cases that are correctly identified	Important for at-risk student detection
F1 Score	Harmonic mean of precision and recall	Balances false positives and false negatives
Confusion matrix	Table of true positive, false positive, false negative, true negative	Visual analysis of class-level performance
AUC-ROC (Area Under the Receiver Operating Characteristic Curve)	Area under the ROC curve	Measures class separability for binary classifiers
Cohen's kappa	Adjusted agreement between predictions and ground truth	Useful for inter-rater or model agreement beyond chance

Source: Author.

Table 6.5 Regression metrics

Metric	Description	Use/benefit in MLPA
Mean Absolute Error	Average of absolute errors	Simple, robust to outliers
Mean Squared Error (MSE)	Average of squared errors	Penalizes large errors more heavily
Root Mean Squared Error (RMSE)	Square root of MSE	More interpretable scale
R^2 Score (coefficient of determination)	Proportion of variance explained	How well features predict the outcome (e.g., test scores)

Source: Author.

CASE STUDIES

In this section, we will provide three case studies that have different educational but the same MLPA setting. The three case studies cover individual debugging, adaptive assessment, and collaborative debugging, but the multimodal data collection procedures remained the same across all three studies. In all three case studies, we collected eye-tracking, facial videos, heart rate variability (HRV), electrodermal activity (EDA) and system logs. For demonstrative purposes, we will show prediction of an outcome variable and one learning process variable.

Case Study 1: Individual Debugging

Dataset 1

Dataset 1 was collected from an experiment conducted with 30 computer science majors (including eight females) in the third semester of ANONYMOUS University's contrived computer lab. Participants were on average 19.5 years old (SD = 1.65 years). All participants took a Python course in the previous semester, where Visual Studio Code (VSCode) was their primary integrated development environment (IDE). Additionally, they were familiar with VSCode's built-in debugging tools.

Participants were assigned the task of debugging two Python codes implementing PacMan and Tetris games, which use the PyGame library. The debugging activity was conducted as part of a collaborative partnership between a European university and the authors. The participants were informed that there were no syntactical errors in the code, and all the bugs were logical and related to the gameplay. For example, PacMan would go through the ghosts without eating them (even when it had the power) or getting killed by them (as would normally occur); or the "walls" of the games would not work. The participants were also informed that they required basic knowledge of Python to solve the task and that knowledge of the PyGame library was not required to debug the code.

Informed consent forms were signed by the participants upon arrival in the laboratory. To ensure accurate facial and physiological tracking, each participant was required to pass an automatic eye-tracking and Empatica E4 calibration routine before the debugging task. During the debugging process, their faces were tracked with a high-quality HD webcam, and their heart rate and EDA were tracked using Empatica E4 wristbands. During the next task, participants had to answer coding questions within ten minutes. Following that, participants had 50 minutes to solve ten debugging tasks presented in the main method of a 100-line Python program for PacMan and a 150-line Python program for Tetris. Participants were informed that the main debugging task's code was free of syntactic errors.

The participants received the equivalent of US$25 as a reward for participating in the study. The number of bugs corrected in the task was used as the learning outcome to be predicted for this study.

Predictables, algorithms, and evaluation metrics

For this case study, we will predict two variables. The first is the performance of the participant in the debugging task. This score was given by analyzing the code that they submitted and finding the bugs that were left. The maximum score one could get was ten, and the minimum possible score was zero. For predicting the debugging performance, we compute the features from the whole interaction and then use them to predict the debugging performance. The second variable we will predict is the cognitive load using the features extracted from remainder of the dataset. For predicting the cognitive load, we choose a one-minute window to compute the features and then use the current minute's features to predict the next minute's cognitive load.

We will compare all the aforementioned algorithms to show which one stands out as the best predicting algorithm. As both our predictables are continuous, we will use the Root Mean Squared Error (RMSE) as an evaluation and comparison metric.

Results

Table 6.6 provides the training and testing RMSE for predicting the two variables for this study (debugging performance and cognitive load). The random

Table 6.6 Comparison of the algorithms

Algorithms	Predicting debugging performance training RMSE	Predicting debugging performance testing RMSE	Predicting cognitive load training RMSE	Predicting cognitive load testing RMSE
SVM-linear	18.81%	18.92%	15.48%	15.95%
SVM-polynomial	14.54%	15.23%	14.24%	14.57%
SVM-radial	7.24%	7.49%	6.37%	6.94%
XGBoost	5.26%	5.32%	4.21%	4.53%
LightGBM	5.13%	5.24%	4.34%	4.67%
k-NN	21.23%	22.26%	20.75%	21.16%

Source: Author.

baseline prediction for debugging performance is 35.32 percent, and for cognitive load it is 29.24 percent.

We can see that in this case, all the algorithms improve the random baseline both for debugging performance and cognitive load predictions. However, the boosting algorithms clearly outperform the others. The SVM-radial is the close second-best performer. This indicates the presence of non-linear relations between MLPA measurements and the outcome variables. For both predictions, k-NN seems to be the worst predictor. Moreover, there is not a significant difference between the training and testing RMSE values for either of the predictions, indicating that there was no case of overfitting the data.

Case Study 2: Adaptive Assessment

Dataset 2

In this course, the instructor typically employed gamified quizzes (Kahoots!) at the beginning of each lecture to link the previous lecture with the current one and engage the classroom in the lecture. When quizzes are gamified, students can often be motivated to improve their learning performance by engaging in competitions that are exciting and fun (Sanchez et al., 2020). Students' scores on the self-assessment tests had no bearing on the students' final course grade (i.e., no rewards as external motivation).

Dataset 2 involved 32 undergraduate students (15 females [46.9 percent] and 17 males [53.1 percent], aged 18–21 years-old [M = 19.24, SD = 0.831]) enrolled in the online adaptive self-assessment procedure. Students' self-assessment and interaction data were collected with a system that consisted of: (1) a testing interface; (2) an adaptation mechanism; (3) a tracker that logs the students' interaction data; and (4) a database storing information about the students and test items.

This dataset is contextualized in adaptive self-assessment settings. As already stated in the introduction, adaptive learning settings are inherently supportive to learners' motivation, and adaptation positively impacts learners' engagement (Walkington, 2013). However, the primary purpose of engaging students in self-assessment is to boost learning and achievement (H. Andrade & Valtcheva, 2009). In fact, self-assessment leads students to greater awareness by training them to self-regulate their motivation and behavior, as well as by fostering reflection on their own progress in knowledge or skills, and finally, by deepening engagement with their learning and their understanding of themselves as learners (Dang et al., 2023; Järvelä, Nguyen, & Molenaar, 2023). In October 2018, the students took the adaptive self-assessment quizzes individually for approximately 45 minutes at a university laboratory, which was specially equipped and organized for the needs of the study. The study was conducted as part of a Web Technologies course (related to front-end development) at a European university.

Each student signed an informed consent form that explained the procedure and gave researchers permission to use their data. Each participant wore a wristband and an EEG cap and was connected to all data collection devices (i.e., eye-tracker, wristband, EEG, cameras). A pre-test questionnaire measured participants' goals and expectations. Afterwards, the adaptive self-assessment test started, and the students had to answer the questions. Only one answer was correct for each item. Students received their test scores, as well as the full test results, at the end of the procedure, which included all the items that they had answered, their responses, their accuracy, and the option to check for correct answers for items they had answered incorrectly. The participants received the equivalent of US$20 as a reward for participating in the study. The score in the adaptive assessment test is used as the learning outcome to be predicted for this study.

Predictables, algorithms, and evaluation metrics

For this case study, we will predict two variables. The first is the performance of the participant in the Adaptive assessment. This score was given by the system itself by adding all the correct answers provided by the participants. The maximum score one could get was ten, and the minimum possible score was zero (this was achieved by using a MinMax scaling). To predict the test performance, we compute the features from the whole interaction and then use them to predict the test performance. The second variable we will predict is the cognitive load, using the features extracted from remainder of the dataset. To predict the cognitive load, we choose a one-minute window to compute the

Table 6.7 Comparison of the algorithms

Algorithms	Predicting test performance training RMSE	Predicting test performance testing RMSE	Predicting cognitive load training RMSE	Predicting cognitive load testing RMSE
SVM-linear	19.12%	19.92%	17.43%	17.95%
SVM-polynomial	15.23%	15.47%	15.27%	15.51%
SVM-radial	7.29%	7.91%	6.76%	6.99%
XGBoost	5.76%	5.95%	4.72%	4.87%
LightGBM	5.43%	5.57%	4.56%	4.79%
k-NN	22.29%	22.76%	22.75%	23.16%

features and then use the current minute's features to predict the next minute's cognitive load.

We will compare all the aforementioned algorithms to show which one stands out as the best predicting algorithm. As both our predictables are continuous, we will use RMSE as an evaluation and comparison metric.

Results

Table 6.7 provides the training and testing RMSE for predicting the two variables for this study (test performance and cognitive load). The random baseline prediction for debugging performance is 39.47 percent, and for cognitive load it is 31.73 percent.

We can see that in this case, all the algorithms improve the random baseline both for test performance and cognitive load predictions. However, the boosting algorithms clearly outperform the others. The SVM-radial is the second-best performer by a narrow margin. This indicates the presence of non-linear relations between MLPA measurements and the outcome variables. For both predictions, k-NN seems to be the worst predictor. Moreover, there is not a significant difference between the training and testing RMSE values for either of the predictions, indicating that there was not any case of overfitting the data.

Case Study 3: Collaborative Debugging

Dataset 3

Dataset 3 was collected from an experiment conducted with 80 computer science majors and professional programmers in the Norwegian University of Science and Technology's (NTNU) contrived computer laboratory. All participants had taken a Python course at the university, where VSCode was their primary IDE. Additionally, they were familiar with built-in debugging tools. This study examines how user-generated multimodal collaborative process data can be used to reinforce students' pair programming practices. Furthermore, the study examined whether students can practice problem-solving strategies (e.g., debugging codes), coupled with reflections and discussions instead of trial and error.

Participants were assigned the task of debugging a Python code implementing a Space Invader game, which uses the PyGame library. The debugging activity was also conducted as part of a collaborative partnership between a European university and the authors. The participants were informed that there were no syntactical errors in the code, and all the bugs were logical and related to the gameplay. For example, the bullets would fly through the aliens, or the "walls" of the games would not work. The participants were also informed that they required basic knowledge of Python to solve the task and that knowledge of the PyGame library was not required to debug the code.

Informed consent forms were signed by the participants upon arrival in the laboratory. To ensure accurate facial and physiological tracking, each participant was required to pass an automatic eye-tracking and Empatica E4 calibration routine before the debugging task. During the debugging process, their faces were tracked with a high-quality HD webcam, and their heart rate and EDA were tracked using Empatica E4 wristbands. During the next task, participants had to answer coding questions within ten minutes. Following that, participants had 30 minutes to solve five debugging tasks presented in the main method of a 150-line Python program. Participants were informed that the main debugging task's code was free of syntactic errors. The participants received the equivalent of US$25 as a reward for participating in the study. The number of bugs corrected in the collaborative task is used as the learning outcome to be predicted for this study.

Predictables, algorithms, and evaluation metrics

For this case study, we will predict two variables. The first is the performance of the participant in the debugging task. This score was given by analyzing the code that they submitted and finding the bugs that were left. The maximum score one could get was ten, and the minimum possible score was zero. For predicting the debugging performance, we compute the features from the whole interaction and then use them to predict the debugging performance. The second variable we will predict is the cognitive load using the features extracted from the remainder of the dataset. To predict the cognitive load, we choose a one-minute window to compute the features and then use the current minute's features to predict the next minute's cognitive load.

Table 6.8 Comparison of the algorithms

Algorithms	Predicting debugging performance training RMSE	Predicting debugging performance testing RMSE	Predicting cognitive load training RMSE	Predicting cognitive load testing RMSE
SVM-linear	17.46%	17.63%	14.42%	15.83%
SVM-polynomial	13.68%	13.72%	13.74%	13.78%
SVM-radial	7.67%	7.82%	6.72%	6.91%
XGBoost	5.76%	5.91%	4.29%	4.47%
LightGBM	5.25%	5.45%	4.51%	4.62%
k-NN	20.23%	22.26%	19.75%	20.06%

We will compare all the aforementioned algorithms to show which one stands out as the best predicting algorithm. As both our predictables are continuous, we will use RMSE as an evaluation and comparison metric.

Results

Table 6.8 provides the training and testing RMSE for predicting the two variables for this study (debugging performance and cognitive load). The random baseline prediction for debugging performance is 36.43 percent, and for cognitive load it is 28.41 percent.

We can see that in this case, all the algorithms improve the random baseline, both for debugging performance and cognitive load predictions. However, the boosting algorithms clearly outperform the others. The SVM-radial is the second-best performer by a narrow margin. This indicates the presence of non-linear relations between MLPA measurements and the outcome variables. For both predictions, k-NN seems to be the worst predictor. Moreover, there is not a significant difference between the training and testing RMSE values for either of the predictions, indicating that there was not any case of overfitting the data.

DISCUSSION AND CONCLUSION

From the case studies, we can observe that the prediction accuracy is very high for the classical ML algorithms. These predictions have several design implications for educational technologies. In the following paragraphs, we briefly present a few of these implications:

Interfaces can dynamically adapt based on predicted performance or cognitive load. For example, if performance is predicted to drop or cognitive load is high, then we can simplify the interface by hiding non-essential information or use progressive disclosure by showing only what is needed, or offer assistive cues such as Tooltips, suggestions, or guided navigation. However, if performance is optimal or cognitive load is low, then we can allow multitasking or power-user features and provide more complex visualizations or interaction paths.

Predictive models could also allow individual-level customization. For example, by adjusting interface layout, color schemes, or control schemes based on user-specific thresholds of cognitive load or by tailoring content complexity (e.g., learning apps adjust reading level or task difficulty). Predictive models can also help us to optimize task sequences based on predicted user strain by reordering tasks to balance cognitive demand (e.g., hard tasks followed by easier ones), by inserting breaks or micro-interactions when high load is predicted, or by delaying notifications or multitasking opportunities during high-load moments.

We can also use predictions to offer just-in-time interventions. For example: (1) notify users when cognitive load is peaking (e.g., "Take a break" alert); (2) adjust pace of information presentation (e.g., delay in augmented reality/virtual reality instructions); and (3) provide confidence indicators when performance might drop. Furthermore, we can use the predictive models as inputs to adaptive agents or recommender systems. For example, virtual assistants might intervene more proactively if user stress is high, or intelligent tutoring systems can pace content or change teaching strategy based on cognitive load.

To summarize, there are several key decisions to be taken when using classical ML techniques to predict the learning outcomes or learning processes. These decisions become even more important when we are considering multiple different data sources. We also presented the three case studies from three different educational settings and compared the different ML algorithms.

7. Deep learning modelling

INTRODUCTION AND BACKGROUND

In recent years, the integration of deep learning (DL) into educational systems has gained considerable attention for its transformative potential (Doleck et al., 2020; Nguyen, Järvelä, et al., 2022). DL, a subfield of artificial intelligence (AI), involves training artificial neural networks with many layers to recognize patterns and make decisions. This technology has already revolutionized domains such as healthcare, finance, and autonomous vehicles, and now it is reshaping education. By enabling machines to analyze vast amounts of data, adapt to individual student needs, and simulate human-like understanding, deep learning is enhancing the way we teach, learn, and assess knowledge. This chapter explores the key benefits of incorporating DL methods into educational settings.

One of the most profound contributions of DL to education is the facilitation of personalized learning experiences (Kurilovas, 2019). Traditional classroom models often adopt a one-size-fits-all approach, which fails to accommodate the diverse learning styles, paces, and needs of students. DL systems, however, can analyze historical student performance data, interaction patterns, and learning behaviors to tailor content delivery in real time. For example, intelligent tutoring systems powered by DL can identify a student's weak areas and dynamically adjust the difficulty of problems or the type of instructional material provided. Platforms like DreamBox Learning and Squirrel AI use DL algorithms to continuously assess student progress and personalize mathematics instruction accordingly. This level of adaptability increases engagement and improves educational outcomes, especially for students who struggle with traditional teaching methods.

DL has made it possible to automate grading and feedback, significantly reducing the workload on educators while providing students with faster responses (Abdi et al., 2023; Pardo et al., 2019). While multiple-choice grading has long been automated, recent advances in Natural Language Processing (NLP)—a key area of DL—allow for the automated evaluation of essays, short answers, and even spoken language. For instance, DL models can assess grammar, coherence, argument structure, and originality in student essays.

Automated writing evaluation tools like Turnitin's Revision Assistant and ETS's e-rater system employ DL to provide constructive feedback on writing quality. These systems not only accelerate the grading process but also support student learning by offering timely, targeted advice for improvement.

Another major application of DL in education is natural language understanding, which enables machines to comprehend, interpret, and generate human language. This has led to the development of advanced AI teaching assistants, chatbots, and voice-activated learning tools. Students can now interact with conversational agents to ask questions, receive explanations, or practice language skills. For example, Duolingo, a language-learning platform, uses DL models to generate adaptive language exercises and offer real-time corrections. Furthermore, AI chatbots embedded in learning management systems (e.g., Canvas or Moodle) can answer student inquiries instantly, improving access to support and reducing reliance on human staff.

Educational institutions are increasingly using DL models for predictive analytics—that is, forecasting future student performance and identifying at-risk individuals (Nguyen et al., 2020). By analyzing variables such as attendance records, assignment completion rates, quiz scores, and online activity, DL systems can flag students who might be likely to fail or drop out. These insights empower educators and administrators to implement early interventions. For instance, Georgia State University has used predictive models to increase graduation rates by proactively supporting students identified as at-risk. DL's ability to process complex and high-dimensional data makes it especially suited for such applications, offering a data-driven approach to student retention and success.

DL models, particularly large language models like GPT, can also assist in content generation (Ali et al., 2023; Kishore et al., 2023). Educators can use AI to automatically generate quizzes, study guides, summaries of textbook chapters, or even entire lesson plans. For example, a teacher could input a scientific article into an AI tool, which then summarizes it and formulates comprehension questions aligned with curriculum standards. These tools are invaluable for educators with limited time and resources. They also benefit students by offering additional learning materials and varied formats (e.g., visual summaries, interactive questions), which reinforce understanding and cater to different learning preferences.

DL is uniquely capable of handling multimodal data—text, audio, images, and video. This opens doors to integrating speech and vision capabilities into educational tools. For example, speech-to-text systems enable real-time transcription of lectures, supporting students with hearing impairments or language barriers. Similarly, image recognition systems can be used in educational apps to evaluate handwritten math problems or detect objects in science experiments.

Additionally, sign language recognition using DL is being developed to support deaf and hard-of-hearing students, making education more inclusive and accessible to all. Understanding students' emotions can significantly enhance teaching effectiveness. DL models can detect emotions from facial expressions, voice tone, or even text responses. By analyzing this data during online or hybrid learning sessions, educational platforms can adapt in real time—for example, offering encouragement if a student appears frustrated or repeating instructions if confusion is detected. This ability to monitor emotional states helps to foster a more empathetic and responsive learning environment. It also equips educators with deeper insight into student well-being and engagement levels, which are crucial for academic success.

As class sizes are growing, and there is increasingly limited access to human tutors, DL enables the creation of scalable AI-powered tutoring systems. These systems, such as Khanmigo from Khan Academy or Socratic by Google, offer instant assistance on a wide range of topics. They can explain concepts, guide problem-solving, and adjust explanations based on the student's input. Such tools provide around-the-clock academic support, which is especially beneficial for students in remote or underserved areas. They complement human instruction, allowing teachers to focus on more complex and interactive classroom activities.

DL also supports language translation and simplification, helping to bridge gaps in multilingual classrooms. Automatic translation tools powered by neural networks allow content to be delivered in multiple languages. Simplification tools can adjust reading complexity based on a student's literacy level. This is especially important in globalized education systems and for refugee or immigrant populations who might face language barriers. DL thus plays a role in democratizing education and making it more inclusive across cultural and linguistic divides.

The adoption of DL methods in educational settings represents a powerful evolution in how learning is delivered and experienced. From personalized instruction and automated feedback to emotion-aware interfaces and scalable tutoring, DL empowers educators and students alike. While challenges such as data privacy, algorithmic bias, and digital infrastructure remain, the benefits of DL—when applied thoughtfully—are profound and far-reaching. As education continues to embrace technology, DL will play an increasingly central role in shaping the future of learning into one that is more personalized, inclusive, efficient, and engaging for all learners. Based on the aforementioned benefits of using DL for prediction purposes using the multimodal data, we can support the claim that DL is a useful tool to be used in the current Multimodal Learning Process Analytics (MLPA) landscape. In this chapter, we will focus on DL approaches to predict/forecast the learning outcomes/processes. The remainder of the chapter is organized as follows. The next section provides the details of feature engineering, models development, evaluation metrics, and how to present and discuss results. The section after that provides three case studies on individual debugging, adaptive assessment, and collaborative debugging. In all three case studies we will show prediction of one performance variable and forecasting of one learning process captured by one of the multimodal data sources.

BUILDING AND EVALUATING DEEP LEARNING MODELS FOR MULTIMODAL LEARNING PROCESS ANALYTICS

Feature Engineering

This is similar to what we have described in Chapter 5.

Model Development

In this section, we will describe three DL algorithms: Visual Geometry Group (VGG) as an example of Convolutional Neural Networks; Long Short-Term Memory (LSTM) as an example of Recurrent Neural Networks; and Transformers as an algorithm that uses attention mechanisms.

Convolutional Neural Network: Visual Geometry Group (VGG)

The Visual Geometry Group (VGG) network is a type of Convolutional Neural Network (CNN) known for its simplicity and effectiveness in image recognition tasks (Simonyan & Zisserman, 2015). The VGG network achieved top results in the ImageNet Large Scale Visual Recognition Challenge (ILSVRC) in 2014. Here is the VGG-16 Architecture:

1. Input: 224 x 224 x 3 RGB image
2. Conv3-64: 2 layers, each with 64 filters of size (3 x 3)
3. Max Pool: (2 x 2) pooling
4. Conv3-128: 2 layers, each with 128 filters of size (3 x 3)
5. Max Pool: (2 x 2) pooling
6. Conv3-256: 3 layers, each with 256 filters of size (3 x 3)
7. Max Pool: (2 x 2) pooling
8. Conv3-512: 3 layers, each with 512 filters of size (3 x 3)
9. Max Pool: (2 x 2) pooling
10. Conv3-512: 3 layers, each with 512 filters of size (3 x 3)
11. Max Pool: (2 x 2) pooling
12. Fully Connected: 4,096 neurons

13. Fully Connected: 4,096 neurons
14. Fully Connected: 1,000 neurons (number of classes in ImageNet)
15. Softmax: Produces probabilities for each class

Below are brief mathematical explanations of the key components and structure of VGG:

Convolutional layers

The VGG network consists of multiple convolutional layers stacked on top of each other. Each convolutional layer performs a convolution operation followed by a non-linear activation function (typically a Rectified Linear Unit, ReLU). Mathematically, for an input image (I) with dimensions (W x H x D) (width, height, depth), a convolutional layer applies a set of (K) learnable filters (or kernels) (F_k) (where k = 1, 2, …, K), each of size (F_W x F_H x D).

The convolution operation for a filter (F_k) on the input (I) produces a feature map (A_k):

$$A_k(x,y) = \sum_{i=0}^{F_W-1}\sum_{j=0}^{F_H-1}\sum_{d=0}^{D-1} I(x+i, y+j, d).F(i,j,d) + b_k$$

where b_k is the bias term for the k-th filter.

After convolution, an activation function σ (typically the ReLU function) is applied element-wise:

$$A'_k(x,y) = \sigma(A_k(x,y))$$

Pooling layers

The VGG network uses max pooling layers to reduce the spatial dimensions of the feature maps while retaining the most important information. Max pooling takes the maximum value from a set of values in a pooling window (typically of size 2 x 2). Mathematically, for a feature map A'_k of dimensions W x H:

$$P_k(x,y) = \max_{0 \le i \le p, 0 \le j \le p} A'_k(px+i, py+j)$$

where P_k is the pooled feature map, and p is the size of the pooling window.

Fully connected layers

After several convolutional and pooling layers, the VGG network flattens the output feature maps into a one-dimensional vector and passes it through one or more fully connected (dense) layers. If the flattened feature vector is v of length N, and the fully connected layer has M neurons with weights W and biases b:

$$\mathbf{u} = \mathrm{W}\mathbf{v} + \mathrm{b}$$

where u is the output of the fully connected layer. An activation function is then applied element-wise to u.

Softmax layer
The final layer in the VGG network is a softmax layer, which converts the output of the last fully connected layer into a probability distribution over the classes. For an output vector u of length C (number of classes):

$$softmax(\boldsymbol{u})_i = \frac{\exp(u_i)}{\sum_{j=1}^{C} \exp(u_i)}$$

where softmax$(\mathbf{u})_i$ is the probability of class i.

Advantages of VGG16
VGG16, with its 16 weight layers (13 convolutional layers and three fully connected layers), has a deep architecture capable of learning rich and hierarchical features from the input images. This depth allows it to capture intricate patterns and details, improving its performance on complex tasks. The network builds hierarchical features layer by layer, starting from simple edges and textures in the initial layers to more complex structures and objects in the deeper layers.

VGG16 uses a consistent architecture with small (3 x 3) convolution filters and (2 x 2) max pooling layers. This uniformity simplifies the network design and reduces the number of hyperparameters. The straightforward and repetitive structure of VGG16 makes it easier to implement and understand compared to more complex architectures. The use of ReLU activation functions introduces non-linearity, which helps in learning complex functions and improving the convergence of the training process. ReLU helps to mitigate the vanishing gradient problem, which is crucial for training deep networks like VGG16. The use of max pooling layers reduces the spatial dimensions of the feature maps, which decreases the computational load and controls overfitting by introducing some translational invariance.

VGG16 pretrained on large datasets like ImageNet provides a robust feature extractor that can be fine-tuned for various other tasks. This transfer learning capability makes it a versatile and widely used backbone in many computer vision applications. The features learned by VGG16 are general and can be adapted to different datasets and tasks, making it a valuable starting point for new projects. In terms of performance, VGG16 has shown excellent performance in benchmark competitions such as the ImageNet Large Scale Visual Recognition Challenge (ILSVRC), establishing its efficacy in image classification tasks. Owing to its proven performance, VGG16 has been widely adopted and validated across various research and practical applications, contributing to its reliability and trustworthiness.

Long Short-term Memory (LSTM)

A single Long Short-term Memory (LSTM) cell comprises four components:

1. Forget gate (f): This is a neural network with a sigmoid activation function. This gate is responsible for what information is propagated to the next time step and what information is discarded. Depending on the previous hidden state h_{t-1} and the current input x_t, the forget gate assigns a value between zero and 1 to every element in the previous cell state C_{t-1}. For all the elements that are assigned a value of 1, the information is retained and all the elements that are assigned a value of zero are discarded. For all the elements that are assigned a value between zero and 1, the value decides how much information is to be retained.
2. Input gate (I): This is also a neural network that uses a sigmoid activation function. To take the decision about what new information is to be stored in the cell state (explained next), there are two different operations:
   a. The input gate decides which values will be updated.
   b. Using a tanh activation function, a set of candidate values are created ($\widetilde{C}_t$). Once $\widetilde{C}_t$ and I_t are computed, the input given to the cell state can be decided.
3. Cell state (C_t): This functions as the memory of the LSTM. Owing to the cell states, LSTMs usually outperform basic recurrent neural networks. For every time window, the C_{t-1} is combined with the forget gate, and it is determined what information is propagated to the next time step and what information is discarded. The retained information is then combined with I_t and $\widetilde{C}_t$ to create the new cell state that will be the new memory of the LSTM.
4. Output gate (O): this is another neural network that uses a sigmoid activation function. The cell state computed from the previous step is passed through a hyperbolic function (tanh), and this creates the cell values that are filtered between -1 and 1.

The schema in Figure 7.1 shows the various gates and their arrangement.

For each gate, the following are the variables (set of weights and biases):

1. W_f, b_f are the forget gate weight and bias, respectively.
2. W_i, b_i are the input gate weight and bias, respectively.
3. W_c, b_c are the candidate cell state weight and bias, respectively.
4. W_o, b_o are the output gate weight and bias, respectively.
5. W_v, b_v are the weight and bias associated with the Softmax layer, respectively.
6. f_t, i_t, $\widetilde{C}_t$, o_t are the outputs of the activation functions for the forget gate, input gate, candidate cell state, and output gate, respectively.
7. a_f, a_i, a_c, a_o are the inputs to the activation functions of the forget, input, cell, and output gates, respectively.
8. CF is the cost function, with respect to which the derivatives are calculated.

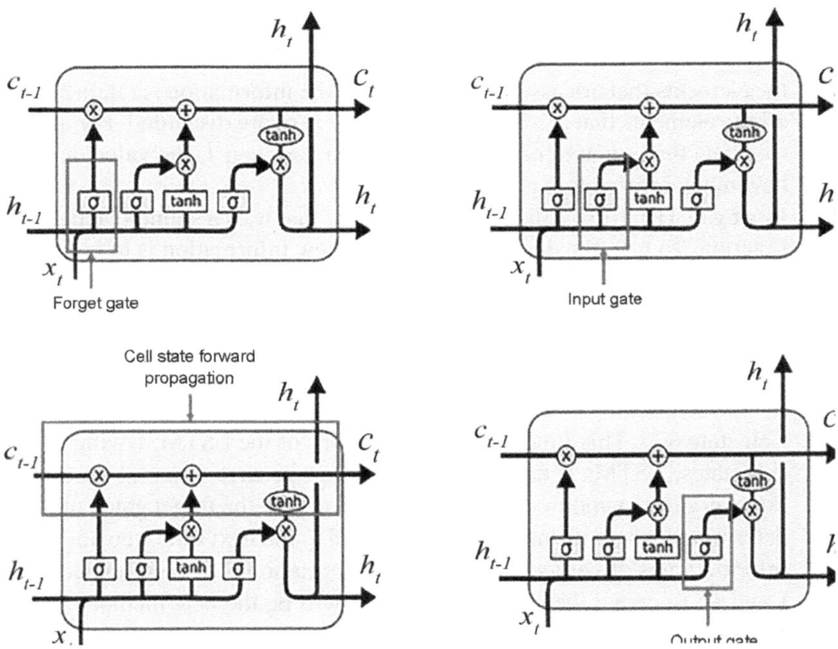

Source: Author's own.

Figure 7.1 *One LSTM cell with all the components marked with light gray boxes*

For each gate, the following equations show how the activation of each gate is calculated:

1. Forget gate: $a_f = W_f.Z_t + b_f f_t = sigmoid(a_f)$
2. Input gate: $a_i = W_i.Z_t + b_i i_t = sigmoid(a_i)$
3. Input gate: $a_c = W_c.Z_t + b_c \widetilde{C_t} = \tanh(a_c)$
4. Cell state: $C_t = f_t \otimes C_{t-1} \oplus i_t \otimes \widetilde{C_t}$
5. Hidden state: $h_t = o_t \otimes \tanh(C_t)$
6. Output equation 1: $V_t = W_V.h_t + b_t$
7. Output equation 2: $y_t = softmax(V_t)$
8. Output gate: $a_f = W_f.Z_t + b_f f_t = sigmoid(a_f)$

The outcome of all the gates is derived in a similar manner. Here, the forget gate calculations are explained as an example. There is a fixed path from the activation of the forget gate to the cost function that is shown as the following:

$f_t \rightarrow C_t \rightarrow h_t \rightarrow CF$

The following is how the derivative is calculated for the cost function with respect to the forget gate:

$$\frac{dCF}{df_t} = \frac{dCF}{dh_t} * \frac{dh_t}{dC_t} * \frac{dC_t}{df_t}$$

All the derivatives of the cost function with respect to the cell state and hidden state are calculated in the same manner. Input to each LSTM are the previous cell state and the concatenated previous hidden state and current input. For simplicity, $[h_{t-1}, x_t]$ Z_t

$$\frac{dCF}{dC_{t-1}} = \frac{dCF}{dC_t} * \frac{dC_t}{dC_{t-1}}$$

$$= \frac{dCF}{dC_t} * f_t$$

$$\frac{dCF}{dZ_t} = \frac{dCF}{da_f} * \frac{da_f}{dZ_t} + \frac{dCF}{da_i} * \frac{da_i}{dZ_t} + \frac{dCF}{da_o} * \frac{da_o}{dZ_t} + \frac{dCF}{da_c} * \frac{da_c}{dZ_t}$$

$$= W_f^T * \frac{da_f}{dZ_t} + W_i^T * \frac{da_i}{dZ_t} + W_o^T * \frac{da_o}{dZ_t} + W_c^T * \frac{da_c}{dZ_t}$$

The forget gate:

$$\frac{dCF}{df_t} = \frac{dCF}{dh_t} * \frac{dh_t}{dC_t} * \frac{dC_t}{df_t}$$

But:

$$\frac{dCF}{dC_t} = \frac{dCF}{dh_t} * \frac{dh_t}{dC_t}$$

So:

$$\frac{dCF}{df_t} = \frac{dCF}{dC_t} * \frac{dC_t}{df_t}$$

$$\frac{dCF}{df_t} = \frac{dCF}{dC_t} * \frac{d\left(f_t \otimes C_{t-1} \oplus i_t \otimes \widehat{C}_t\right)}{df_t}$$

$$\frac{dCF}{df_t} = \frac{dCF}{dC_t} * C_t$$

And:

$$\frac{dCF}{da_f} = \frac{dCF}{df_t} * \frac{df_t}{da_f}$$

$$\frac{dCF}{da_f} = \frac{dCF}{dC_t} * C_{t-1} * f_t\left(1 - f_t\right)$$

The other derivatives can be computed with respect to the inputs and outputs to the cost function. For example, for the input gate:

$$\frac{dCF}{di_t} = \frac{dCF}{dC_t} * \widehat{C}_t$$

$$\frac{dCF}{da_i} = \frac{dCF}{dC_t} * \widehat{C}_t * i_t\left(1 - i_t\right)$$

For the cell state:

$$\frac{dCF}{dC_t} = \frac{dCF}{dh_t} * O_t * \left(1 - \tanh^2\left(C_t\right)\right)$$

$$\frac{dCF}{d\hat{C}_t} = \frac{dC_t}{d\hat{C}_t} * i_t$$

$$\frac{dCF}{da_c} = \frac{dCF}{dC_t} * i_t * \left(1 - \hat{C}_t^2\right)$$

Output gate:

$$\frac{dCF}{dO_t} = \frac{dCF}{dh_t} * \tanh(C_t)$$

$$\frac{dCF}{da_o} = \frac{dCF}{dh_t} * \ tanh\left(C_t\right) * O_t\left(1 - O_t\right)$$

And finally, the hidden state:

$$\frac{dCF}{dh_t} = \frac{dCF}{dV_t} * \frac{d\left(W_V * h_t\right)}{dh_t} = W_V^T * \frac{dCF}{dV_t}$$

The weights for all the gates are below:

Forget gate:

$$\frac{dCF}{dW_f} = \frac{dCF}{da_i} * \frac{da_f}{dW_f}$$

Input gate:

$$\frac{dCF}{dW_i} = \frac{dCF}{da_i} * \frac{da_i}{dW_i}$$

Output:

$$\frac{dCF}{dW_V} = \frac{dCF}{dV_t} * \frac{dV_t}{dW_V}$$

Output gate:

$$\frac{dCF}{dW_o} = \frac{dCF}{da_o} * \frac{da_o}{dW_o}$$

Transformers

Mathematically, Transformers leverage linear transformations, attention mechanisms, and feed-forward networks to process sequences in parallel, capturing local and global dependencies alike effectively. The model leverages multi-head attention to capture various aspects of the sequence in parallel, with each layer building a more refined representation of the input data. In a typical NLP task (where the Transformers have shown excellent performance) the first step is to input embedding. This step transforms the words/sentences into quantitative vectors. In our case, we are dealing with quantitative measurements. Therefore, we do not need word embedding. In this subsection, we will describe the Transformer process from after the word embeddings.

Positional encoding

Transformers lack the inherent ability to understand the order of the elements in the time series, so positional encodings are added to the input to provide this information. Positional encodings are defined as:

$$PE(pos, 2i) = \sin\left(\frac{pos}{10000^{2i/d}}\right)$$

$$PE(pos, 2i+1) = \cos\left(\frac{pos}{10000^{2i/d}}\right)$$

For a position *pos* and dimension *2i* or *2i+1*, these functions provide a unique encoding. The input to the transformer is then:

$$z_i = x_i + PE_i$$

Self-attention

The self-attention mechanism computes the relevance of each word to every other word in the sequence. This is done through the following steps:

1. Calculating queries, keys, and values

For each input z_i, we compute three vectors: query Q, key K, and value V. These vectors are obtained by multiplying the input by learned weight matrices:

$$Q = ZW^Q$$

$$K = ZW^K$$

$$V = ZW^V$$

Where, W^Q, W^K, and W^V are matrices of dimensions $d \times d_q$, $d \times d_k$, and $d \times d_v$, respectively.

2. Scaled dot-product attention

The attention score for a pair of words is calculated as the dot product of their query and key vectors, scaled by the square root of the dimension of the key vectors: $Attention(Q,K,V) = softmax\left(\frac{QK^T}{\sqrt{d_k}}\right)V$

The softmax function ensures that the attention weights are positive and sum to 1.Multi-head attention

Instead of performing a single attention function, multi-head attention runs multiple attention mechanisms in parallel, allowing the model to jointly attend to information from different representation subspaces. Each head i is computed as:

$$head_i = \left(QW_i^Q, KW_i^K, VW_i^V\right)$$

The results of these attention heads are then concatenated and linearly transformed:

$$MultiHead(Q,K,V) = Concat\left(head_1 \ldots head_n\right)W^O$$

Where W_i^Q, W_i^K, W_i^V are the learned projections for the ith-*head*, and W^O is a weight matrix for the output.

Feed-forward network

After the multi-head attention layer, the output passes through a feed-forward neural network, which consists of two linear transformations with a ReLU activation in between:

$$FFN(x) = \max\left(0, xW_1 + b_1\right)W_2 + b_2$$

Here W_1 and W_2 are weight matrices, and b_1 and b_2 are biases.

Layer normalization and residual connections
Each sub-layer (multi-head attention and feed-forward network) is followed by layer normalization and a residual connection, which helps in stabilizing and accelerating the training process:

$$Output = LayerNorm\left(x + SubLayer\left(x\right)\right)$$

Stacking layers
Transformers consist of multiple layers stacked on top of each other. Each layer takes the output of the previous layer as its input and processes it through the attention and feed-forward sub-layers.

Output layer
The final output is often projected back into the space of predictable variable using a linear layer, followed by a Softmax function to get the probability distribution over the predictable variable:

$$Output = softmax\left(ZW^{O} + b^{O}\right)$$

Where W^O and b^O are learned parameters.

Evaluation metrics
This is similar to what we described in Chapter 6.

Explainable AI (XAI)
It is very important to understand that all the models that we are using in this chapter, are "black box" models. Therefore, it is essential to make sure that we use XAI methods with these DL methods. In this chapter, we will focus on two of the most used methods LIME (Local Interpretable Model-agnostic Explanations) and SHAPley values (SHapley Additive exPlanations from cooperative game theory to estimate the contribution of each feature to a model's prediction).

LIME
Many machine learning models (like deep neural networks, gradient boosting machines, etc.) are accurate but not interpretable. It is often hard to understand why a model made a specific prediction. LIME helps by providing a local explanation of individual predictions. Let us define the following:

$f : R^d \rightarrow R$: The **black-box model** we want to explain

$x \in R^d$: The **instance** we want to explain (a single prediction)

$g \in G$: The **interpretable model** (e.g., linear model) used for explanation. G is the family of such models

$\pi_x(z)$: A **proximity measure** between the original input x and a perturbed sample z, to define a local neighborhood

$L(f,g,\pi_x)$: The **loss function** measuring how well the explanation model g approximates f locally

$\Omega(g)$: The **complexity measure** of the explanation model g, encouraging interpretability (e.g., sparsity)

$$\arg\min_{g \in G} \mathcal{L}(f, g, \pi_x) + \Omega(g)$$

This means finding a simple model g that approximates f well *locally* around x, while keeping g interpretable. The following are the steps to compute LIME for a ML model:

Choose a prediction to explain: Say a model predicts that an email is spam with 92 percent confidence. Create perturbed samples: LIME generates new data points by slightly modifying the original input (e.g., changing some words in the email or features in a tabular dataset).

Generate a dataset $Z=\{z_1,z_2,\ldots,z_N$, where each $z_i \in R^d$ is a perturbed version of x.

For each zi ∈ Z:

- Compute the black-box prediction: $f(z_i)$
- Compute the proximity to:

$$x : \pi_x(z_i) = \exp\left(-\frac{D(x, z_i)^2}{\sigma^2}\right)$$

where $D(\cdot,\cdot)$ is a distance metric (e.g., cosine or Euclidean distance), and σ controls the neighborhood width.

Get model predictions: The black-box model is used to predict outcomes for these perturbed inputs.

Fit an interpretable model locally: A simple, human-understandable model (like linear regression or decision tree) is trained on the perturbed data and their corresponding predictions. This model is a local approximation around the original input. For models like text or images, the original input x might be high-dimensional or not directly interpretable. LIME uses a simplified, interpretable binary representation $x' \in \{0,1^d$, indicating presence/absence of components. A mapping $h_x:\{0,1\}^d \rightarrow R^d$ reconstructs the original feature from interpretable space. Use the weighted dataset $\{(z_i, f(z_i), \pi_x(z_i))\}$ to fit an interpretable model gg. If g is linear (e.g., ridge regression or Lasso), then:

$$g(z') = w^T z' + b$$

We solve:

$$\arg\min_{w,b} \sum_{i=1}^{N} \pi_x(z_i) \cdot \left(f(z_i) - g(z_i')\right)^2 + \Omega(g)$$

Where:

- z_i' is the interpretable version of z_i
- $\Omega(g)$ can be a $\ell 1$ or $\ell 0$ norm on w, encouraging sparsity (to limit the number of features shown in explanation)

Explain the prediction: The simple model's weights (like feature importances in linear regression) are used to explain what features influenced the original prediction the most. The weights w_j from the sparse linear model g correspond to the importance of feature j in explaining f(x). Typically, the top-k features with the largest magnitude weights $|w_j|$ are presented as the explanation.

SHAP

SHAP (SHapley Additive exPlanations) is a unified framework for interpreting predictions of machine learning models, based on *cooperative game theory*—specifically the concept of *Shapley values*. SHAP assigns each *feature* a value that represents its *contribution* to a particular prediction. The idea is to fairly distribute the total "payout" (prediction) among "features" (players) depending on their contribution. Let:

- f(x): The output of the model for input $x \in R^d$
- $f(x) \in R$: A scalar prediction (e.g., probability of a class)
- ϕ_j: The SHAP value for feature j, representing how much j contributes to the prediction
- $x' \in \{0,1\}^d$: A binary vector indicating which features are "present" in a coalition (subset of features)

The explanation model is *additive*:

$$f(x) \approx \phi_0 + \sum_{j=1}^{d} \phi_j$$

Where:

- ϕ_0: The expected prediction (baseline, e.g., average over all data)
- ϕj: The marginal contribution of feature j

The SHAP value for feature jj is:

$$\phi_j = \sum_{S \subseteq N \setminus \{j\}} \frac{|S|!(|N|-|S|-1)!}{|N|!} \left[f_{S \cup \{j\}}(x) - f_S(x) \right]$$

Where:

- N is the set of all features
- $S \subseteq N \setminus \{j$: A subset of features not including j
- $f_S(x)$: The model's prediction using only the features in subset S
- The weights are the Shapley kernel: They ensure fair averaging across all possible orderings

SHAP satisfies these *desirable axioms*:

1. Local accuracy (Additivity):

$$f(x) = \phi_0 + \sum_{j=1}^{d} \phi_j$$

2. Missingness
3. If a feature is missing (i.e., never used), then its SHAP value is 0
4. Consistency
5. If a model changes so that a feature has a larger effect, its SHAP value should not decrease

CASE STUDIES

In this section, we will provide three case studies that have different educational settings but the same MLPA setting. The three case studies examine individual debugging, adaptive assessment, and collaborative debugging, but the multimodal data collection was the same. In all the three case studies, we collected eye-tracking, facial videos, heart rate variability (HRV), electrodermal activity (EDA), and system logs. For demonstrative purposes, we will show prediction of an outcome variable and one learning process variable.

Case Study 1: Individual Debugging

Dataset 1

Same Dataset 1 as in Case Study 1: Individual Debugging in Chapter 6.

Predictable, algorithms, and evaluation metrics

For this case study, we will predict two variables. The first is the performance of the participant in the debugging task. This score was given by analyzing the code they submitted and finding the bugs that were left. The maximum score one could get was ten, and the minimum possible score was zero. For predicting the debugging performance, we compute the features from the whole interaction and then use them to predict the debugging performance. The second variable we will predict is the cognitive load using the features extracted from remainder of the dataset. For predicting the cognitive load, we choose a one-minute window to compute the features and then use the current minute's features to predict the next minute's cognitive load.

We will compare all the aforementioned algorithms to show which one stands out as the best predicting algorithm. As both our predictables are

Table 7.1 Comparison of the algorithms

Algorithms	Predicting debugging performance training RMSE	Predicting debugging performance testing RMSE	Predicting cognitive load training RMSE	Predicting cognitive load testing RMSE
CNN	3.45%	3.72%	2.63%	2.97%
LSTM	3.13%	3.37%	2.36%	2.61%
Transformer	3.24%	3.61%	2.84%	2.91%
Best from Chapter 6	5.13%	5.24%	4.21%	4.53%

continuous, we will use the Root Mean Squared Error (RMSE) as an evaluation and comparison metric.

Results

Table 7.1 provides the training and testing RMSE for predicting the two variables for this study (debugging performance and cognitive load). The random baseline prediction for debugging performance is 35.32 percent, and for cognitive load it is 29.24 percent.

We observe that all three models provide similar RMSE values for debugging performance and cognitive load predictions alike. Moreover, they also improve slightly over the best classical machine learning performance. Once again, there are no signs of overfitting in either of the algorithms.

XAI results

In this subsection, we will present the SHAP results, as they provide local and global explanations alike (Figure 7.2). We can observe that the top 20 most important features originate from cognitive load, confusion, frustration, fixation duration, saccade velocity, HRV, and EDA. The left panel shows the global importance (How important is the feature?), and the right panel shows the local importance (How do the feature values correspond to the feature importance?).

Case Study 2: Adaptive Assessment

Dataset 2

Same Dataset 2 as in Case Study 2: Adaptive Assessment in Chapter 6.

Predictable, algorithms, and evaluation metrics

For this case study, we will predict two variables. The first is the performance of the participant in the adaptive assessment task. This score was given by the system that added the correct answers provided by the participants. The maximum score one could get was ten, and the minimum possible score was zero (this was achieved by using a MinMax scaling). To predict the test performance, we compute the features from the whole interaction and then use them to predict the debugging performance. The second variable we will predict is the cognitive load using the features extracted from remainder of the dataset. To predict the cognitive load, we choose a one-minute window to compute the features and then use the current minute's features to predict the next minute's cognitive load.

We will compare all the aforementioned algorithms to show which one stands out as the best predicting algorithm. As both our predictables are continuous, we will use RMSE as an evaluation and comparison metric.

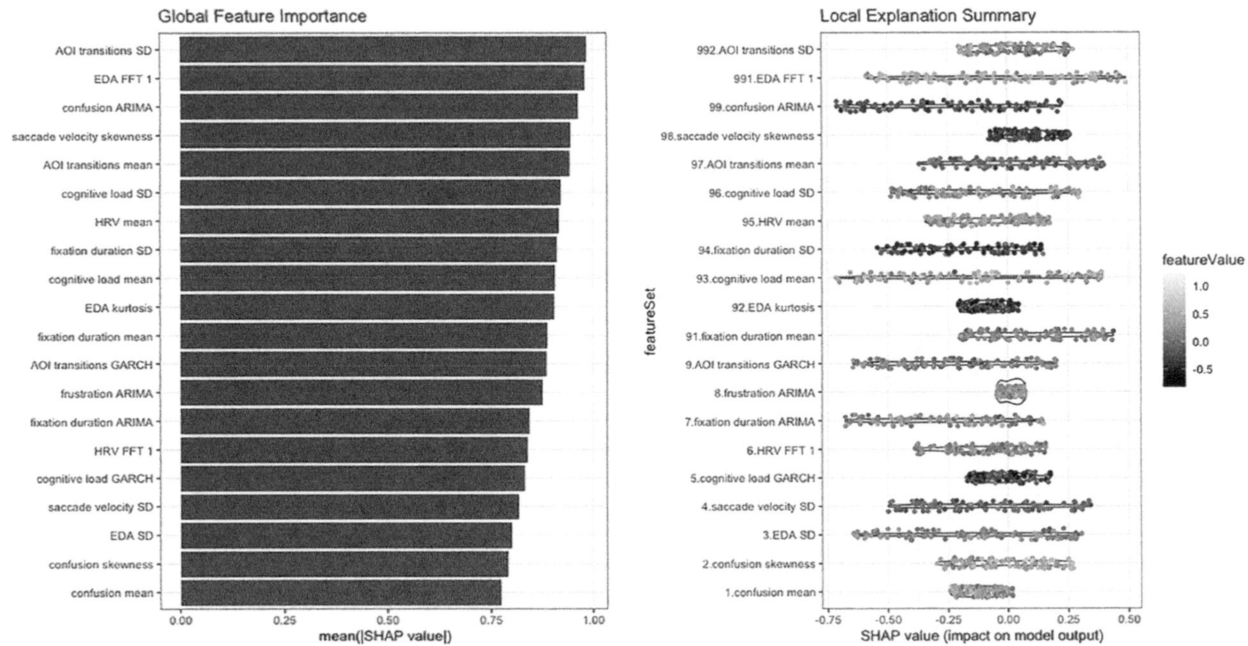

Note: The numbers on the y axis of the right panel are just to force the feature names to appear in a particular order; they do not hold a semantic value for the case study.
Source: Author's own.

Figure 7.2 SHAP global and local explanations

Table 7.2 Comparison of the algorithms

Algorithms	Predicting Test performance training RMSE	Predicting test performance testing RMSE	Predicting cognitive load training RMSE	Predicting cognitive load testing RMSE
CNN	4.42%	4.95%	3.86%	4.03%
LSTM	4.46%	4.61%	3.54%	3.59%
Transformer	4.58%	4.94%	3.43%	3.92%
Best from Chapter 6	5.43%	5.57%	4.56%	4.79%

Results

Table 7.2 provides the training and testing RMSE for predicting the two variables for this study (test performance and cognitive load). The random baseline prediction for test performance is 39.47 percent, and for cognitive load it is 31.73 percent.

We observe that all three models provide similar RMSE values for test performance and cognitive load predictions alike. Moreover, they also improve slightly over the best classical machine learning performance. Once again, there are no signs of overfitting in either of the algorithms.

XAI results

In this subsection, we will present the SHAP results, as they provide local and global explanations alike (Figure 7.3). We can observe that the top 20 most important features originate from cognitive load, confusion, frustration, fixation duration, saccade velocity, HRV, and EDA. The left panel shows the global importance (How important is the feature?), and the right panel shows the local importance (How do the feature values correspond to the feature importance?).

Case Study 3: Collaborative Debugging

Dataset 3

Same Dataset 3 as in Case Study 3: Collaborative Debugging in Chapter 6.

Predictable, algorithms, and evaluation metrics

For this case study, we will predict two variables. The first is the performance of the participant in the debugging task. This score was given by analyzing the code they submitted and finding the bugs that were left. The maximum score one could get was ten, and the minimum possible score was zero. To predict

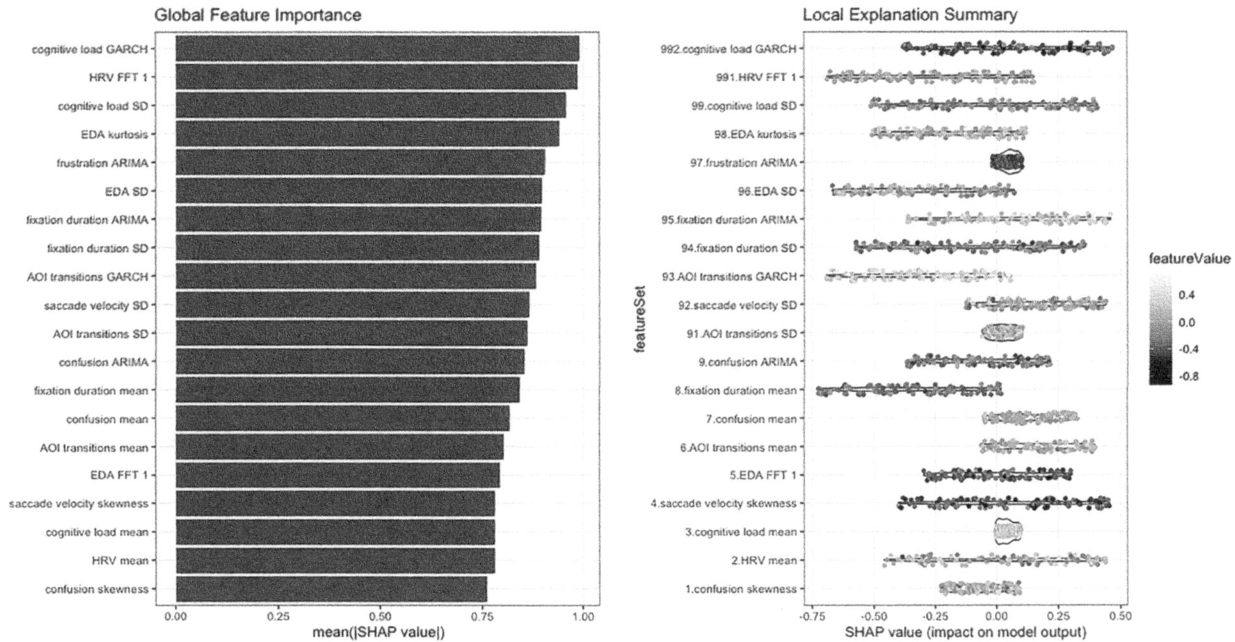

Note: The numbers on the y axis of the right panel are just to force the feature names to appear in a particular order; they do not hold a semantic value for the case study.
Source: Author's own.

Figure 7.3 SHAP global and local explanations

the debugging performance, we compute the features from the whole interaction and then use them to predict the debugging performance. The second variable we will predict is the cognitive load using the features extracted from remainder of the dataset. To predict the cognitive load, we choose a one-minute window to compute the features and then use the current minute's features to predict the next minute's cognitive load.

We will compare all the aforementioned algorithms to show which one stands out as the best predicting algorithm. As both our predictables are continuous, we will use RMSE as an evaluation and comparison metric.

Results

Table 7.3 provides the training and testing RMSE for predicting the two variables for this study (debugging performance and cognitive load). The random baseline prediction for debugging performance is 36.43 percent, and for cognitive load it is 28.41 percent.

We observe that all three models provide similar RMSE values for debugging performance and cognitive load predictions alike. Moreover, they also improve slightly over the best classical machine learning performance. Once again, there are no signs of overfitting in either of the algorithms.

XAI results

In this subsection, we will present the SHAP results, as they provide local and global explanations alike (Figure 7.4). We can observe that the top 20 most important features originate from cognitive load, confusion, frustration, fixation duration, saccade velocity, HRV, and EDA. The left panel shows the global importance (How important is the feature?), and the right panel shows the local importance (How do the feature values correspond to the feature importance?).

Table 7.3 Comparison of the algorithms

Algorithms	Predicting debugging performance training RMSE	Predicting debugging performance testing RMSE	Predicting cognitive load training RMSE	Predicting cognitive load testing RMSE
CNN	4.64%	4.72%	3.53%	3.95%
LSTM	4.34%	4.47%	3.62%	3.51%
Transformer	4.29%	4.91%	3.67%	3.99%
Best from Chapter 6	5.25%	5.45%	4.29%	4.47%

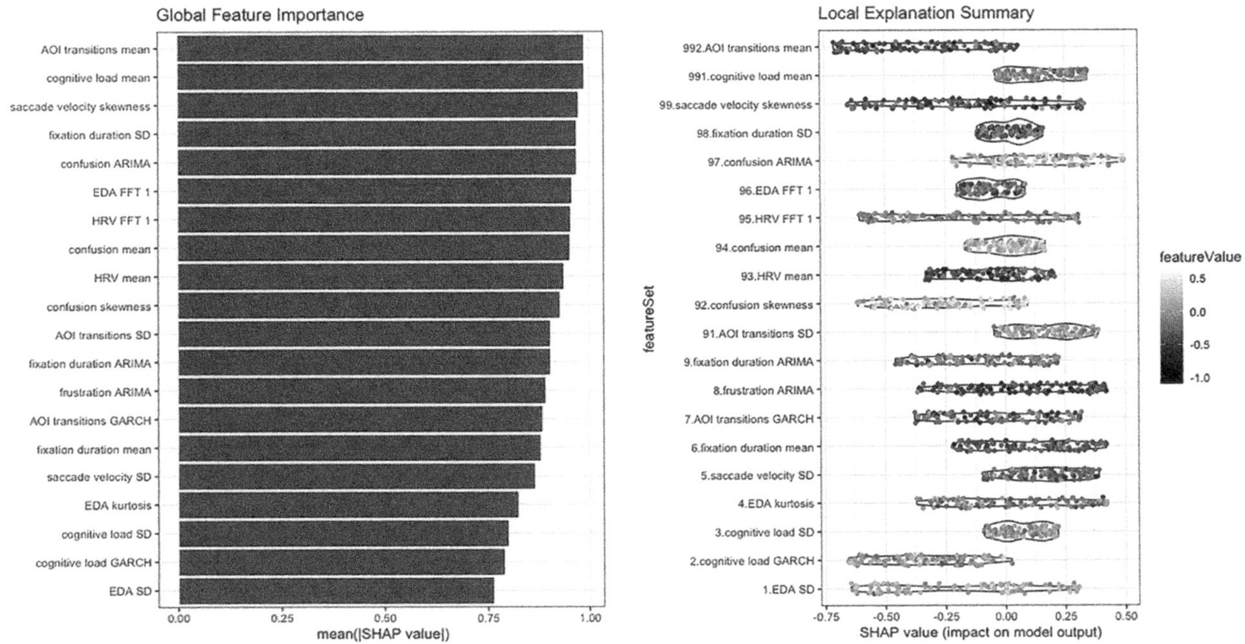

Note: The numbers on the y axis of the right panel are just to force the feature names to appear in a particular order; they do not hold a semantic value for the case study.
Source: Author's own.

Figure 7.4 SHAP global and local explanations

DISCUSSION AND CONCLUSION

In all the three case studies, we observe that the DL algorithms slightly outperform the best classical machine learning models. This shows the better structure of information processing by the DL algorithms. However, the training times for DL algorithms were significantly higher (a few thousand times) than the training time for classical machine learning algorithms. Therefore, we should consider the trade-off between using these two classes of algorithms. Another important aspect of DL models is the additional XAI component. DL models, such as CNNs, LSTMs, or Transformers, are powerful but opaque. Their complexity makes it hard for humans to understand how they arrive at their conclusions. Feature attribution techniques (like SHAP and LIME) highlight which inputs influenced the model's decision. This increases confidence in the model's decision-making and reduces blind trust in algorithms. DL models can learn shortcuts or spurious correlations that do not generalize well. XAI models can reveal whether the model is attending to meaningful features. This enables model auditing and root-cause analysis and helps to improve generalization and reduce overfitting. In summary, XAI is essential to make DL useful, trustworthy, and safe—especially as these models are deployed in more critical, regulated, and high-impact educational interventions. Without explanation capabilities, we risk building systems that are powerful but unpredictable, biased, or even harmful.

8. Generative artificial intelligence methods for multimodal learning process analytics

INTRODUCTION

Analyzing multimodal learning data often requires substantial methodological expertise, computational resources, and advanced analytical techniques to manage and interpret the complexity of heterogeneous data streams. Generative AI has recently emerged as a transformative technology with potential to address some of these challenges. Generative AI refers to models that can produce complex data outputs, fluent text, detailed images, realistic audio, and even video—often by learning from large-scale unlabeled datasets. In particular, the advent of Large Language Models (LLMs) such as GPT-3 and GPT-4 has demonstrated unprecedented capacity to interpret and generate human-like text (Kishore et al., 2023; Nguyen et al., 2024). Modern LLMs can answer questions, summarize documents, translate languages, and perform various reasoning tasks, all through a natural language interface. Building on these advances, Multimodal Large Language Models (MLLMs) have extended the input and output capabilities of LLMs beyond text, enabling them to process images, audio, and other modalities in addition to text. For example, GPT-4 is capable of analyzing visual inputs and producing textual descriptions or answers about them (Whitehead et al., 2025). Such models effectively combine vision or auditory understanding with language generation, providing a single interface to interpret complex multimodal data (Yan et al., 2024). Meanwhile, other classes of generative models—including diffusion models for image generation and transformation, Generative Adversarial Networks (GANs), and advanced audio generation models—have also matured. These models can produce high-fidelity synthetic images, videos, and sounds, potentially serving as tools to augment datasets or simulate learning scenarios.

This chapter provides a technical overview of how Generative AI methods can be applied within multimodal learning process analytics (MLPA). We focus on the pipelines and methods by which MLPA researchers and practitioners can leverage MLLMs, diffusion models, GANs, and audio generation models to collect, preprocess, analyze, and interpret multimodal learning data. Importantly, while we acknowledge relevant learning theories, our emphasis is on the technical integration: how to move from theoretical constructs (such as "socially shared regulation of learning") to concrete analytical measures using Generative AI. As an illustrative centerpiece, a detailed case study is included, adapted from a recent empirical study (Whitehead et al., 2025) in which a MLLM (GPT-4 with vision capabilities) was used to analyze video data of student posture during collaborative learning. This case study illustrates a pipeline—from operationalizing a learning theory construct (socially shared regulation) into observable categories, through prompt engineering and model selection, to validation of the AI-generated annotations—and offers critical reflections and lessons learned. We then broaden the discussion to consider the implications of Generative AI for MLPA, including reliability, ethical considerations, and the evolving role of human experts. The chapter concludes with forward-looking perspectives on future directions for research and practice, envisioning how Generative AI might further transform multimodal analytics of learning processes in the coming years.

By the end of this chapter, the reader, whether an advanced graduate student, early-career researcher, education consultant, or educational technologist, should have an understanding of the major types of Generative AI methods applicable to MLPA, the practical steps for integrating these methods into an analytics pipeline, and the considerations to keep in mind (from prompt design to validation to ethical use). The advent of Generative AI in education offers exciting opportunities to capture and interpret the richness of learning as it happens, but realizing this potential requires marrying new AI capabilities with sound methodological rigor and theoretical grounding. This chapter aims to chart that path in a clear and technically detailed manner.

POTENTIAL ADVANTAGES OF GENERATIVE AI FOR MLPA

As a reminder, a key step in any MLPA study is operationalizing theoretical constructs into observable metrics. Learning sciences offer many theories about how learning occurs (or fails to occur) in social and individual contexts. For example, in self-regulated learning (SRL) theory, effective learners plan, monitor, and regulate their cognition, motivation, and behavior. In collaborative settings, the construct of socially shared regulation of learning (SSRL) has been proposed to describe how groups co-regulate these processes together. SSRL involves the coordination of cognitive, behavioral, and emotional processes among group members to achieve shared learning goals (Järvelä & Hadwin, 2024). Such a construct is abstract—one cannot measure "SSRL" directly with a sensor. Instead, researchers identify *proxy indicators* or behavioral manifestations of SSRL that can be observed and logged. For instance, group planning might manifest in sequences of speech turns where students agree on goals, or socioemotional regulation might manifest in supportive gestures or posture mirroring among teammates. In a recent example, Whitehead et al. (2025) connected the SSRL construct to a set of nine posture-related behaviors hypothesized to be relevant to regulation in collaborative learning (e.g., whether a student is sitting vs standing, leaning on the table, hands on lap, engaged with a task object, etc.). By defining such categories, the researchers created an observational coding scheme that maps an aspect of theory (group regulatory engagement) to something tangible in video data (students' postures and actions) (Whitehead et al., 2025). This step of construct mapping is crucial in MLPA—it ensures that the multimodal data analysis is theoretically meaningful and not just a fishing expedition. Other examples of theoretical constructs operationalized via multimodal measures include cognitive load (e.g., measured via facial confusion expressions or physiological arousal), attention (e.g., via gaze dispersion or head position), and collaboration quality (e.g., via speaking turn patterns, overlap, and body orientation).

Traditionally, once constructs are defined, data collection involves capturing the relevant modalities with appropriate tools: video cameras for physical behaviors, microphones for speech, log files for digital interactions, wearable sensors for physiological data, etc. These raw data streams often require substantial preprocessing: e.g., synchronizing timestamps across devices, segmenting continuous recordings into meaningful episodes (such as turns of talk or problem-solving phases), filtering noise from audio, detecting and tracking faces or bodies in video frames, and so on. In early MLPA research, extracting features from these modalities often relied on bespoke algorithms or classical machine learning models. For instance, computer vision techniques might be used to estimate body pose (joint positions) from video or to recognize facial expressions; or Natural Language Processing (NLP) might be applied to transcripts to detect questions or cognitive words. These approaches, while effective in controlled settings, demanded specialized expertise and often considerable interdisciplinary collaboration—teams of learning scientists working with computer vision experts to tailor models for educational data (Whitehead et al., 2025). Moreover, many such methods were not easily generalizable: a model trained to detect "confusion" on one dataset might not work on another without retraining, owing to differences in context or behavior (Cukurova et al., 2020). Data heterogeneity and contextual nuance in learning environments remained challenging for these earlier techniques.

This is where Generative AI offers a new paradigm. The latest generative models are often large pretrained models that have learned from vast and varied data (for example, vision-language models trained on millions of image-caption pairs, or language models trained on internet-scale text). They come equipped with a broad (if implicit) understanding of the world and can be adapted to specific tasks through prompting or fine-tuning without needing task-specific training from scratch. In other words, they carry powerful representational capabilities that can potentially be harnessed for feature extraction and pattern recognition in multimodal data. If properly directed, a single large model might perform many of the analytical steps that previously required separate algorithms—for example, looking at a video frame and identifying meaningful actions or objects in educational context, or reading a student's written response and both grading it and providing feedback. The promise of MLLMs and related Generative AI methods in MLPA is to *lower the technical barriers* and *increase the scalability* of multimodal analysis: even researchers or practitioners without advanced programming or machine learning skills could leverage these models (through natural language prompts) to interpret complex data (Yan et al., 2024). The next sections provide an overview of the major classes of Generative AI and how each can contribute to MLPA, before diving into technical integration details and the case study.

OVERVIEW OF GENERATIVE AI METHODS FOR MLPA

Generative AI encompasses a variety of model architectures and approaches. Here we highlight four categories especially relevant to multimodal analytics of learning: (1) Multimodal Large Language Models, (2) Diffusion models, (3) Generative Adversarial Networks, and (4) Audio Generation Models. Each category represents a different way of generating and/or interpreting data, with unique strengths for addressing MLPA tasks.

Multimodal Large Language Models (MLLMs)

Multimodal Large Language Models (MLLMs) are an extension of text-based large language models that can accept and produce multiple types of data. A prototypical example is OpenAI's GPT-4, which has the ability to take images as inputs in addition to text. In essence, an MLLM combines advanced language understanding with vision (and potentially audio) processing capabilities within one unified model. Some MLLMs are trained via multimodal training objectives (e.g., image + caption pairs), while others attach pretrained vision encoders to language model decoders. The result is a model that can, for instance, look at a picture or video frame and generate a detailed description in natural language, or conversely take a textual query and find relevant image regions.

In the context of MLPA, MLLMs offer a powerful and flexible tool for interpreting raw multimodal data. An MLLM can effectively play the role of a human observer or annotator, but at scale and speed. For example, given a video still or a series of frames from a classroom recording, an MLLM can be prompted to "Describe what the students are doing and how they are positioned." It might output something like, "Student A is sitting and leaning on the table with their chin on their hand, looking at the worksheet, while Student B is standing and pointing at the laptop screen." Such a description encapsulates several observable features (posture, gaze direction, gesture) that an analyst might be interested in. Importantly, because the model is *generative*, we can tailor its output via prompts to focus on what we care about. We can instruct the model to categorize an image into predefined codes (e.g., "sitting" vs "standing") or to fuse information (e.g., "Is the group physically engaged in the task? Answer yes or no based on their body language."). This flexibility makes MLLMs akin to an adaptable sensor or coder that can be re-purposed for different constructs without retraining—one needs only to craft an appropriate prompt or set of instructions.

Several early studies and applications have begun to demonstrate the value of MLLMs for analyzing learning situations. Whitehead et al. (2025) showed that a multimodal LLM (GPT-4) could reliably annotate certain student postures from video data, as will be detailed in the case study. Others have used similar models to annotate non-verbal behaviors like facial expressions or gestures in educational videos, finding that the model-generated labels can reach moderate to high agreement with human coders (Khan et al., 2024; Zeng et al., 2024). MLLMs have also been explored for analyzing classroom images or lab setup images to detect affordances in the environment (e.g., identifying lab equipment present, seating arrangements) which can contextualize student actions. The generative nature of these models means that they can provide rich contextual descriptions; not just labeling that "hands are on table" but also noting relevant context such as "the student appears to be writing" or "two students are facing each other," if prompted appropriately. This contextual awareness is particularly relevant in learning environments, where the interpretation of a behavior often depends on surrounding activity (for instance, a student standing might indicate leadership if others are seated, or off-task behavior if standing away from the group).

It is important to note that while MLLMs are extremely powerful, they are not infallible. They might sometimes produce plausible-sounding but incorrect interpretations, a phenomenon known as hallucination (Kishore et al., 2023). For instance, if an image is ambiguous or partially cropped, the model might "fill in" details that are not actually there. Ensuring that prompts are specific and that input data contains sufficient detail (more on this in the technical pipeline section) can mitigate this issue. Moreover, MLLMs' performance depends on the quality of their training such GPT-4's vision capability is state-of-the-art as of 2026, but open-source alternatives (like earlier CLIP-based models or smaller vision-language models) might be less accurate in nuanced educational scenes. Nonetheless, the advent of MLLMs represents a significant step forward in MLPA: they serve as generalist analyzers that can be directed to many tasks, shifting much of the effort from model development to prompt engineering and interpretative guidance.

Diffusion Models for Image and Video Generation

Diffusion models are a class of generative models that have revolutionized image synthesis and editing. A diffusion model learns to generate data (often images) by iteratively denoising random noise, essentially learning the inverse of a gradual noising process (Ho, Jain, & Abbeel, 2020). Well-known examples include OpenAI's DALL-E 2 and the Stable Diffusion model, which can produce highly detailed images from text prompts (Rombach et al., 2022). While diffusion models are most famous for creating original images (e.g., "generate a picture of a classroom with students collaborating at a round table"), they can also be used for tasks like image inpainting (filling in missing parts of an image), super-resolution (increasing image quality), and even generating short video clips when extended to the time dimension.

In MLPA, diffusion models have several potential uses focused on data augmentation and transformation. One straightforward application is synthetic data generation for model training or scenario simulation. Suppose we want to train a computer vision classifier to recognize specific student postures or classroom configurations, but we have limited labeled examples. A diffusion model, guided by text prompts, could generate additional realistic images of students exhibiting those postures in various settings. For instance, by prompting a model with "a top-down view of four students around a table, two are standing and leaning in, two are sitting back with arms crossed," we might obtain multiple synthetic images that exhibit those features. These images (if sufficiently realistic) could be used to augment a training dataset, improving the robustness of detectors for engagement or disengagement postures. Diffusion models can thus help to overcome the data scarcity problem in educational contexts, where collecting large, diverse datasets is often difficult.

Another use is visualization and extrapolation. MLPA researchers might use diffusion models to visualize abstract analytics findings. For example, if analysis reveals a certain pattern (like a "typical" arrangement of people during high-engagement moments), one could prompt a diffusion model to create an illustrative image of that scenario for presentation or hypothesis generation. In a more interactive sense, generative models could allow "what-if" explorations: *What might this classroom look like if arranged differently?* or *Generate a sequence showing a student becoming increasingly frustrated.* These are speculative uses, but they highlight that generative models do not only analyze existing data—they can help to imagine or simulate new data, which might be a part of design-based research or communicating insights.

Diffusion models also enable data preprocessing enhancements. One practical issue in multimodal data is sensor imperfections: a camera might miss part of the action, or an important detail might be obscured. With diffusion-based inpainting, one could attempt to recover or guess missing visual information. For instance, if whiteboard content is partially occluded by a person, a generative model could be tasked to reconstruct the hidden text (although accuracy might vary). If video frame resolution is low (blurry faces or text), super-resolution diffusion models could clarify them. These uses must be done cautiously—one does not want to introduce false data—but as assistive steps (e.g., improving legibility of materials or slightly correcting poor lighting), they might be valuable.

It is worth noting that diffusion models primarily handle visual modalities (images, and by extension, videos, if temporal diffusion is used). Typically they are not used to interpret data (that is the realm of MLLMs or discriminative models), but rather to generate or enhance data. Thus, in an MLPA pipeline, diffusion models might be auxiliary tools: for example, generating additional training images for a deep learning model that will later analyze real classroom video, or creating illustrative figures of student behavior patterns to accompany an analysis. They might also contribute to *content creation* for educational interventions (like generating scenarios for students to respond to), which, while an application of Generative AI in education, goes slightly beyond "analytics" into the design realm. However, the line is blurring—a generative model could be part of a learning analytics-driven adaptive system that not only measures student state but also generates new multimodal content (like hint messages with images or adaptive simulations) based on that state.

Generative Adversarial Networks (GANs)

Generative Adversarial Networks (GANs) are another prominent category of generative models (Goodfellow et al., 2020). A GAN consists of two components—a generator and a discriminator—which are trained in tandem in a competitive process. The generator tries to produce fake data (e.g., images) that can fool the discriminator, and the discriminator learns to distinguish the generator's fakes from real data. Through this adversarial training, GANs have been able to produce remarkably realistic outputs, especially in image domains (such as photorealistic human faces, which did not actually belong to any real person). Over the past decade, various GAN architectures (DCGAN, StyleGAN, CycleGAN, etc.) have been developed for tasks ranging from image generation and style transfer to data augmentation.

For MLPA purposes, GANs can serve many of the same roles as diffusion models in terms of synthetic data creation and augmentation. Prior to the recent rise of diffusion models, GANs were frequently used to generate synthetic images to balance datasets. For example, if an educational dataset had few examples of a certain important event (say, a student raising a hand), a GAN could be trained to generate more images of hand-raising in class by learning the distribution of poses from the limited data and sampling new examples. Researchers have used GANs to generate artificial classrooms or learners in simulations for testing algorithms. One interesting application is using CycleGAN or similar frameworks for modality translation—for instance, translating sketches to images or generating realistic lip movements for an avatar given an audio track. In an analytics scenario, one could imagine using a GAN to anonymize video by generating artificial student faces that preserve expressions but remove identity (by training a GAN to map real faces to a set of synthetic faces). This could address privacy concerns while retaining emotional information.

GANs have also been used for upscaling and refining sensor data. Before diffusion models took the lead in super-resolution, GAN-based models (like ESRGAN) were common for cleaning up images or even for denoising signals. In an MLPA pipeline, a GAN-based filter might improve the quality of an infrared camera feed or fill gaps in an eye-tracking signal by learning from context. Another potential use is anomaly detection: if a GAN is trained on typical patterns of behavior, it might struggle to generate or discriminate unusual patterns. Those anomalies—such as an unexpected type of interaction—could flag moments of interest for an analyst.

Compared to diffusion models, GANs can be trickier to train and sometimes suffer issues like mode collapse (where they generate limited varieties of outputs). In terms of direct use by educational researchers, GANs historically required more machine learning expertise (one needed to set up neural network training with the adversarial loss, requiring a lot of data and tuning). However, as many pre-trained GAN models and simpler frameworks are available today, users can often leverage GANs without training from scratch. For instance, StyleGAN models pre-trained on face datasets can be fine-tuned to generate faces with certain characteristics, or tools like Nvidia's GauGAN can generate scenes from sketches via a trained GAN. For a non-technical MLPA practitioner, using GANs might involve tapping into such tools to, say, generate classroom background scenes or new variations of an image by instructing the model ("make this student's posture more slouched").

In summary, GANs in MLPA can be viewed as generators of synthetic but realistic data that can fill needs in analysis (whether for augmentation, anonymization, or enhancement). While perhaps less directly "analytic" than MLLMs (which interpret data), GANs and diffusion models empower the analytics process by ensuring that the data we work with is richer, more balanced, and more flexible than what raw collection alone provides. They enable a form of "imagination" in our analytical systems—producing possible data that align with learned patterns. As with all generative outputs, caution is warranted: synthetic data should be clearly separated from observed data, and its impact on analyses should be carefully validated (we would not want conclusions driven by artifacts of generated data). When used judiciously, though, GANs can strengthen the robustness and scope of multimodal analytics.

Audio Generation Models

While images and text often steal the spotlight in Generative AI discussions, **audio generation models** form another important piece of the Generative AI landscape, especially relevant for learning environments rich in verbal communication. Audio generation can refer to a few different capabilities: text-to-speech (TTS) synthesis (converting written text into spoken voice), voice cloning or style transfer (making one person's voice sound like another or altering prosody), music generation, and more generally any model that creates or continues audio waveforms. A landmark in audio generation was WaveNet by van den Oord et al. (2016), a deep generative model that produced exceptionally natural-sounding speech by modeling audio waveforms directly. Since then, transformer-based models and diffusion models have also been applied to audio; for example, models like Tacotron and FastSpeech improved the controllability and speed of TTS, and more recent diffusion-based vocoders further enhanced quality. In addition, LLMs have begun to be extended to audio in modalities such as automatic speech recognition (ASR) or even spoken dialog generation (where the model produces both text and a corresponding waveform).

In MLPA, audio is a central modality, because so much learning process data are conversational (think of classroom discussions, collaborative group talk, tutor-student dialogs, etc.). Audio generation models can support MLPA in a variety of ways such as:

- **Transcription and data augmentation**: Although transcription itself is a recognition task, once we have transcripts, we might use generative models to create variations of speech data. For instance, to test a speech emotion detection system, one could use a TTS model to generate spoken utterances with specific emotions or intonations (by manipulating input text and perhaps an emotion control vector) to expand the training data. Similarly, if we have only a few examples of off-task conversation, we could prompt a LLM to *generate additional dialog lines* that are off-task (text generation), and then use TTS to synthesize them into audio, creating a larger corpus of "off-task speech" audio for analysis or model training.

- **Voice anonymization and translation**: Using voice cloning or TTS, one can anonymize student voices by re-synthesizing their speech in a uniform, artificial voice. This can be important for privacy—the content of what students say is preserved (or could even be translated into another language via intermediate text), but their identifiable vocal characteristics are removed. For example, an English transcript from a collaborative learning session could be fed to a Spanish TTS or to an English TTS with a generic voice to produce audio that is safe to share with international collaborators or to use in a demo without exposing real identities. Audio generation can also convert written teacher feedback into spoken feedback automatically, which ties into interventions but also could be analyzed (e.g., analyzing different tones of voice in feedback by generating them purposefully).
- **Simulating acoustic environments**: Another angle is generating background noise or environmental audio to test the robustness of audio analytics pipelines. If an algorithm to detect questions in student conversations works well in a quiet lab recording, we might want to know if it still works in a noisy classroom. Rather than trying to record many noisy variations, we could take our clean audio and use generative noise models to overlay varying levels of cafeteria noise or chatter. This is more of a data augmentation for testing analytic models, ensuring that our features or algorithms are not overly sensitive to particular acoustic conditions.
- **Interactive agents and personalized feedback**: In emerging applications, generative audio models could be part of multimodal analytic-feedback loops. Imagine a system that analyzes a student's engagement via video and audio; if it detects, say, confusion or frustration from those signals, it might generate an immediate spoken prompt like, "I notice you seem stuck, would you like a hint?" to support the learner. This requires the system to not only analyze but also produce a response. The production of that response in a natural and situationally appropriate way is where generative models come in. A carefully tuned TTS voice (perhaps even a familiar voice to the student, cloned with permission) can deliver support messages in an empathetic tone, which might be more effective than plain text feedback. While this crosses into adaptive learning systems design, it is enabled by analytics recognizing a state and generative models creating a multimodal output (spoken language) to intervene.

In summary, audio generation models enrich MLPA by enabling flexible use and reuse of speech data. They allow us to transform and generate the auditory channel as needed—whether to create synthetic examples, protect privacy, or engage users. As with other Generative AI, there are caveats: TTS voices, if not clearly disclosed, could mislead participants; generated speech could convey unintended nuances if not carefully controlled (for example, a supportive message delivered in a flat or robotic tone might not have the desired effect). Ensuring quality and appropriateness of generated audio is key. However, given that much of learning is communicated through speech, the ability to algorithmically generate and manipulate speech is a powerful complement to the analysis of speech. It essentially lets us test hypotheses (e.g., how would a different intonation affect student perception?) and implement interactive analytical applications that were not feasible before.

Having reviewed the main categories of Generative AI relevant to MLPA, we now turn to the practical question: how do we integrate these tools into the research pipeline? The next section outlines technical pipelines and methodological considerations for deploying generative models in multimodal analytics, from data preprocessing and prompt engineering to validation strategies.

TECHNICAL PIPELINES AND METHODOLOGICAL INTEGRATION

Applying Generative AI in multimodal learning analytics requires thoughtful design of the end-to-end pipeline. This section breaks down the typical steps and considerations of integrating generative models into MLPA research. We focus on practical guidance: how to prepare data for generative models, how to craft prompts and select models, how to adjust parameters, and how to validate and interpret the outputs. Throughout, we emphasize that while generative models can automate parts of analysis, *human oversight and iterative refinement* remain critical to ensuring the outcomes are trustworthy and meaningful.

Data Collection and Preprocessing

Before generative models can be applied, one must ensure the multimodal data are captured and formatted appropriately. Data collection in MLPA often involves multiple devices and sensors; for instance, video cameras capturing group interactions, microphones recording speech, screenshots or log files from online learning platforms, etc. A first challenge is aligning these streams in time and context. If using a multimodal LLM to analyze an event, you might need to feed it an image (or a series of images) along with related text (perhaps a transcript excerpt). This requires synchronizing audio and video—e.g., identifying the video frame that corresponds to a particular utterance. Tools like video editing software or specialized sync programs can help to align transcripts with video timestamps. In some cases, you might break a continuous recording into segment files (like one image per second, or one snippet per conversation turn) to feed into a model piecewise.

Preprocessing steps are often needed to improve the quality and relevance of data for analysis. For video/image data, this might include resolution adjustments and framing. The case study by Whitehead et al. (2025) found that the performance of GPT-4's vision analysis improved when images contained sufficient context—for example, an image should include the student's full upper body and relevant surroundings (desk, computer) to accurately judge if they are sitting or standing. Cropping too tightly or having other people's limbs in the frame led to errors (Whitehead et al., 2025). Thus, as a rule, one should ensure that images are preprocessed to maximize relevant information and minimize confounding details. This could involve writing a script to detect faces or bodies and crop around them appropriately, or conversely to ensure a full body is in view. If certain known issues exist (like "limb intrusion," where a bystander's arm appears in the target student's frame), manual or automated editing might be needed to mask those extraneous parts. Generative inpainting could even be used here: if a person's arm intrudes, one could replace that region with a neutral background using a diffusion model to avoid confusing the MLLM. Whitehead et al. (2025) recommend careful camera positioning and data selection to mitigate these issues from the outset—e.g., using camera angles that clearly separate individuals and capture their posture completely.

For text and speech data, preprocessing might involve transcription (using ASR for audio to get text), segmentation (splitting a long transcript into relevant chunks, such as for each speaker turn or each topic), and possibly noise reduction (for audio, if feeding it into an audio-generative system or if the presence of noise might affect analysis). If one plans to use an LLM to analyze conversation, it might help to format the input with clear markers (like speaker labels or timestamps) or to include only the necessary portions of text to stay within token limits. Current LLMs have context length limits (e.g., a few thousand tokens), so one might not feed an entire hour-long transcript at once; instead, a sliding window or an extractive summary can be used.

It is also often beneficial to incorporate any domain knowledge at the preprocessing stage. For example, if we know we want to analyze when students handle lab equipment, we might use computer vision object detection (a pretrained model or even a prompt to an MLLM focusing on objects) to annotate frames with the presence of "lab apparatus." This kind of pre-annotation can then be included as text along with an image to the generative model (effectively giving it more info to work with). Another example: if analyzing collaborative problem solving where certain phases are well defined (like "planning phase" vs "implementation phase"), we might segment the data by task phase and run separate analyses for each in order to let the model focus on the behaviors relevant to that phase.

Finally, data privacy and security must be considered in preprocessing. Many generative models (like GPT-4) run on cloud services, meaning that data are sent to external servers. If the multimodal data include video of students or sensitive audio, ethical guidelines (Cukurova, Giannakos, & Martinez-Maldonado, 2020) and possibly institutional regulations require that we handle these carefully. Options include: blurring faces in images (if identity is not needed for analysis), stripping or encoding personal identifiers in text (replace names with pseudonyms), or even using local/offline models if available (to avoid sending data off-site). In Whitehead et al.'s (2025) study, for instance, they obtained ethical approval and likely ensured that video data sent to the OpenAI application programme interface (API) did not contain any direct student identifiers beyond physical behavior (Whitehead et al., 2025). It is good practice to document how data was sanitized or secured at this stage, both for compliance and for transparency in research reporting.

Prompt Engineering for Generative Models

One of the most critical new skills required when using Generative AI in MLPA is prompt engineering—the craft of writing inputs or instructions to the generative model to elicit the desired output. Unlike traditional analysis methods where the algorithm's behavior is relatively fixed once set up, generative models like LLMs are highly flexible, and their outputs depend heavily on how you ask your question or frame the task. In an MLLM context, a "prompt" might include a textual instruction plus (optionally) some examples or context, and possibly a special format if using an API (like a system message to instruct the model's role).

Key principles of prompt engineering for MLLMs in analytics include:

- **Clarity of the task**: Explicitly tell the model what you want it to do. If you need it to classify an image into categories, say so directly: e.g., "Analyze the image and list which of the following categories apply: [list categories]." In the posture case study, the prompt began by establishing the overarching goal: to categorize visible actions and postures according to predefined categories (Whitehead et al., 2025). This sets the stage and reduces ambiguity.
- **Step-by-step guidance**: Often, breaking the task into steps or giving a structured procedure in the prompt improves the consistency of results. For instance, the case study prompt included sequential instructions: first determine if the person is sitting or standing, then check arm positions, etc., and finally produce an output in a specified format (Whitehead et al., 2025). This mirrors how one would instruct a human coder to follow a

codebook: it ensures the model does not jump to conclusions and covers all aspects systematically.

- **Inserting domain knowledge (codebooks)**: A particularly effective approach, as demonstrated by Whitehead et al. (2025) and supported by Xiao et al. (2023), is to incorporate a *codebook* or definitions of categories into the prompt. Essentially, you feed the model the expert knowledge that defines each category or construct. For example, you might write in the prompt: "The relevant posture categories are: (1) *Sitting (SIT)*—individual's bottom is on a seat; (2) *Standing (STD)*—individual is upright on feet; (3) *Leaning on table* (LTB)—individual's arms or torso are resting on the table surface, ..."; and so on, covering all categories with short definitions. This serves as a guideline for the model, much like training data would in a supervised classifier. Studies have found that using predetermined codebooks in prompts can enhance the reliability of LLM-based coding, as the model aligns its interpretations with the provided definitions (Xiao et al., 2023).
- **Output formatting**: It is important to tell the model exactly how you want the answer. If the goal is to integrate with a data analysis pipeline, you might want outputs in a Comma-Separated Values (CSV)-friendly format or JSON. In the case study, the prompt concluded with: "Output as the following example: SIT, HTR, LTB," meaning that the model should output comma-separated category abbreviations (Whitehead et al., 2025). By providing an example output template, the researchers ensured consistency—the model was less likely to respond with a full sentence or extraneous commentary. Many LLMs are quite capable of returning well-structured outputs if asked, which saves effort on the parsing side.
- **System messages and role**: If using an API like OpenAI's, one often has a "system message" parameter to set the role or persona of the AI. In analytical use, a neutral or instructive system message (e.g., "You are a data analysis assistant.") can help. Whitehead et al. (2025) kept the default "You are a helpful assistant" system message, which is generic. In some cases, one might fine-tune this: for example, "You are an expert learning analytics researcher. You observe classroom images and code student behaviors according to research guidelines." Such a system prompt can potentially make the model's style more analytical and less fanciful.

It often takes *iteration and testing* to refine prompts. A sensible practice is to pilot the prompt on a small subset of data, examine where the model's outputs deviate from expectations, and then adjust the wording or detail of instructions. Whitehead et al. (2025) describe using a pilot process where they tried various prompt phrasings and subsets of categories to see what the model could accurately interpret. From an initial 30 candidate behaviors, they narrowed down to nine that the model handled well, tweaking the prompt along the way to maximize performance. This iterative prompt design—sometimes called *prompt tuning* (though done manually)—is a crucial methodological step. In effect, the prompt becomes part of your *method*, akin to a coding scheme in qualitative research. Documenting the final prompt in publications (perhaps in an appendix or supplemental material, as Whitehead et al. did) is important for transparency and reproducibility.

Another tactic is using *few-shot prompting*—giving a few examples of input-output pairs in the prompt to demonstrate the task. For instance, you could include: "Example: [image of student with hands on lap] -> Output: SIT, HRL (meaning hands resting on lap)." Then: "Now analyze the following new image: [image]." In the posture case, they ended up using zero-shot prompting (no explicit examples, just instructions), because GPT-4 was already quite capable. But for smaller models or more complex/nuanced tasks, providing a couple of correctly coded examples can calibrate the model.

Finally, when prompt engineering, one must be mindful of *token limits and cost*. Long prompts (with many category definitions and examples) consume a lot of the model's context window and also cost more if using a paid API (as cost often scales with token count). There is a balance between giving enough detail and keeping the prompt concise. Often definitions can be brief bullet points rather than lengthy prose. Also, one can offload some information to the "system" message or assume some base knowledge (for a powerful model like GPT-4, you do not need to explain basic terms like "table" or "standing").

To illustrate a simplified prompt structure for a hypothetical MLLM task, consider analyzing video frames for student emotional expression:

> System: You are a data analyst assistant helping to identify students' emotional states from images.
>
> User: You will be given an image from a classroom. Analyze the image and identify the emotion displayed by the student in the image, using these categories: Happy (smiling or positive expression), Confused (furrowed brow, squinting eyes, or looking at others for help), Focused (neutral but attentive expression, eyes on task), Frustrated (frowning, head in hands or negative expression). Provide the category name that best fits.
>
> Image: [embedded image] This prompt clearly states the task and categories. We would expect a one-word answer like "Confused" or "Focused" from the model. If the model instead gave a sentence, we might refine by saying "Output only the single category name."

In summary, prompt engineering translates our analytic needs and domain knowledge into a form the generative model can act on. It is an interactive process that often determines the success of using Generative AI in MLPA more than anything else. With a well-crafted prompt, even a general model can perform quite specialized analytic tasks (Xiao et al., 2023). Conversely, a poorly specified prompt might lead the model astray or produce inconsistent results. Thus, investing time in this stage is paramount.

Model Selection and Parameter Tuning

Choosing which Generative AI model to use is another important decision. The landscape of models is expanding rapidly, with options ranging from proprietary state-of-the-art models to open-source models that can be run locally. Key factors to consider in *model selection* include: modality support, performance, cost, accessibility, and any constraints such as data privacy or allowed usage.

For tasks heavily involving image understanding + text, for example in 2025, *GPT-4 (Vision)* is currently a top performer (OpenAI, 2023), as evidenced by Whitehead et al. (2025), who selected it for their posture analysis owing to its high reported multimodal capabilities. Alternatives to GPT-4 include models like Google's PaLM-E (a large multimodal model for embodied reasoning) or open models like CLIP-GPT combinations (e.g., BLIP-2; LLaVA, which connects a vision encoder to LLaMA). If fine-grained accuracy is needed and the domain is specialized (say analyzing scientific diagrams or handwriting), a specialized model or a fine-tuned version might outperform a general model. For instance, an optical character recognition (OCR)-based model might be better for reading text from images than GPT-4 is. Therefore, consider the nature of your data: if it contains a lot of printed text (like slides or documents in video frames), you might pair an OCR system with an LLM rather than rely on the LLM's vision alone.

Cost and access cannot be ignored. GPT-4 via API costs money for each image and token; if your study involves thousands of images, this could become expensive. Some cloud providers have quotas or require proposals for large-scale research use. In contrast, open-source models that you can run on a local GPU cluster (if you have one) might have no incremental cost beyond electricity but could require technical setup and might run more slowly or with memory limits. For example, Stable Diffusion (for image generation) can be run on a decent GPU locally, whereas DALL-E 3 might be accessible only via an API. An education researcher might start prototyping with a free or low-cost model and use the expensive model only if needed for final analysis.

Once a model is chosen, there are often *parameters to tune* to optimize its behavior for our use case:

- **Temperature**: This is a common parameter for generative models, especially LLMs, that controls the randomness of token selection during generation. A low temperature (near 0) makes the output more deterministic and focused (the model will more likely give the highest-probability answer), while a higher temperature introduces more variability (potentially more creative or diverse outputs). In analytic coding tasks, we typically want consistency and accuracy over creativity. Thus, a low temperature is usually preferred. Whitehead et al. (2025) set the temperature to 0.1 for GPT-4 when classifying images in order to reduce stochastic variation in the model's outputs. This helped with reliability, as the model would be more likely to produce the same output for the same image across runs (minimizing random fluctuations). If you notice an LLM giving sometimes one label, sometimes another for the same input, turning down the temperature will reduce that jitter, although it does not guarantee perfectly identical outputs in all cases.

- **Level of detail**: Some multimodal APIs (like the Azure OpenAI Vision service used by Whitehead et al., 2025) have parameters to control how detailed the analysis is. In the case of Whitehead et al., they used a "detail" parameter on high, which internally caused the model to do a two-pass analysis (first a broad look, then zooming into image regions for finer details) (Whitehead et al., 2025). If such options exist, it is often worthwhile to maximize detail for analytic tasks, as missing a subtle cue could cause a misclassification. The trade-off might be speed: high detail could be slower or more expensive. If a quick real-time response were needed (like in a live classroom support tool), one might sometimes dial down detail to gain speed, but for research analysis, accuracy is usually paramount.
- **Top-k or Top-p (nucleus) sampling**: These are other generation parameters controlling how the model samples from its probability distribution. In classification-oriented use, one might disable these (or set top-k=1), so that the model always picks the single most likely outcome. In tasks where a bit of elaboration is okay (like summarizing a discussion), one could keep moderate settings. But in analytics, unpredictability is typically not desired.
- **Multimodal-specific settings**: If using diffusion models, parameters include the number of inference steps (more steps yield better quality up to a point, at the cost of time) and guidance scale (how strongly the model follows a text prompt for text-to-image generation). For instance, to generate synthetic images closely matching a description, a higher guidance weight might be used. If using a diffusion model to inpaint missing data, one might need to tune the mask and prompt carefully to avoid artifacts. If training or fine-tuning a generative model (like fine-tuning a GAN on your dataset), then of course training hyperparameters (learning rate, epochs) are part of the pipeline—although increasingly researchers try to use pre-trained models to avoid heavy training.
- **API or SDK specifics**: Each service might have its own extra toggles. It is good to read the documentation. In Whitehead et al.'s (2025) pipeline, they

accessed GPT-4 via the Azure Software Development Kit (SDK), which allowed customization and automation not possible through the standard chat interface. This highlights a point: using the API directly (via Python, etc.) is often necessary for scaling to large datasets and for systematic control of parameters. Interactive web demos (like ChatGPT's interface) are fine for experimentation but not for processing hundreds of files reliably.

A practical tip is to create a *small validation set* or a known-answer test set and try different models and parameter settings on it to see what yields the best results. For example, if you have ten images where you know the "ground truth" labels (from human coding), run your prompt on those with GPT-4, with an open-source model like LLaVA, and maybe with different temperature settings, then compare. This pilot test can prevent costly mistakes of running a huge analysis only to find out later a certain setting was suboptimal.

It is also worth considering *model updates and versions*. AI providers occasionally update models (for example, a new version of GPT-4 or a completely new model like GPT-5 in the future). These updates might improve quality but could also change behavior slightly. Keeping track of which model version was used (e.g., GPT-4 version from March 2025) is important for reproducibility. If extremely high stability is needed for longitudinal use, one might need to stick to a frozen model or offline model, as API models can be a moving target.

In summary, model selection and tuning is about picking the right tool for the job and configuring it to behave in line with the analytic goals. The good news is that many generative models, especially LLMs, work quite well out-of-the-box for a range of tasks if prompted correctly; heavy "tuning" is often not needed as it was with older machine-learning approaches. However, attention to these details can lead to better performance and fewer headaches down the line.

Validation and Evaluation Strategies

Using Generative AI in analysis does not remove the need for rigorous validation—in fact, it necessitates new forms of validation to ensure that the AI-driven results are credible. As generative models can occasionally produce convincing but erroneous outputs, researchers must implement checks to differentiate correct analyses from AI "imagination." Several strategies can be employed:

- **Inter-rater reliability with human coders**: If the generative model is used to annotate or code data (as in our case study with posture categories), one of the strongest validation methods is to have human experts independently code a sample of the data and then compare the AI's codes to the human codes. Metrics like Cohen's kappa, as used by Whitehead et al. (2025), quantify the level of agreement beyond chance between AI and human. In their study, they found substantial agreement for some categories (e.g., $\kappa \approx 0.95$ for "sitting") but lower agreement for others (e.g., $\kappa \approx 0.33$ for "arms resting on table"), indicating where the model's performance was strong versus where it struggled. They also compared two human coders' agreement to understand the upper bound of consistency—if even humans only moderately agree on a category, expecting the AI to match humans perfectly would be unrealistic. For our purposes, reaching "substantial" agreement (commonly, $\kappa > 0.6$) with human coders on critical categories could be a reasonable benchmark for the AI's utility (Landis & Koch, 1977 criteria as referenced in Whitehead et al., 2025). If the AI falls short in certain categories, those could be flagged for either exclusion, prompt refinement, or further interpretation with caution.

- **Test–retest consistency**: A somewhat unique concern with generative models (especially stochastic ones) is consistency. If you run the model on the same input twice, do you get the same result? Ideally yes, especially for deterministic classification tasks. Whitehead et al. (2025) evaluated test–retest reliability by giving the model the same images on two different passes and checking agreement. They found near-perfect consistency (the model gave the same output across all categories on repeated trials) when using a low temperature setting, which is reassuring. If one did see differences, it might suggest that the model is hovering between two interpretations; in such cases, one might average multiple runs or choose the most frequent output as the final. But generally, for analysis, you want to eliminate that randomness. Ensuring that the model environment and parameters are fixed (e.g., set random seeds if possible) is one approach. In published results, demonstrating high test–retest reliability strengthens the argument that the method is scientific and reproducible (Yan et al., 2024, found GPT-4 to outperform other models on this consistency aspect, which aligns with Whitehead et al.'s, 2025, findings that hallucinations or random changes were minimal in their specific context).
- **Error analysis and qualitative validation**: Beyond numeric measures, it is important to qualitatively inspect where the model goes wrong. Whitehead et al. (2025) did an in-depth error analysis by sampling instances where the AI's annotation did not match the human's and categorizing the reasons (limb intrusion, insufficient context, insufficient guidance). Conducting such an error analysis in your study can reveal systematic biases or blind spots in the model. For example, you might notice that the model consistently misidentifies "writing on paper" as "hands on lap," because from a certain angle those look similar. By understanding these failure modes, you can potentially address them (e.g., adjust camera angles, or add clarifying

instructions in the prompt like "if a person is writing, do not classify it as hands resting").

- **Comparison with alternate methods**: If possible, compare the Generative AI approach against a conventional baseline. For instance, if analyzing sentiment in student feedback, one could compare an LLM's sentiment judgments to a classic sentiment analysis tool or a simple dictionary-based method. If results align, this builds confidence; if they diverge, one should investigate which seems more plausible. In posture analysis, a baseline could have been a pre-trained pose estimation algorithm or a convolutional neural network (CNN) classifier for posture—Whitehead et al. (2025) note that their approach is a feasible alternative to traditional joint-position based methods which often require constrained settings (e.g., motion capture suits or calibrated multi-camera setups). Showing that Generative AI can achieve comparable results to those specialized methods (or highlighting its advantages, such as working in unconstrained settings) is a valuable form of validation by comparison.
- **Cross-modal and construct validation**: In learning analytics, one might also validate AI-derived measures by correlating them with other indicators or outcomes. For example, if an AI model measures "engagement level" from video via generative descriptions, one could check if those engagement scores correlate with known quantities such as task performance, self-reported engagement, or teacher ratings. If the AI says that a group was highly engaged in segments A and B and not in C, and indeed the group's learning outcome was better in A and B, that triangulates some validity for the AI measure. In Whitehead et al.'s (2025) case, as it was a methodological study, they did not necessarily correlate posture frequencies with learning gains—but in an applied scenario, one might see if the posture patterns identified by the model relate to, say, successful versus unsuccessful groups or episodes of regulation (SSRL) observed through other means. If the generative analytics align well with theoretical expectations, that boosts confidence in their utility.
- **Human review of outputs**: Especially when generative models produce richer output (like summaries or narratives rather than discrete codes), a human expert should review a sample to ensure factual accuracy. For instance, if GPT-4 were used to summarize a discussion, one would want to check that it did not fabricate any points that were not actually said (a kind of hallucination). In many cases, generative models might subtly alter wording—an expert can judge whether the summary still faithfully represents the conversation. One might quantify this by having humans rate the fidelity of AI-generated summaries or explanations.
- **Ethical and bias audit**: Part of validation involves checking for biases or ethical issues. Does the model systematically misinterpret certain students

(e.g., along demographic lines)? This is hard to fully assess, but one can test the model on diverse examples or even synthetic variations (like overlaying different gender-presenting faces on the same posture) to see if the outputs differ. Ensuring that the generative model is not injecting stereotypes or skew (for example, labeling assertive behavior differently for different genders) is important for fairness. If any such issues are found, mitigation strategies might include rephrasing prompts to be neutral or using a different model less prone to those biases.

Finally, it is important to integrate validation *into* the pipeline, not just as a post-hoc step. For example, one might design the analysis to have a "verification" stage—say, after the model labels all data, you pick a random 10 percent of the instances and have a human double-check them. If more than a certain percentage of those are wrong, you might decide that the model is not ready and revise the approach. This kind of on-the-fly validation guard can prevent proceeding with unreliable data.

In conclusion, while Generative AI can automate much of the heavy lifting in feature extraction and analysis, the role of the researcher shifts to being a *critical evaluator* of the AI's contributions. By employing rigorous validation strategies—quantitative reliability measures, qualitative error analysis, cross-checks with theory and human judgment—we ensure that the integration of Generative AI into MLPA yields scientifically sound conclusions. The next section will exemplify many of these points by diving into a concrete case study of using an MLLM for posture coding in collaborative learning, illustrating successes and challenges in a real research context.

CASE STUDY: POSTURE ANNOTATION USING MLLMs IN COLLABORATIVE LEARNING

To ground the discussion in a real-world scenario, we present a detailed case study based on the work of Whitehead, Nguyen, and Järvelä (2025). This study exemplifies how a MLLM can be incorporated into an MLPA pipeline to extract meaningful non-verbal features from video data. We will describe the context and goals of the study, the methodology (including Generative AI integration), the results obtained, and the lessons learned. This case provides a concrete example of operationalizing a learning theory construct (socially shared regulation of learning, SSRL) into observable data via Generative AI, along with reflections on reliability and methodological considerations.

Context and Goals

The study by Whitehead et al. (2025) was motivated by a need to analyze non-verbal behavior in collaborative learning settings efficiently. The context was a co-located collaborative learning task: 52 pre-service teacher education students working in groups on a physics-based learning activity. These group sessions were video-recorded to capture the rich interaction data. Prior research in collaborative learning emphasized the importance of non-verbal cues, like how students position themselves, gesture, or physically engage with materials, for understanding group dynamics and regulation of learning (Järvelä & Hadwin, 2013). However, manually coding such behaviors from video is extremely time-consuming, and traditional automated approaches (like pose estimation) often require controlled conditions or do not directly yield high-level behavioral categories (Radu et al., 2020).

The specific theoretical lens was SSRL, which involves group members collectively managing their learning processes (planning, monitoring, motivation control, etc.). SSRL is not directly visible, but certain physical behaviors might indicate that these regulatory processes are happening. For instance, a student leaning in towards the group might signal engagement and shared focus (a regulatory behavior), whereas a student slouching or turning away might signal disengagement or a breakdown in coordination. Whitehead et al. (2025) aimed to extract postural behaviors as a window into these SSRL processes. By doing so, they hoped to illustrate how Generative AI (an MLLM in this case) could augment the MLPA process, making it feasible to include such non-verbal features in analysis without excessive cost.

The key research questions they posed were:

1. How can MLLMs be reliably used as a scientific research tool in the MLPA process to extract posture behaviors?
2. What are the considerations, including strengths and weaknesses, for using MLLMs for image annotation in a collaborative learning context? (Whitehead et al., 2025)

In simpler terms, they wanted to know whether an AI like GPT-4 could take over the role of coding videos for posture behaviors (RQ1) and what one must keep in mind when doing this—where it works well, where it might fail, and what that implies for research (RQ2).

Methodology

Data and construct mapping

The researchers recorded 14 video sessions of the collaborative learning activity. As a first step, they identified which posture-related behaviors to focus on. Using a constant comparison method (iteratively reviewing video to inductively surface behaviors, then refining them), they initially noted about 30 distinct postural actions or states (Whitehead et al., 2025). Through expert discussion and pilot testing with the AI, they narrowed these down to nine categories that were theoretically relevant to SSRL as well as within the AI's capacity to recognize reliably. The nine posture categories were (paraphrased from the study): Sitting (SIT); Standing (STD); Engaged with computer peripherals (ECP)—e.g., hands on mouse/keyboard; Hands touching each other (HTC) or self-clasping; Holding a task-related object (HTR)—e.g., holding a lab apparatus or worksheet; Hands near face/head (HFN)—possibly thinking pose; Hands resting on laps (HRL); Leaning on the table (LTB)—weight on arms on table; and Arms resting on the table (ART) (Whitehead et al., 2025). Each of these was theorized to connect to aspects of regulation or engagement. For example, "engaged with computer" might indicate that a student is focusing on a specific task tool (an element of task regulation), whereas "arms resting on table" might sometimes indicate a relaxed or passive stance, depending on context.

These categories formed the *codebook* for analysis. Notably, researchers were not claiming SSRL is *measured* directly by any single category, but rather that these behaviors are proxies or pieces of evidence that, combined with other data, could reflect SSRL processes (Whitehead et al., 2025). The study explicitly did not go as far as correlating these with learning outcomes or delving into the SSRL processes—the aim was to demonstrate the extraction method.

Integration of the MLLM

The heart of the methodology was using GPT-4's multimodal capabilities to label images from the videos with the above categories. The team used the Microsoft Azure OpenAI service to access GPT-4, which allowed them to automate the process via Python and set certain parameters (Whitehead et al., 2025). They extracted video frames at a certain interval (the exact sampling rate is not stated in the excerpt, but presumably they took periodic frames or frames at key moments to code—let's assume it could be one frame per second or one frame each time a posture changed noticeably). Each frame image was then sent to GPT-4 with a carefully engineered prompt containing instructions and the codebook definitions.

The *prompt* (summarizing from Whitehead et al., 2025) included the following elements:

- **Task directive**: e.g., "Analyze the image provided and categorize the visible actions and postures of the individuals according to the predefined categories."
- **Observation guidance**: Reminding the model to focus on body language and only list relevant categories observed, without guessing or adding extra details.
- **Category list with abbreviations**: The nine categories were listed with short descriptions as given above, each paired with its abbreviation (e.g., "Sitting (SIT)—person's bottom is on a chair or seat.", "One or two arms resting on table (ART)—...", "Hands touching each other or clasped (HTC)—...", etc.).
- **Step-by-step instruction**: E.g., "Begin by determining if they are sitting or standing. Then check if they are leaning on the table. Next, look at the hands: are they touching each other, near face, on lap, holding an object, or on the table? Identify all that apply."
- **Output format**: "Output as the following example: SIT, HTR, LTB." (They provided an example of a possible combination of codes in the required format.)

By giving this prompt along with the image, GPT-4 would return a response like "SIT, LTB, HTC," if, say, the image showed a student sitting, leaning on the table, with hands clasped together. The choice to output abbreviations made it easy to parse and tally the results.

The *parameters* used were chosen to maximize reliability. They set the detail level to "high," so that GPT-4 would thoroughly analyze the image (in Azure's implementation, high detail means the model looks at the image in tiles for fine features) (Whitehead et al., 2025). They set temperature to 0.1 (very low) to ensure consistent outputs. They used "zero-shot" prompting (no exemplar Q&A pairs, just instructions), as the task was clearly defined by the codebook.

After the API returned outputs for all frames, the responses (in JSON via the API) were parsed into a structured dataset (CSV). Each frame now had machine-generated labels indicating which of the nine behaviors were present.

Reliability testing

The researchers did a focused reliability test on a subset of the data. They had human raters annotate a random sample of frames (approximately 2.5 percent of the dataset, which was a few hundred frames, given the large video corpus) with the same categories (Whitehead et al., 2025). They calculated Cohen's kappa between the MLLM's annotations and a human rater, as well as between two independent human raters on that sample. Additionally, they conducted a power analysis to confirm that even a 2.5 percent sample was statistically sufficient to detect agreement levels (and it was, given the effect sizes observed) (Whitehead et al., 2025).

Error analysis

To address RQ2 (strengths and weaknesses), they performed a systematic analysis of instances where the MLLM disagreed with humans. They randomly sampled ten mismatched cases per category and examined why the model might have erred (Whitehead et al., 2025). They categorized these errors into the three themes mentioned earlier: limb intrusion, insufficient context, and insufficient guidance. They also presented examples (with images) of each type of error for illustration.

Results

The results can be summarized in terms of (1) reliability metrics, and (2) qualitative insights into model performance:

Inter-rater reliability: Overall, the MLLM (GPT-4) showed a mix of high and moderate agreement with human coding, varying by category. The reported Cohen's kappa values ranged from about 0.96 (almost perfect) to 0.33 (fair agreement) across the nine categories (Whitehead et al., 2025). For example, categories like Sitting (SIT) and Standing (STD) were identified with very high reliability by the model—these are unambiguous, relatively easy distinctions, and indeed the model matched the human coder ~96 percent of the time (κ ~0.95). However, categories such as Arms resting on table (ART) and Leaning on table (LTB) had much lower agreement—around $\kappa = 0.3$–0.4, which is not much better than chance. These are more nuanced behaviors that can be ambiguous in a single image (is the person leaning forward to engage, or just stretching? Are their arms "resting," or are they actively using something on the table?). The human–human agreement for such categories was higher than the model's (e.g., humans might have κ ~0.6–0.7 on them, indicating moderate agreement), implying the model struggled more. The mean kappa across all categories was about 0.625, which falls in the substantial range overall but with high variation (Whitehead et al., 2025).

It is noteworthy that for every category, the model was at least consistent with itself (test–retest κ ~1.0 within model outputs). So, any "errors" were systematic rather than random. This consistency was considered a positive sign, because it means that the model could be a dependable coder, if calibrated—it will not flip-flop in its interpretation unpredictably (Whitehead et al., 2025).

Error patterns: The error analysis shed light on *why* the model missed some categories:

- *Limb intrusion*: In some frames, another person's arm or leg would appear in the scene in a misleading way. For instance, the target student might be sitting, but a standing neighbor's arm crosses into the frame at an angle that makes it look like the target has an arm raised. The model, not having persistent identity tracking, might attribute that limb to the target student and thus output an incorrect category (Whitehead et al., 2025). They found this most affected categories like ECP (hands on computer) or SIT/STD confusion when a stray limb suggested a different posture. The recommendation was to avoid or preprocess such frames (perhaps excluding frames where multiple people overlap in weird ways, or use multi-angle cameras to distinguish individuals).
- *Insufficient context*: GPT-4 analyzes each image independently with no memory of previous frames. Thus, if an image is cropped or does not show the entire person, the model might misinterpret. Whitehead et al. (2025) gave an example: a student was actually sitting, but the frame captured only their torso and above (no chair or lap visible), so the model misclassified them as standing. The fix here is to ensure images have enough of the scene—e.g., include chairs, full body if possible. If not, some context might be provided in prompt (like "the camera is top-down, consider that they may be seated even if legs aren't visible"). They observed insufficient context issues across many categories—basically whenever the image was too zoomed-in or ambiguous without background knowledge.
- *Insufficient guidance*: Some categories were conceptually fuzzy or overlapping, and the model might not have had clear rules to decide. For example, differentiating Hands near face (HFN) vs Hands touching each other (HTC) vs Hands on lap (HRL) can be tricky, because a person might be doing a bit of both (one hand touching the other near the face!). Or the posture might be borderline leaning vs sitting upright. Whitehead et al. (2025) noted that the less concrete categories with more variation (ART, HFN, HRL, HTC, HTR, LTB) were often where the model's guidance was insufficient. The prompt definitions might not have captured every scenario, so the model was left to guess. They suggest that more precise definitions or even adding clarifying sub-questions could help (e.g., define how much leaning counts as "leaning on table," or instruct the model in such cases to choose one consistently).

Implications of results: Despite the imperfections, the study highlighted that using an MLLM was indeed *feasible and efficient* for extracting posture data. The model processed hundreds of hours of video into coded data far more quickly than a human could. The high agreement on certain categories (like sitting/standing) shows that even out-of-the-box GPT-4 can do straightforward physical classification with scientific reliability. This is encouraging for those kinds of features—one could confidently automate detection of who is seated vs standing at any given time in a classroom, which itself is a useful interaction metric (e.g., teachers often ask groups to stand up when presenting, etc., and one could track if that happened). For more complex categories, the results advise caution: the AI-derived data might need cleaning or filtering. For example, one might use the AI's output but drop the categories that were below a reliability threshold, or use them only in aggregate ways.

Reflections and Lessons from the Case

Several critical reflections emerged from Whitehead et al.'s (2025) experience that are valuable for anyone looking to use Generative AI in MLPA:

- **Generative AI can substantially reduce manual coding load**, but it is not a plug-and-play replacement for humans in all respects. The study's pipeline drastically accelerated feature extraction (imagine coding thousands of frames by hand—the AI did it in a fraction of the time). However, the human had to be in the loop initially (to develop the codebook and prompt) and afterward (to validate reliability and interpret errors).
- **Prompt engineering and domain knowledge are key:** The success in extracting those posture categories was largely due to the careful prompt that embedded the codebook (Whitehead et al., 2025). If one had just asked GPT-4 "What is happening in this picture?," the answers would be too free-form and inconsistent for quantitative analysis. By giving it a structure grounded in learning theory (SSRL-informed categories), they constrained the model to produce analytically useful outputs. This indicates that generative models work best in analysis when guided by theory and expert knowledge, rather than being left open-ended.
- **Model consistency can make up for lower accuracy** in some use-cases. As GPT-4 was internally consistent (reliable with itself), one could treat its output as a distinct lens—for example, maybe GPT-4 always underestimates "leaning on table" unless it is very obvious. A researcher could recalibrate or adjust thresholds, effectively *learning the model's behavior* and possibly correcting for it. In classical test theory, one might think of the AI as another rater with certain biases; if those biases are systematic, one can adjust or at least be aware of them in interpretation. Whitehead et al. noted that beyond simple accuracy, the consistency is what allows the method to be scientifically usable (Whitehead et al., 2025).

- **Identification of edge cases and failure modes is necessary for trustworthy deployment**: The three types of errors (limb intrusion, context, guidance) are likely not unique to this study—they might appear in other vision-based LLM analyses (any context where images have occlusion, limited field of view, or ambiguous criteria). Knowing these, future researchers can preempt some problems: e.g., designing data collection to minimize occlusions, or including multiple frames to provide context (maybe feed two subsequent frames instead of one, to give a sense of motion or position). Also, "insufficient guidance" points to the potential benefit of *iteratively improving the prompt* or even fine-tuning the model if possible on a few examples where it got it wrong.
- **Scalability and novel feature extraction**: This approach allowed for extracting relatively high-level behavior ("hands on lap" is something a typical pose estimation algorithm would not directly output—it would give joint coordinates, and one would have to infer hands-on-lap via some geometric reasoning). Models such as GPT-4 in effect provided a shortcut for that by doing the interpretation itself. This suggests that generative models can expand the toolkit of what we measure. We are not limited to what classical sensors can detect; we can ask the model to detect *conceptual* things if they manifest in the data. Whitehead et al. (2025) even mention that the MLLM approach made it possible to work with more "meaningful and high-level behavioral categories without additional algorithms or sensors," citing how something like "hands task-related (HTR)" is hard to get from raw pose data, but GPT-4 could infer it from context (like seeing a student holding a pen and writing—it knows that that is task-related).
- **Integration with existing frameworks**: The authors relate their work as extending Ochoa et al.'s (2022) MLPA framework by adding prompt engineering as a new step in the feature extraction process (Whitehead et al., 2025). This is an interesting conceptual point: Generative AI does not remove the need for frameworks; it adds a new component to them. One must manage prompts and AI interactions just like one manages sensor calibration or feature selection in traditional pipelines.
- **Considerations for research adoption**: From a practical viewpoint, the case study shows promise but also some barriers. To use GPT-4 on images, the team had to use Azure's service with appropriate settings—not something every education researcher might be immediately familiar with. There are also costs (they did not detail cost, but GPT-4 image analysis is not free). This implies that while the method is powerful, developing user-friendly tools or workflows, for example a plugin for widely used video analysis software that calls an API in the background, could help more researchers to adopt it. On the positive side, the method did not require them to collect new kinds of data or lab setups; they used ordinary video

recordings from a classroom—so the barrier to data collection was low, and the AI did the heavy analysis.

- **Ethical and privacy reflection**: Although not deeply discussed in the excerpt, one can reflect that sending video frames to a cloud AI involves privacy considerations. The study had ethical clearance and presumably participant consent (Whitehead et al., 2025). For broader use, especially in real-time classroom tools, one would need strict data agreements or on-premises models to ensure that student privacy is maintained (Cukurova, Giannakos, & Martinez-Maldonado, 2020 mention privacy as a core concern). This is a general point for Generative AI in MLPA—the convenience of API services must be balanced with privacy or else a push toward secure, possibly offline deployment of models for sensitive data.

In conclusion, this case study demonstrates that a multimodal LLM (GPT-4) can serve as an effective tool in multimodal learning analytics for coding complex behaviors like posture. The integration of Generative AI allowed the researchers to obtain granular, time-series data of group posture dynamics with relatively modest effort once the pipeline was set up. The reliability was good for many categories, although not uniformly so, highlighting the need for careful validation. The methodological lessons—about prompt design, data preparation, and understanding model limitations—provide a roadmap for others attempting similar projects. This case also shows how linking analytics to learning constructs (SSRL here) guides the entire process, ensuring that even when using cutting-edge AI, the analysis remains grounded in educational significance.

Next, we distill the broader lessons learned from this case and other experiences and discuss their implications for researchers and practitioners interested in leveraging Generative AI in multimodal analytics.

LESSONS LEARNED AND REFLECTIONS

Integrating Generative AI into multimodal learning process analytics is a promising yet challenging endeavor. Based on the above case study and the growing body of research in this space, we summarize key lessons and reflections that can inform future projects. These lessons highlight what has worked well, what pitfalls to watch out for, and how the role of researchers and educators is evolving in the age of Generative AI.

- **Generative AI can *augment* and/or *enhance*, not replace, human analysts**: One clear lesson is that Generative AI methods are powerful assistants for feature extraction and pattern finding, but they are not a silver bullet that makes human expertise obsolete. In the case study, the MLLM automated the detection of posture features with reasonable reliability, drastically reducing manual coding effort. However, human experts were still crucial for designing the coding scheme (categories derived from SSRL theory), crafting the prompts, and validating the outputs. Generative models do not inherently know what is pedagogically relevant—they must be guided to it. Thus, researchers and educators still define the problems and interpret the results; the AI handles the grunt work of processing and initial labeling. This human–AI collaboration can lead to more efficient analytics pipelines, but it requires thoughtful setup and oversight. As a reflection, we should embrace Generative AI as a collaborator that can handle scale and complexity while maintaining our role in asking the right questions and ensuring quality (Järvelä et al., 2023).

- **Importance of careful pipeline design (from data to prompt to output)**: The technical pipeline needs to be well orchestrated to harness Generative AI effectively. From the lessons above, every step matters: capturing good quality data, preprocessing to avoid known issues (e.g., occlusions or missing context), writing precise prompts, choosing stable model settings, and planning validation. Skipping or rushing any of these can undermine the whole analysis. For instance, if one fed raw, unfiltered video frames to an LLM without considering camera angles, one might get a lot of garbage in the output (because the model is confused by irrelevant visual features). Or if one used a poorly chosen prompt, the model might ignore key aspects (like failing to mention a category, meaning the model might never output it). The case study underscored the value of iterative refinement—they did not get the prompt and categories perfect on the first try; these evolved through pilot tests. A broader lesson is the benefit of *incremental development*: start with a small subset of data, experiment and refine, then scale up to the full dataset once confident. This saves time and ensures the final pipeline is robust.
- **Generative models show high *consistency* even when accuracy is imperfect**: An interesting finding from using GPT-4 was that while it had difficulty with some nuanced categories, it was internally consistent and systematically biased rather than random (Whitehead et al., 2025). This is important, because consistency (reliability) is a foundation for any scientific measurement—a consistent tool can often be calibrated or its results interpreted with known margins of error. If a model is inconsistent (one day it labels something one way, the next day differently with no reason), it is very hard to use. Generative AI models, when configured with low stochasticity, tend to be very consistent. This suggests that for analytics purposes, one should run models in deterministic modes (low temperature, fixed seeds) to maximize repeatability. The high test–retest reliability observed in GPT-4's outputs is encouraging—it means that once we trust

the process, we can generate data, and even if the model has some bias, that bias will be the same across the dataset, which might cancel out or be adjusted. Reliability is as crucial as validity; ensure your generative approach is giving stable results, then tackle improving validity through better prompts or model choice.

- **Error analysis is invaluable for improving model prompts and interpretation**: The identification of error types (limb intrusion, context, guidance issues) in our case study was not just an academic exercise—it points directly to remedies and cautions. For example, knowing about "insufficient context" errors suggests always including enough background in images or even feeding sequences of frames to give context. Knowing about "insufficient guidance" suggests adding more detailed definitions to the prompt or splitting a complex category into simpler ones. Future users of Generative AI in MLPA should incorporate an error analysis step: take a sample of outputs, especially the borderline or mismatched ones, and analyze them. Often, a pattern will emerge that can inform a tweak to the methodology. Over time, as a community, collecting these common pitfalls can lead to best practices (perhaps a "troubleshooting guide" for using LLMs to annotate educational data).
- **The role of learning theory and constructs remains central**: One might wonder, with such powerful models, can we not just throw the raw data at them and have them tell us what's interesting? The answer from current experience is largely no—or at least, doing so is risky if we want meaningful, theory-aligned insights. Generative models do not have an inherent understanding of "learning" or "collaboration quality," unless we prompt them in those terms. In our case, SSRL theory guided what categories to measure and how to interpret them (e.g., hands on a task object indicates engagement in joint task work). Without that theoretical framing, the model might still describe the video (e.g., "Person is holding a pen"), but we might not know why that matters or how to use it. By embedding theory into analytics (like using SSRL to choose posture codes, or using self-regulated learning theory to define indicators like "planning gestures" vs "impulsive actions"), we ensure that the output is actionable and insightful. Generative AI, in fact, might allow us to operationalize more nuanced constructs than before because we can ask the model to detect things that lack precise sensor equivalents (like "curiosity in tone of voice" or "group attention alignment"). But we must define those constructs and verify the model's capability to detect them. The takeaway is that multidisciplinary collaboration—between learning scientists (to bring theory/constructs) and AI specialists (to implement them with Generative AI)—is still very much needed, and Generative AI can actually strengthen that bridge by

making it easier to test whether a theoretical construct has observable signals in data.

- **Scalability and efficiency come with new cost structures and technical needs**: Using Generative AI is often computationally heavy. Instead of training one model to do one thing, we might be invoking a huge model hundreds or thousands of times. The cost might be in API usage fees or in needing a machine with a strong graphics processing unit (GPU) if running locally. Also, handling large data outputs (the model might output a lot of text or JSON) requires new data management. Researchers should plan for resource usage by budgeting both money (for cloud APIs if needed) and time (generative models might take several seconds per analysis, which over tens of thousands of data points could be hours of compute). In the posture study, the authors processed quite a lot of images—using the Azure cloud presumably made it manageable, but such infrastructure is a consideration. For practitioners in schools, this raises issues of how to deploy—e.g., running a simplified local model for quick feedback vs using cloud services with sensitive student data. From a lesson perspective: plan your infrastructure early and perhaps start with smaller data to estimate how the approach scales. Fortunately, as technology advances, these models could become faster and more accessible (the cost of AI inference tends to drop over time as hardware and optimization improve).
- **Ethical considerations are amplified**: MLPA already had to deal with privacy (video and audio of students are sensitive). Introducing Generative AI adds layers: potential biases in models could inadvertently introduce fairness issues (e.g., if a model misinterprets the behavior of some demographic groups more than others, leading to skewed analytics). Also, using external services means trusting third-party AI providers with data security. Lesson learned: any Generative AI-enhanced analytic pipeline should undergo an ethical review. If a model is found to have bias, consider mitigation (maybe adjust the training data or prompt it to be more neutral, or at least report the limitations). If using cloud services, ensure that data are encrypted, agreements are in place, or use anonymization techniques (like face blurring or voice masking as mentioned earlier) to protect identities. Moreover, transparency is key: stakeholders (teachers, students) should know that an AI system is being used to analyze their behaviors and agree to it. In the research context, Whitehead et al. (2025) noted ethical procedures, owing to using sensitive video with MLLMs, highlighting that even researchers need to be aware that sending student data to an AI system is something to be handled carefully and reported.
- **Interpreting Generative AI outputs requires critical thinking**: Another reflection is that we, as researchers, need to avoid being lulled by the fluent and confident outputs of generative models. Just because an AI labels

something or produces a nice summary does not make it true. We must maintain a healthy skepticism and examine consistency with other evidence. For instance, if an AI-coded analysis suggests "Group X exhibited high engagement throughout," cross-check that with perhaps the video itself or other measures (did Group X actually complete tasks successfully?). The classic "trust but verify" approach applies. We should treat AI outputs as one source of evidence that can be triangulated. Also, keep in mind that generative models might have some training data biases—e.g., GPT-4 is trained on a lot of internet images, which might affect how it interprets body language in certain contexts (maybe it has seen more images of people at work than at school, etc.).

To summarize these lessons in a few key points for practitioners and researchers:

- **Start small and iterate**: Pilot your Generative AI approach on a small dataset to refine prompts and parameters.
- **Ground in theory**: Use learning theories to define what you ask the AI to detect—this ensures relevance and guides interpretation.
- **Validate thoroughly**: Do not assume the AI is correct—use human judgment and other data to check its outputs.
- **Document and report methods transparently**: Others will want to know your prompt, model version, etc., to replicate or critique—be open about it.
- **Stay aware of limitations**: Be upfront about categories or situations where the model did not do well; suggest that findings in those areas be taken cautiously or need further study.

With these lessons in mind, we now look ahead. How might this field evolve? What developments in AI or educational practice could further shape the use of Generative AI in multimodal analytics? The final section explores future directions and open questions for research and practice.

FUTURE DIRECTIONS

The intersection of Generative AI and multimodal learning analytics is a rapidly developing frontier. As AI technology and educational practices both evolve, several future directions and opportunities emerge:

More Integrated Multimodal Foundation Models

Currently, we often feed one modality at a time to models (e.g., an image or a block of text). Future AI models are likely to handle multiple streams simultaneously—imagine an AI that can watch a video with audio and read associated text (like chat or slides) all at once and draw insights. Early steps in this direction exist (e.g., research on models like Meta's ImageBind, which creates joint embeddings for image, audio, text, etc.). In an MLPA context, this could enable a single model to take in raw multimodal data (video + audio + perhaps sensor data encoded in text) and directly output analyses or classifications that account for cross-modal cues. For example, it might understand that a student's posture plus a long silence in conversation plus a confused facial expression together indicate a breakdown in understanding. Currently, we handle these signals separately then merge; a future model might reason over them holistically, possibly capturing complex interactions that human analysts could miss.

Real-time Analytics and Feedback Loops

As generative models become faster and deployable on local devices (which is happening as optimized versions and hardware improvements roll out), we might see real-time applications. For instance, an augmented classroom system could use an on-site model to monitor collaborative groups and give instant, adaptive support. If a group is stuck (sitting idle, not talking) and the model detects this, it could generate a prompt or hint via an embodied agent or display. Some projects are already exploring "AI in the loop" for classrooms (Holstein et al., 2019's real-time dashboards for teachers, etc.), and generative models could supercharge this by providing context-aware suggestions or even simulating a peer or tutor. However, implementing this will require robust analytics (we cannot have too many false alarms or inappropriate help), which means that the models must be well-tuned and validated in real settings. There is also the need for *user interface and experience design* how to deliver AI-generated insights or feedback to teachers and students in a non-disruptive, supportive way.

Domain-specific Fine-tuning and Custom Models

While GPT-4 and similar general models are impressive, there is space for models specifically tailored to educational contexts. We might see the rise of "EduGPT" or other foundation models trained on data from classrooms, textbooks, educational dialogs, etc. Such models could potentially understand educational jargon, student behaviors, and pedagogical strategies more deeply than a general model. Fine-tuning or instruction-tuning general models on multimodal educational datasets (videos of classrooms, transcripts of tutoring sessions, etc.) might yield models that are better at subtle tasks like identifying when a teacher is using a certain instructional method or when a student group has reached a particular phase of problem solving. Researchers like Yan et al. (2024) have called for exploring human–AI collaboration frameworks; part of that could involve adapting AI to better align with educational research needs. We anticipate more interdisciplinary datasets being created to enable this (multimodal corpora labeled for things like engagement, confusion, SSRL episodes, etc., which can be used to train or evaluate models).

Enhanced Prompt Engineering Tools and Automation

The reliance on prompt engineering currently is both a strength (flexible control) and a weakness (it is somewhat an art and not always systematic). In the future, we might have tools that assist researchers in generating effective prompts. For example, an interactive system could allow a researcher to highlight parts of an image and label them and then automatically generate a prompt for the model focusing on those elements; or one AI model could be used to help to optimize the prompt for another (there is already work on using LLMs to critique or refine prompts). We might also see *prompt libraries*—collections of validated prompts for common analytics tasks (e.g., "prompt to identify on-task vs off-task behavior from chat," "prompt to code debate discourse moves from text", etc.). Sharing these could reduce duplication of effort and standardize how Generative AI is applied, much like validated questionnaires are shared in educational research. Moreover, as prompt-based use grows, we might formalize prompt engineering as a methodology such as guidelines on how to translate constructs into prompts, how to test prompts systematically (Whitehead et al., 2025 provides such insights in an AI context). The community can move from ad-hoc prompting to more principled approaches (perhaps even an "APA style" for prompts in research papers, ensuring completeness and clarity).

Addressing Ethical, Privacy, and Bias Issues: Frameworks and Policies

As Generative AI becomes more embedded in educational analytics and potentially interventions, the stakes for ethical use get higher. We might see frameworks developed specifically for responsible use of AI in classrooms, akin to data privacy laws but encompassing AI's unique challenges. For example, policies might require that any AI-generated feedback to students be vetted or that models used on student data be audited for bias. There is an opportunity for the learning analytics community to lead in proposing such frameworks (perhaps extending work like Cukurova et al., 2020 who outlined MLPA concerns to directly tackle Generative AI). Techniques like federated learning or on-device analysis might be emphasized to keep student data local. Another aspect is "explainable AI"—future research might demand that generative models provide some rationale for their analytics decisions to be acceptable in educational settings. There is emerging research on prompting models to explain their classification (e.g., "Explain why you labeled this image as off-task"), which could be invaluable for trust. We foresee more work on how to integrate human judgment with AI suggestions in analysis—for instance, maybe an interactive platform where an AI codes data but flags low-confidence cases for a human analyst to review, achieving both efficiency and accuracy with a human-in-the-loop approach.

Expanding MLPA to New Frontiers

Generative AI might also push the boundaries of *what* we analyze. For example, with advanced audio models, we could analyze tone of voice and prosody (not just transcription of words) by having a model categorize the emotional tone or confidence level in a student's voice. With video generation and analysis, we might analyze micro-gestures or posture shifts that were previously too subtle to code (maybe an AI could detect patterns of fidgeting as a proxy for disengagement). Also, as augmented reality/virtual reality learning environments rise, multimodal data could include 3D interactions, and generative models could help summarize those (e.g., describing a student's actions in a virtual lab in natural language for a teacher's dashboard). The tools and methods we developed could apply there with some adaptation.

With scalable Generative AI coding, one can analyze much larger datasets—perhaps years of classroom video or data across multiple schools—something that was impractical with manual coding. This opens up research on questions of generalizability: will an AI model trained/tuned in one context (say, a physics class in Finland) work well in another (say, a history class in Japan)? We can test this by sharing models or prompts and seeing how behavior definitions transfer. Generative AI might help normalize some differences (because it has broad knowledge), but there will always be local nuances. Future research can explore how to adapt models to local contexts, possibly by a small amount of fine-tuning on context-specific data (few-shot learning on new class examples). The hope is that some analytics (like detecting obvious engagement vs disengagement behaviors) might generalize well, allowing cross-comparisons and bigger meta-analyses of learning processes across contexts—something that traditionally has been very hard, owing to differing coding schemes and labor demands.

Collaboration Between AI Developers and Education Researchers

Finally, a future direction is simply deeper collaboration. As AI labs develop new generative models, involving educational researchers in the process could ensure that the models are better suited for educational data and tasks. Conversely, education researchers might work with AI experts to hack existing models for their needs. The case study was a nice example of applying a general model to an educational setting; future projects might involve co-developing a model with features specifically for MLPA (perhaps a vision model that has been taught what a "raising hand" looks like, or a text model aware of common student answer errors). Workshops, shared datasets (with privacy-respecting measures), and interdisciplinary initiatives will likely increase.

In conclusion, the future of Generative AI in multimodal learning analytics is bright but will require careful navigation. The potential to greatly enhance our understanding of learning through rich data is clear—we can capture dimensions of learning that were once hidden in the "video archives" or lost in translation. But we must proceed in a way that maintains rigor, equity, and privacy. By building on the technical foundations and lessons discussed in this chapter, future work can create analytics tools that are not only more powerful, but also more adaptive, transparent, and aligned with educational values. As Generative AI becomes more ingrained, it might even shift how we conceptualize learning processes (for instance, if an AI can identify a pattern across thousands of classroom videos that humans had not noticed, it could lead to new theories of interaction). Thus, the partnership between human insight and AI will continue to deepen, ideally leading to both scientific advances and practical innovations that benefit learners and educators.

PART IV

Future directions and final remarks

9. Future directions for multimodal learning process analytics

ENVISIONING THE FUTURE OF MLPA

In this concluding chapter, we adopt an exploratory and forward-looking stance, focusing on key areas poised to shape the future of multimodal learning process analytics (MLPA). Building on the theoretical foundations and methodological innovations described in earlier chapters, we discuss emerging directions in multimodal analytics rather than immediate practical implementations. The sections below outline major avenues for future research, including innovations in data fusion and temporal modeling, next-generation sensing modalities, and real-time adaptive analytics for formative feedback. We then consider the integration of large-scale multimodal datasets alongside ethical and privacy implications, followed by the development of cross-disciplinary frameworks and standards to unify the field. Recognizing the importance of context, we discuss culturally responsive approaches to MLPA that ensure inclusivity and equity. We also explore how advances in generative artificial intelligence (AI) could transform learning process modeling and envision new forms of human–AI collaboration in learning analytics. Finally, we address open challenges related to the scalability, reliability, and interpretability of MLPA systems. Throughout, our aim is to articulate a research agenda that will guide the community toward MLPA solutions that are technically robust, pedagogically meaningful, and ethically sound. By anticipating these future directions, researchers and practitioners can work proactively to design the next generation of multimodal learning analytics that truly enhance educational outcomes.

A cornerstone of MLPA is the ability to fuse heterogeneous data streams (e.g., facial expressions, speech, physiological signals, eye gaze, and log files) into a coherent picture of the learning process. Future research will need to develop more sophisticated data fusion techniques and temporal modeling approaches to fully leverage complementary information in multimodal data. One critical challenge is the alignment of data from different modalities and time scales. For instance, sensor data can be captured at high frequency (e.g., heart rate variability measured in milliseconds), while observational data such as video are sampled at lower frame rates; combining these meaningfully is non-trivial.

Beyond alignment, multimodal data fusion techniques will evolve to integrate information both within each modality and across modalities in a more principled way. Traditional early fusion (concatenating features) or late fusion (combining separate model outputs) can give way to deep fusion approaches, where learning algorithms discover cross-modal interactions. Future work might draw on advances in machine learning such as cross-modal transformers and graph neural networks, which can model relationships between modalities over time. Indeed, an important methodological question is how to fuse multimodal data so that inter-modality and cross-modality correlations are effectively integrated. Future research can extend these by incorporating attention mechanisms that attend to salient moments across modalities, or by using multiscale temporal modeling (capturing micro-patterns within an activity and macro-patterns across multiple sessions).

Ultimately, advancing data fusion and temporal modeling will require addressing current limitations head-on. Many existing MLPA models struggle when faced with fragmented or missing data, which is common when integrating multiple sensors (owing to signal dropouts, varying participation, or privacy filters). Making fusion techniques robust to sporadic data availability is a key research direction. For example, if a student opts out of video recording for privacy reasons, the system should still function by relying on other signals (wearables, logs)—possibly by imputing missing modalities or dynamically re-weighting sources. Moreover, as multimodal datasets grow in size and complexity, scalable data integration pipelines will be needed. This might involve distributed computing frameworks that handle high-frequency, high-volume streams in real time, or federated data fusion approaches that allow combining insights from separate datasets without pooling raw sensitive data. In summary, innovations in data fusion and temporal modeling will form the technical backbone of next-generation MLPA, enabling more accurate and nuanced interpretations of learning processes. By developing algorithms that synchronize multimodal data, capture cross-modal patterns, and model temporal dynamics, researchers will pave the way for MLPA systems that mirror the true complexity of learning as it unfolds over time.

NEXT-GENERATION SENSING TECHNOLOGIES AND DATA MODALITIES

The future of multimodal analytics will be heavily influenced by advances in sensing technologies and the emergence of new data modalities. Early MLPA research has largely focused on modalities such as video (for facial expressions and gestures), audio (speech and paralinguistic cues), interaction logs (click-streams, keystrokes), and physiological signals (heart rate, skin conductance) that can be collected with today's devices. Going forward, next-generation sensors promise to expand both the breadth and depth of data available for learning analytics. A wide range of sensors can already be classified into motion sensors, biosensors, and environmental sensors, as well as camera and microphone inputs for recognizing actions and affect. These provide a baseline, but emerging technologies will push beyond the current state of the art. One important category is wearable and ubiquitous sensors, which are becoming more miniaturized, affordable, and sophisticated. Wearable devices (e.g., smartwatches, fitness bands, electroencephalogram [EEG] headbands) can continuously capture fine-grained physiological and behavioral data in natural learning settings. For instance, motion sensors such as accelerometers and gyroscopes can detect subtle movements or fidgeting; biosensors can monitor heart rate variability, skin conductance, or even brain activity (via EEG) as proxies for cognitive load or emotional arousal. Environmental sensors embedded in classrooms or mobile devices can log contextual factors, such as ambient noise, light, or location, that influence learning.

Future classrooms might integrate a network of such sensors to create "intelligent learning spaces" that respond to learners in context. A notable trend is the development of in-sensor computing capabilities—sensors and wearables that not only collect data but also perform on-device processing. By analyzing signals locally (e.g., a smartwatch app inferring stress levels from pulse data in real time), these devices reduce the need for continuous raw data transmission, thereby minimizing latency and preserving privacy. Research should explore how such edge-computing approaches can be harnessed for instantaneous analytics and feedback within learning environments.

Beyond wearables, novel modalities are on the horizon for MLPA. Brain–computer interfaces (BCI), such as EEG or functional near-infrared spectroscopy headsets, could provide real-time measures of cognitive states (attention, workload) that were previously inaccessible in classroom settings. While still experimental, these neurophysiological sensors are becoming more user-friendly and could enable a deeper integration of neuroscience and education research. In fact, future work is expected to examine higher-order brain signals and their interplay with other modalities to better infer complex states like mental effort or confusion. Likewise, tactile and haptic data represent an under-explored modality that could be relevant in domains such as skills training or collaborative learning—for example, pressure sensors in pens or tablets to gauge uncertainty, or haptic feedback devices that measure and respond to student actions. Eye-tracking and gaze technology, already used in controlled studies, might become more ubiquitous (e.g., built into augmented reality [AR]/virtual reality [VR]/mixed reality headsets or standard classroom equipment) to capture attention distribution and joint attention in collaborative settings. AR/VR environments themselves offer new streams of data: detailed logs of 3D interactions, head and hand movements, and immersive context information. However, integrating AR/VR data into MLPA is still nascent; future research can develop analytics that span the physical and virtual learning spaces. A recent outlook notes that modalities like tactile data, BCIs, and AR are emerging but remain under-explored in current MLPA studies. Incorporating these into mainstream research will broaden the scope of which learning processes can be observed and supported.

Another frontier is multi-party sensing—capturing data not just from individual learners but from groups and social interactions. For example, positioning systems or proximity sensors can track how students physically cluster during group work; wearable microphones for each student can disentangle contributions in a discussion; synchronized wearable data across group members can reveal patterns of social coordination or emotional contagion. These richer multimodal interaction datasets will enable analysis of collaborative learning processes in unprecedented detail. However, they also pose technical challenges (synchronizing data across individuals, dealing with interference among devices) and ethical challenges (managing consent and privacy in group data).

As next-generation sensors proliferate, it will be crucial to ensure that their data are not only collected but meaningfully used. Raw data from complex sensors like EEG or motion capture are often noisy and high-dimensional, requiring advanced preprocessing and feature extraction techniques. Future MLPA research must devise methods to distill interpretable features from these modalities (e.g., recognizing meaningful brain wave patterns correlating with mind wandering or extracting posture dynamics from motion data). Moreover, each new modality added to the analytics pipeline introduces questions of validity: what aspect of learning does this signal actually reflect? For instance, does a particular EEG pattern truly indicate engagement, or might it be confounded by unrelated factors? Cross-disciplinary collaboration with domain experts (neuroscientists, kinesiologists, etc.) will be needed to correctly interpret novel sensor data in educational terms. There is also a risk of information overload—more data are not automatically better if they are not integrated well. Thus, a parallel direction for future work is sensor selection and context-aware data reduction: identifying which combination of modalities yields the most useful information for a given educational question and filtering out extraneous data. Research might investigate adaptive sensing, where the system intelligently toggles or weights sensors based on the context (e.g., focusing on audio and gesture during a group dialog, but on eye-tracking and EEG during quiet reading).

CROSS-DISCIPLINARY FRAMEWORKS AND METHODOLOGICAL STANDARDIZATION

Multimodal learning analytics inherently draws from multiple disciplines—computer science, learning sciences, psychology, data science, neuroscience, and more. As the field progresses, there is a growing recognition that fostering cross-disciplinary frameworks and achieving methodological standardization are critical for sustained advancement. Future research directions include developing integrative frameworks that bridge theoretical perspectives with computational methods and establishing standards that enable researchers to build cumulatively on each other's work.

A key challenge for MLPA has been that studies often operate within their own disciplinary silos or conceptual paradigms. For example, a computer science-driven study might focus on algorithm performance without deeply engaging with educational theory, while an education-driven study might collect rich multimodal data but use relatively simple analytics methods. Bridging these gaps is a priority. One future direction is the creation of unified conceptual frameworks that map how data from various modalities relate to learning constructs across different theories. This could involve explicit alignment of constructs: e.g., linking the concept of "cognitive load" from educational psychology with specific multimodal indicators (such as gaze dispersion or EEG patterns) identified by data science within a single framework. By aligning computational methods with well-established learning theories, MLPA systems can be both technologically advanced and pedagogically meaningful.

Grounding multimodal analytics in frameworks like constructivism, sociocultural learning, or self-regulated learning can yield richer interpretations and more effective interventions. For instance, an MLPA framework could incorporate an embodied learning perspective, positing that gestures and posture (captured via motion sensors) are not just ancillary data but core components of cognitive processing—thus encouraging analytics to treat them as such. Developing these cross-disciplinary frameworks will likely require collaborative teams of experts. We could see more joint efforts, such as workshops or special interest groups, where learning scientists and AI specialists co-create models of the learning process that explicitly inform what data to collect and how to interpret them.

In parallel, there is a need for methodological standardization to advance MLPA from a collection of isolated studies to a coherent scientific domain. Currently, variations in experimental design, data collection instruments, feature extraction techniques, and analytic models make it difficult to compare results across studies or replicate findings. Progress in this area will require community-driven standards established on several fronts. First, standard data formats and ontologies for multimodal data can be established. Just as the biomedical field has standards for data reporting (e.g., for clinical trials), MLPA could benefit from agreed descriptions of datasets—listing the modalities, sampling rates, measures of learning outcomes, etc. Shared benchmarks and challenge problems could be instituted to spur progress on common tasks (for example, a benchmark dataset for "multimodal emotion recognition in classrooms" or "multimodal collaboration success prediction"). Indeed, scholars have pointed out the pressing need for shared datasets and evaluation frameworks to support replication and cross-study comparisons. If the community were to assemble a few high-quality multimodal datasets, make them open-access, and collectively focus on them, it could accelerate algorithmic improvements and reveal which methods generalize. We might also see the emergence of standardized evaluation metrics for MLPA. Beyond accuracy, metrics such as robustness, response time (for real-time systems), or user acceptance of interventions could become part of the standard evaluation battery. Establishing such benchmarks will help in objectively identifying the best performing techniques and areas needing improvement.

Another dimension of standardization is developing best-practice methodologies for conducting multimodal studies. This includes guidelines on experimental design (e.g., how to incorporate multimodal data collection without disrupting learning), data preprocessing (how to synchronize modalities—perhaps a standard tool for multimodal timestamp alignment), and feature selection (ensuring that features used across studies are comparable or interpretable). Efforts by the community to publish methodological primers or protocol papers can be valuable. For instance, a *Multimodal Learning Analytics Handbook* (some initial efforts exist in that direction) can compile recommended practices. In the long run, these standards and protocols contribute to what one review called a "systematic theoretical framework" for MLPA built through multidisciplinary convergence. By integrating expertise from multiple fields, researchers should aim to construct unified theories and methods for understanding learning with multimodal data. This could manifest as a reference model describing, say, how attentional, emotional, and collaborative processes interact during learning, and what multimodal indicators correspond to each—a model that both theorists and data analysts agree upon.

Cross-disciplinary work also extends to methodological innovation. As new techniques from one field become available (e.g., transformer neural networks from AI, or novel statistical models from psychometrics), integrating them into MLPA often requires adapting them to educational contexts and aligning them with pedagogical interpretation. An interesting future direction is hybrid methodologies that combine qualitative and quantitative, human and machine analysis. For example, mixed-methods approaches might use AI to crunch large multimodal datasets to identify patterns and then involve human experts (teachers or psychologists) to interpret or validate these patterns in context. The interplay of qualitative insights (from classroom observations, student interviews) with quantitative sensory data could lead to more credible and ecologically valid findings. Encouraging multidisciplinary teams to work together from project inception—rather than sequential handoff—will help to ensure that the questions asked of the data are grounded in learning theory, and that the technological solutions are applicable in practice. Notably, future research should also prioritize professional development and teacher involvement as part of cross-disciplinary integration. Teachers are key stakeholders who can provide practical perspectives about what analytics are useful or how feedback should be delivered. Engaging educators in the design of MLPA systems (co-design) will help to bridge the gap between computational possibilities and classroom realities.

Finally, building a cohesive field of MLPA requires investment in community and capacity building. This might include cross-disciplinary training programs for emerging scholars (so a Ph.D. student might be equally comfortable discussing deep learning algorithms and educational psychology theories), and collaborative venues where researchers from different backgrounds converge. If successful, the field will move toward a state where studies not only report their own results but also contribute to a larger, interoperable ecosystem of knowledge. In summary, the future of MLPA relies on breaking down silos and establishing common ground—through unified frameworks that incorporate multi-faceted understandings of learning, and through standardized methods that allow cumulative progress. These efforts will ensure that as the field grows, it does so cohesively, with shared language and tools enabling researchers to build on each other's insights rather than reinventing the wheel for each new study.

ADVANCES IN GENERATIVE AI AND THEIR POTENTIAL IN LEARNING PROCESS MODELING

The rise of Generative AI—systems capable of producing human-like text, images, simulations, and more—represents a transformative development in technology with significant implications for learning analytics. Large Language Models (LLMs), such as GPT-4, image generators, and other generative models, offer new capabilities that future MLPA research can leverage to model learning processes in novel ways. In this section, we explore how Generative AI might be integrated into multimodal analytics and what potential benefits and challenges this entails.

One immediate application of Generative AI is in handling unstructured data that traditional analytics struggle with. Educational settings produce rich unstructured data: think of open-ended responses in text, student discussions in audio, handwritten work, or diagrams drawn on paper. LLMs and related models excel at interpreting and generating natural language and could be used to analyze classroom discourse or written reflections at scale. For example, a generative model fine-tuned on educational dialog might automatically summarize a group discussion, extracting key points or misunderstandings to inform an instructor. In fact, researchers posit that Generative AI can play pivotal roles in analyzing unstructured data within the learning analytics cycle. This might involve converting raw transcripts into meaningful indicators (such as detecting arguments or questions asked by students) or even translating between modalities (converting a diagram drawn by a student into a textual description that can be analyzed by a Natural Language Processing pipeline).

Generative AI also opens the door to creating synthetic data to augment learning analytics. One perpetual challenge in MLPA is the scarcity of labeled multimodal data for training complex models—it is expensive and time-consuming to collect thousands of hours of synchronized video, audio, and sensor data with ground truth labels of learning outcomes. Generative models could alleviate this by simulating realistic multimodal data. For instance, an advanced generative system might create synthetic student interaction scenarios: simulated sensor feeds (heart rate, gaze patterns, etc.) paired with generated student dialogs that reflect certain emotional or cognitive states. By carefully blending real and synthetic data, researchers could train more robust models or explore scenarios that are rare in actual data (such as simulating how a student might behave when extremely stressed without needing to ethically induce that state in real life). Of course, synthetic data must be used cautiously—it should be validated to ensure that it truly mimics reality and does not inadvertently introduce bias. This is an active area of research in other domains (e.g., using Generative Adversarial Networks to generate image data for training vision models), now making its way into educational data.

Generative models can also enhance interactive and explanatory analytics for instructors and researchers. An LLM could be used to generate natural language explanations of complex multimodal analytics results, making them more interpretable. Instead of a teacher seeing a confusing dashboard, they might get a narrative report like "The class discussion on Topic X saw high engagement from most students, but two students (Alice and Bob) were relatively quiet and showed signs of confusion in facial expressions. Perhaps consider checking in with them." This kind of summary, produced by combining analytic data with generative text, could make MLPA insights more actionable. Moreover, explainable AI techniques could incorporate generative methods to provide rationales for model decisions (e.g., generating a hypothetical example to illustrate why a system thinks a student is frustrated).

10. Conclusion and final remarks

Multimodal learning process analytics (MLPA) represents a significant advancement in educational research and practice, bridging the fields of learning sciences, educational technology, and artificial intelligence (AI). This book has outlined critical theoretical foundations, methodological advancements, and applied examples that illustrate the potentials and complexities of integrating AI-driven multimodal analytics into educational contexts.

A central message throughout the book emphasizes that learning is a deeply contextual, dynamic, and multimodal phenomenon. Traditional assessment methods, which rely largely on static, single-modality data such as tests or surveys, inadequately capture the real-time interplay of cognitive, affective, social, and behavioral processes that underpin learning. MLPA addresses this gap by systematically integrating diverse data streams—such as facial expressions, physiological responses, speech patterns, eye movements, digital interactions, and gestures—to provide a richer, temporally nuanced perspective of learning processes.

Key theoretical contributions highlighted in this book include frameworks drawn from cognitive, metacognitive, affective, and social learning theories. The interplay between theory and multimodal data collection has been crucial, as demonstrated by numerous empirical studies cited throughout this volume. Notably, theories such as cognitive load, SRL, SSRL, and achievement emotions have provided critical lenses to interpret multimodal analytics data, ensuring alignment between analytical insights and educational objectives.

From a methodological standpoint, the integration of classical machine learning, deep learning, and Generative AI methods in processing multimodal data has significantly expanded the analytical capabilities within educational research. Chapters dedicated to preprocessing multimodal data, applying classical and deep learning models, and leveraging Generative AI have underscored both the sophistication and technical rigor required in MLPA research. In particular, recent advancements in deep learning and Generative AI have introduced powerful tools capable of capturing complex, nuanced patterns within multimodal datasets. These technologies, however, require careful ethical consideration, given their implications for privacy, fairness, transparency, and learner autonomy.

Ethical considerations emerged as a significant theme throughout this book. While MLPA offers substantial opportunities for enhancing educational practices, it simultaneously raises critical ethical questions concerning data privacy, algorithmic bias, learner agency, and cultural sensitivity. This book highlights that ethical practices in MLPA research must be proactive rather than reactive, embedded systematically within research design, data management, model development, and deployment phases. Adhering to ethical guidelines such as transparency, accountability, and inclusive representation is imperative for ensuring the responsible advancement and application of MLPA technologies.

Several promising avenues for future research were identified, particularly around the integration of analytics techniques, the development of more interpretable and transparent AI models, and the expansion of multimodal analytics methodologies to broader, more diverse educational settings. Future MLPA research must also consider scalability, sustainability, and equitable access, particularly in resource-constrained educational environments. Enhancing interdisciplinary collaboration—bringing together educators, technologists, data scientists, ethicists, and learners—is essential for addressing these complex challenges effectively.

Finally, this book serves as both an academic resource and a practical guide for researchers and practitioners interested in adopting MLPA methodologies. By demonstrating how theoretical constructs can be operationalized through sophisticated multimodal data collection and analytical techniques, it provides a foundation for new researchers entering the field while also offering comprehensive insights for experienced practitioners.

MLPA stands at the intersection of technology, learning theory, and educational practice. As AI technologies evolve and educational contexts become increasingly multimodal and digitally enhanced, the relevance and applicability of MLPA methodologies will only grow. It is our hope that this book not only advances scholarly understanding of multimodal learning analytics but also inspires further innovations and ethical considerations that improve educational outcomes and learner experiences globally.

Bibliography

Abdi, A., Sedrakyan, G., Veldkamp, B., van Hillegersberg, J., & van den Berg, S. M. (2023). Students feedback analysis model using deep learning-based method and linguistic knowledge for intelligent educational systems. *Soft Computing*, *27*(19), 14073–14094. https://doi.org/10.1007/s00500-023-07926-2

Abrahamson, D. & Lindgren, R. (2014). *Embodiment and Embodied Design*. https://escholarship.org/uc/item/4917v8ds

Abrahamson, D., Tancredi, S., Chen, R. S. Y., Flood, V. J., & Dutton, E. (2023). Embodied design of digital resources for mathematics education: Theory, methodology, and framework of a pedagogical research program. In B. Pepin, G. Gueudet, & J. Choppin (Eds), *Handbook of Digital Resources in Mathematics Education* (pp. 1–34). Springer International Publishing. https://doi.org/10.1007/978-3-030-95060-6_8-1

Ahn, B. "Tony" & Harley, J. M. (2020). Facial expressions when learning with a queer history app: Application of the control value theory of achievement emotions. *British Journal of Educational Technology*, *51*(5), 1563–1576. https://doi.org/10.1111/bjet.12989

Alexander, P. A., Schallert, D. L., & Reynolds, R. E. (2009). What Is learning anyway? A topographical perspective considered. *Educational Psychologist*, *44*(3), 176–192. https://doi.org/10.1080/00461520903029006

Ali, F., Choy, D., Divaharan, S., Tay, H. Y., & Chen, W. (2023). Supporting self-directed learning and self-assessment using TeacherGAIA, a generative AI chatbot application: Learning approaches and prompt engineering. *Learning: Research and Practice*, *9*(2), 135–147. https://doi.org/10.1080/23735082.2023.2258886

Alwahaby, H. & Cukurova, M. (2024). Navigating the ethical landscape of multimodal learning analytics: A guiding framework. In S. Caballé, J. Casas-Roma, & J. Conesa (Eds), *Ethics in Online AI-based Systems* (pp. 25–53). Elsevier. https://www.sciencedirect.com/science/article/pii/B9780443188510000147

Alwahaby, H., Cukurova, M., Papamitsiou, Z., & Giannakos, M. (2022). The evidence of impact and ethical considerations of multimodal learning analytics: A systematic literature review. In M. Giannakos, D. Spikol, D. Di Mitri, K. Sharma, X. Ochoa, & R. Hammad (Eds), *The Multimodal Learning Analytics Handbook* (pp. 289–325). Springer International Publishing. https://doi.org/10.1007/978-3-031-08076-0_12

Andersen, M. S., & Makransky, G. (2021). The validation and further development of a multidimensional cognitive load scale for virtual environments. *Journal of Computer Assisted Learning*, *37*(1), 183–196. https://doi.org/10.1111/jcal.12478

Andrade, A., Danish, J. A., & Maltese, A. V. (2017). A measurement model of gestures in an embodied learning environment: Accounting for temporal dependencies. *Journal of Learning Analytics*, *4*(3), 18–46.

Andrade, H. & Valtcheva, A. (2009). Promoting learning and achievement through self-assessment. *Theory Into Practice*, *48*(1), 12–19. https://doi.org/10.1080/00405840802577544

Antonenko, P., Paas, F., Grabner, R., & van Gog, T. (2010). Using electroencephalography to measure cognitive load. *Educational Psychology Review*, *22*(4), 425–438. https://doi.org/10.1007/s10648-010-9130-y

Axelrod, R. (1973). Schema theory: An information processing model of perception and cognition. *American Political Science Review*, *67*(4), 1248–1266. https://doi.org/10.2307/1956546

Azevedo, R. (2015). Defining and measuring engagement and learning in science: Conceptual, theoretical, methodological, and analytical issues. *Educational Psychologist*, *50*(1), 84–94. https://doi.org/10.1080/00461520.2015.1004069

Azevedo, R. & Gašević, D. (2019). Analyzing multimodal multichannel data about self-regulated learning with advanced learning technologies: Issues and challenges. *Computers in Human Behavior*, *96*, 207–210. https://doi.org/10.1016/j.chb.2019.03.025

Baker, R. S. (2019). Challenges for the future of educational data mining: The Baker Learning Analytics Prizes. *Journal of Educational Data Mining*, *11*(1), 1–17. https://doi.org/10.5281/ZENODO.3554745

Baltrušaitis, T., Ahuja, C., & Morency, L.-P. (2019). Multimodal machine learning: A survey and taxonomy. *IEEE Transactions on Pattern Analysis and Machine Intelligence*, *41*(2), 423–443. https://doi.org/10.1109/TPAMI.2018.2798607

Becerra, Á., Daza, R., Cobos, R., Morales, A., Cukurova, M., & Fierrez, J. (2023). M2LADS: A system for generating multimodal learning analytics dashboards. *2023 IEEE 47th Annual Computers, Software, and Applications Conference (COMPSAC)*, 1564–1569. https://doi.org/10.1109/COMPSAC57700.2023.00241

Bernacki, M. L., Yu, L., Kuhlmann, S. L., Plumley, R. D., Greene, J. A., Duke, R. F., Freed, R., Hollander-Blackmon, C., & Hogan, K. A. (2024). Using multimodal learning analytics to validate digital traces of self-regulated learning in a laboratory study and predict performance in undergraduate courses. *Journal of Educational Psychology*, 117(2), 176–205. https://psycnet.apa.org/record/2025-32400-001

Birt, J., Clare, D., & Cowling, M. (2019). Piloting multimodal learning analytics using mobile mixed reality in health education. *2019 IEEE 7th International Conference on Serious Games and Applications for Health (SeGAH)*, 1–6. https://doi.org/10.1109/SeGAH.2019.8882435

Blikstein, P. (2013). Multimodal learning analytics. *Proceedings of the Third International Conference on Learning Analytics and Knowledge*, 102–106. https://doi.org/10.1145/2460296.2460316

Blikstein, P. & Worsley, M. (2016). Multimodal learning analytics and education data mining: Using computational technologies to measure complex learning tasks. *Journal of Learning Analytics*, *3*(2), Article 2. https://doi.org/10.18608/jla.2016.32.11

Csikszentmihalyi, M. (1997). *Flow and the psychology of discovery and invention*. HarperPerennial.

Cukurova, M. (2024). The interplay of learning, analytics and artificial intelligence in education: A vision for hybrid intelligence. *British Journal of Educational Technology*, *56*(2), 469–488. https://doi.org/10.1111/bjet.13514

Cukurova, M., Giannakos, M., & Martinez-Maldonado, R. (2020). The promise and challenges of multimodal learning analytics. *British Journal of Educational Technology*, *51*(50), 1441–1449. https://doi.org/10.1111/bjet.13015

Dang, B., Huynh, L., Gul, F., Rosé, C., Järvelä, S., & Nguyen, A. (2025). Human-AI collaborative learning in mixed reality: Examining the cognitive and socio-emotional interactions. *British Journal of Educational Technology, 56*(5). https://doi.org/10.1111/bjet.13607

Dang, B., Nguyen, A., & Järvelä, S. (2024). Deliberative interactions for socially shared regulation in collaborative learning: An AI-driven learning analytics study. *Journal of Learning Analytics, 11*(3), Article 3. https://doi.org/10.18608/jla.2024.8393

Dang, B., Vitiello, R., Nguyen, A., Rose, C., & Järvelä, S. (2023). How do students deliberate for socially shared regulation in collaborative learning? A process-oriented approach. *Proceedings of International Conference on Computer Supported Collaborative Learning (CSCL).* https://doi.org/10.22318/cscl2023.280974

DeLeeuw, K. E. & Mayer, R. E. (2008). A comparison of three measures of cognitive load: Evidence for separable measures of intrinsic, extraneous, and germane load. *Journal of Educational Psychology, 100*(1), 223. https://psycnet.apa.org/doi/10.1037/0022-0663.100.1.223

Di Mitri, D., Scheffel, M., Drachsler, H., Börner, D., Ternier, S., & Specht, M. (2017). Learning pulse: A machine learning approach for predicting performance in self-regulated learning using multimodal data. *Proceedings of the Seventh International Learning Analytics & Knowledge Conference*, 188–197. https://doi.org/10.1145/3027385.3027447

Dindar, M., Alikhani, I., Malmberg, J., Järvelä, S., & Seppänen, T. (2019). Examining shared monitoring in collaborative learning: A case of a recurrence quantification analysis approach. *Computers in Human Behavior, 100*, 335–344. https://doi.org/10.1016/j.chb.2019.03.004

Dindar, M., Järvelä, S., Ahola, S., Huang, X., & Zhao, G. (2020). Leaders and followers identified by emotional mimicry during collaborative learning: A facial expression recognition study on emotional valence. *IEEE Transactions on Affective Computing, 13*(3), 1390–1400. https://doi.org/10.1109/TAFFC.2020.3003243

Dindar, M., Järvelä, S., Nguyen, A., Haataja, E., & Çini, A. (2022). Detecting shared physiological arousal events in collaborative problem solving. *Contemporary Educational Psychology, 69*, 102050. https://doi.org/10.1016/j.cedpsych.2022.102050

D'Mello, S., Dieterle, E., & Duckworth, A. (2017). Advanced, analytic, automated (AAA) measurement of engagement during learning. *Educational Psychologist, 52*(2), 104–123. https://doi.org/10.1080/00461520.2017.1281747

D'Mello, S. K. & Graesser, A. (2012). Dynamics of affective states during complex learning. *Learning and Instruction, 22*(2), 145–157. https://doi.org/10.1016/j.learninstruc.2011.10.001

D'Mello, S. K., Tay, L., & Southwell, R. (2022). Psychological measurement in the information age: Machine-learned computational models. *Current Directions in Psychological Science, 31*(1), 76–87. https://doi.org/10.1177/09637214211056906

Doleck, T., Lemay, D. J., Basnet, R. B., & Bazelais, P. (2020). Predictive analytics in education: A comparison of deep learning frameworks. *Education and Information Technologies, 25*(3), 1951–1963. https://doi.org/10.1007/s10639-019-10068-4

Doyle, P. R., Gessinger, I., Edwards, J., Clark, L., Dumbleton, O., Garaialde, D., Rough, D., Bleakley, A., Branigan, H. P., & Cowan, B. R. (2025). The Partner Modelling Questionnaire: A validated self-report measure of perceptions toward machines as dialogue partners. *ACM Transactions on Computer-Human Interaction, 32*(4), 1–33. https://doi.org/10.1145/3729170

Drachsler, H. & Greller, W. (2016). Privacy and analytics: It's a DELICATE issue a checklist for trusted learning analytics. *Proceedings of the Sixth International Conference on Learning Analytics & Knowledge*, 89–98. https://doi.org/10.1145/2883851.2883893

Du, X., Dai, M., Tang, H., Hung, J.-L., Li, H., & Zheng, J. (2023). A multimodal analysis of college students' collaborative problem solving in virtual experimentation activities: A perspective of cognitive load. *Journal of Computing in Higher Education*, *35*(2), 272–295. https://doi.org/10.1007/s12528-022-09311-8

Edwards, J., Nguyen, A., Lämsä, J., Sobocinski, M., Whitehead, R., Dang, B., Roberts, A.-S., & Järvelä, S. (2025). Human-AI collaboration: Designing artificial agents to facilitate socially shared regulation among learners. *British Journal of Educational Technology*, *56*(2), 712–733. https://doi.org/10.1111/bjet.13534

Efklides, A. (2011). Interactions of metacognition with motivation and affect in self-regulated learning: The MASRL model. *Educational Psychologist*, *46*(1), 6–25. https://doi.org/10.1080/00461520.2011.538645

Emerson, A., Cloude, E. B., Azevedo, R., & Lester, J. (2020). Multimodal learning analytics for game-based learning. *British Journal of Educational Technology*, *51*(5), 1505–1526. https://doi.org/10.1111/bjet.12992

Fan, Y., Matcha, W., Uzir, N. A., Wang, Q., & Gašević, D. (2021). Learning analytics to reveal links between learning design and self-regulated learning. *International Journal of Artificial Intelligence in Education*, *31*(4), 980–1021. https://doi.org/10.1007/s40593-021-00249-z

Fan, Y., Tang, L., Le, H., Shen, K., Tan, S., Zhao, Y., Shen, Y., Li, X., & Gašević, D. (2025). Beware of metacognitive laziness: Effects of generative artificial intelligence on learning motivation, processes, and performance. *British Journal of Educational Technology*, *56*(2), 489–530. https://doi.org/10.1111/bjet.13544

Gebru, T., Morgenstern, J., Vecchione, B., Vaughan, J. W., Wallach, H., Daumé III, H., & Crawford, K. (2021). Datasheets for datasets. *Communications of the ACM*, *64*(12), 86–92. https://doi.org/10.1145/3458723

Giannakos, M. & Cukurova, M. (2023). The role of learning theory in multimodal learning analytics. *British Journal of Educational Technology*, *54*(5), 1246–1267. https://doi.org/10.1111/bjet.13320

Goodfellow, I., Pouget-Abadie, J., Mirza, M., Xu, B., Warde-Farley, D., Ozair, S., Courville, A., & Bengio, Y. (2020). Generative adversarial networks. *Communications of the ACM*, *63*(11), 139–144. https://doi.org/10.1145/3422622

Greene, J. A. & Azevedo, R. (2010). The measurement of learners' self-regulated cognitive and metacognitive processes while using computer-based learning environments. *Educational Psychologist*, *45*(4), 203–209. https://doi.org/10.1080/00461520.2010.515935

Greene, J. A., Deekens, V. M., Copeland, D. Z., & Yu, S. (2017). Capturing and modeling self-regulated learning using think-aloud protocols. In P. A. Alexander, D. H. Schunk, & J. A. Greene (Eds),*Handbook of Self-Regulation of Learning and Performance* (pp. 323–337). Routledge. https://www.taylorfrancis.com/chapters/edit/10.4324/9781315697048-21/capturing-modeling-self-regulated-learning-using-think-aloud-protocols-jeffrey-greene-victor-deekens-dana-copeland-seung-yu

Hadwin, A., Järvelä, S., & Miller, M. (2017). Self-regulation, co-regulation, and shared regulation in collaborative learning environments. In P. A. Alexander, D. H. Schunk, & J. A. Greene (Eds), *Handbook of Self-regulation of Learning and Performance* (pp. 83–106). Routledge. https://www.taylorfrancis.com/chapters/edit/10.4324/9781315697048-6/self-regulation-co-regulation-shared-regulation

-collaborative-learning-environments-allyson-hadwin-sanna-j%C3%A4rvel%C3%A4-mariel-miller
Hall, E. T. (1966). *The Hidden Dimension.*. Anchor Books.
Hall, E. T., Birdwhistell, R. L., Bock, B., Bohannan, P., Diebold, A. R., Durbin, M., Edmonson, M. S., Fischer, J. L., Hymes, D., Kimball, S. T., La Barre, W., McClellan, J. E., Marshall, D. S., Milner, G. B., Sarles, H. B., Trager, G. L., & Vayda, A. P. (1968). Proxemics [and comments and replies]. *Current Anthropology*, *9*(2/3), 83–108. https://doi.org/10.1086/200975
Henrie, C. R., Bodily, R., Larsen, R., & Graham, C. R. (2018). Exploring the potential of LMS log data as a proxy measure of student engagement. *Journal of Computing in Higher Education*, *30*, 344–362.
Ho, J., Jain, A., & Abbeel, P. (2020). Denoising diffusion probabilistic models. *Advances in Neural Information Processing Systems, 33*, 6840–6851. https://arxiv.org/abs/2006.11239
Holmes, W., Porayska-Pomsta, K., Holstein, K., Sutherland, E., Baker, T., Shum, S. B., Santos, O. C., Rodrigo, M. T., Cukurova, M., Bittencourt, I. I., & Koedinger, K. R. (2021). Ethics of AI in education: Towards a community-wide framework. *International Journal of Artificial Intelligence in Education, 32,* 504–526. https://doi.org/10.1007/s40593-021-00239-1
Holstein, K., McLaren, B. M., & Aleven, V. (2019). Co-designing a real-time classroom orchestration tool to support teacher-AI complementarity. *Grantee Submission*. https://eric.ed.gov/?id=ED618924
Huang, A. Y. Q., Lu, O. H. T., Huang, J. C. H., Yin, C. J., & Yang, S. J. H. (2020). Predicting students' academic performance by using educational big data and learning analytics: Evaluation of classification methods and learning logs. *Interactive Learning Environments*, *28*(2), 206–230. https://doi.org/10.1080/10494820.2019.1636086
Ifenthaler, D. & Widanapathirana, C. (2014). Development and validation of a learning analytics framework: Two case studies using support vector machines. *Technology, Knowledge and Learning*, *19*(1), 221–240. https://doi.org/10.1007/s10758-014-9226-4
Järvelä, S., & Hadwin, A. F. (2013). New frontiers: Regulating learning in CSCL. *Educational Psychologist*, *48*(1), 25–39. https://doi.org/10.1080/00461520.2012.748006
Järvelä, S. & Hadwin, A. (2024). Triggers for self-regulated learning: A conceptual framework for advancing multimodal research about SRL. *Learning and Individual Differences*, *115*, 102526. https://doi.org/10.1016/j.lindif.2024.102526
Järvelä, S., Malmberg, J., Haataja, E., Sobocinski, M., & Kirschner, P. A. (2021). What multimodal data can tell us about the students' regulation of their learning process? *Learning and Instruction*, *72*, 101203. https://doi.org/10.1016/j.learninstruc.2019.04.004
Järvelä, S., Nguyen, A., & Hadwin, A. F. (2023). Human and AI collaboration for socially shared regulation in learning. *British Journal of Educational Technology*, *54*(5), 1057–1076. https://doi.org/10.1111/bjet.13325
Järvelä, S., Nguyen, A., & Molenaar, I. (2023). Advancing SRL research with artificial intelligence. *Computers in Human Behavior*, *147*, 107847. https://doi.org/10.1016/j.chb.2023.107847
Jennett, C., Cox, A. L., Cairns, P., Dhoparee, S., Epps, A., Tijs, T., & Walton, A. (2008). Measuring and defining the experience of immersion in games. *International*

Journal of Human-Computer Studies, 66(9), 641–661. https://doi.org/10.1016/j.ijhcs.2008.04.004

Junokas, M. J., Lindgren, R., Kang, J., & Morphew, J. W. (2018). Enhancing multimodal learning through personalized gesture recognition. *Journal of Computer Assisted Learning, 34*(4), 350–357. https://doi.org/10.1111/jcal.12262

Kalina, C., & Powell, K. C. (2009). Cognitive and social constructivism: Developing tools for an effective classroom. *Education, 130*(2), 241–250.

Kauffeld, S., Lehmann-Willenbrock, N., & Meinecke, A. L. (2018). The Advanced Interaction Analysis for Teams (act4teams) coding scheme. In E. Brauner, M. Boos, & M. Kolbe (Eds), *The Cambridge Handbook of Group Interaction Analysis* (pp. 422–431). Cambridge University Press.

Khan, M. S. U., Naeem, M. F., Tombari, F., Van Gool, L., Stricker, D., & Afzal, M. Z. (2024). *Human pose descriptions and subject-focused attention for improved zero-shot transfer in human-centric classification tasks.* arXiv. https://doi.org/10.48550/arXiv.2403.06904

Khosravi, H., Shum, S. B., Chen, G., Conati, C., Tsai, Y.-S., Kay, J., Knight, S., Martinez-Maldonado, R., Sadiq, S., & Gašević, D. (2022). Explainable Artificial Intelligence in education. *Computers and Education: Artificial Intelligence, 3*, 100074. https://doi.org/10.1016/j.caeai.2022.100074

Kishore, S., Hong, Y., Nguyen, A., & Qutab, S. (2023). Should ChatGPT be banned at schools? Organizing visions for Generative Artificial Intelligence (AI) in education. *International Conference on Information Systems (ICIS),* December 11. https://aisel.aisnet.org/icis2023/learnandiscurricula/learnandiscurricula/5/

Kizilcec, R. F., Piech, C., & Schneider, E. (2013). Deconstructing disengagement: Analyzing learner subpopulations in massive open online courses. *Proceedings of the Third International Conference on Learning Analytics and Knowledge*, 170–179. https://doi.org/10.1145/2460296.2460330

Knight, S., & Shum, S. (2017). Theory and learning analytics. In C. Lang, G. Siemens, A. Wise, & D. Gašević (Eds), *Handbook of Learning Analytics* (pp. 17–22). Society for Learning Analytics Research (SoLAR). https://doi.org/10.18608/hla17.001

Kosmas, P., Ioannou, A., & Retalis, S. (2018). Moving bodies to moving minds: A study of the use of motion-based games in special education. *TechTrends, 62*(6), 594–601. https://doi.org/10.1007/s11528-018-0294-5?urlappend=%3Futm_source%3Dresearchgate.net%26utm_medium%3Darticle

Kurilovas, E. (2019). Advanced machine learning approaches to personalise learning: Learning analytics and decision making. *Behaviour & Information Technology, 38*(4), 410–421. https://doi.org/10.1080/0144929X.2018.1539517

Lahat, D., Adali, T., & Jutten, C. (2015). Multimodal data fusion: An overview of methods, challenges, and prospects. *Proceedings of the IEEE, 103*(9), 1449–1477. https://doi.org/10.1109/JPROC.2015.2460697

Lämsä, J., Edwards, J., Haataja, E., Sobocinski, M., Peña, P., Nguyen, A., & Järvelä, S. (2024). Learners' linguistic alignment and physiological synchrony: Identifying trigger events that invite socially shared regulation of learning. *Journal of Learning Analytics, 11*(2), 197–214. https://doi.org/10.18608/jla.2024.8287

Landis, J. R., & Koch, G. G. (1977). The measurement of observer agreement for categorical data. *Biometrics, 33*(1), 159–174. https://doi.org/10.2307/2529310

Lane, H. C. & D'Mello, S. K. (2019). Uses of physiological monitoring in intelligent learning environments: A review of research, evidence, and technologies. In T. D. Parsons, L. Lin, & D. Cockerham (Eds), *Mind, Brain and Technology: Learning in the Age of Emerging Technologies* (pp. 67–86). Springer International Publishing. https://doi.org/10.1007/978-3-030-02631-8_5

Larmuseau, C., Cornelis, J., Lancieri, L., Desmet, P., & Depaepe, F. (2020). Multimodal learning analytics to investigate cognitive load during online problem solving. *British Journal of Educational Technology, 51*(5), 1548–1562. https://doi.org/10.1111/bjet.12958

Li, Y., Liu, Y., Nguyen, A., Shi, H., Vuorenmaa, E., Järvelä, S., & Zhao, G. (2024). Interactions for socially shared regulation in collaborative learning: An interdisciplinary multimodal dataset. *ACM Transactions on Interactive Intelligent Systems, 14*(3), 1–34. https://doi.org/10.1145/3658376

Li, S., & Tang, H. (2025). Multimodal alignment and fusion: A survey. *International Journal of Computer Vision, 134*(3). https://doi.org/10.1007/s11263-025-02667-1

Lubold, N. & Pon-Barry, H. (2014). Acoustic-prosodic entrainment and rapport in collaborative learning dialogues. *Proceedings of the 2014 ACM Workshop on Multimodal Learning Analytics Workshop and Grand Challenge*, 5–12. https://doi.org/10.1145/2666633.2666635

Malmberg, J., Fincham, O., Pijeira-Díaz, H. J., Järvelä, S., & Gašević, D. (2021). Revealing the hidden structure of physiological states during metacognitive monitoring in collaborative learning. *Journal of Computer Assisted Learning, 37*(3), 861–874. https://doi.org/10.1111/jcal.12529

Malmberg, J., Järvelä, S., Holappa, J., Haataja, E., Huang, X., & Siipo, A. (2019). Going beyond what is visible: What multichannel data can reveal about interaction in the context of collaborative learning? *Computers in Human Behavior, 96*, 235–245. https://doi.org/10.1016/j.chb.2018.06.030

Mangaroska, K., Sharma, K., Gašević, D., & Giannakos, M. (2022). Exploring students' cognitive and affective states during problem solving through multimodal data: Lessons learned from a programming activity. *Journal of Computer Assisted Learning, 38*(1), 40–59. https://doi.org/10.1111/jcal.12590

Martinez-Maldonado, R., Schulte, J., Echeverria, V., Gopalan, Y., & Shum, S. B. (2020). Where is the teacher? Digital analytics for classroom proxemics. *Journal of Computer Assisted Learning, 36*(5), 741–762. https://doi.org/10.1111/jcal.12444

Mayer, C. W., Rausch, A., & Seifried, J. (2023). Analysing domain-specific problem-solving processes within authentic computer-based learning and training environments by using eye-tracking: A scoping review. *Empirical Research in Vocational Education and Training, 15*(1), 2. https://doi.org/10.1186/s40461-023-00140-2

Mayer, R. E. (1992). Cognition and instruction: Their historic meeting within educational psychology. *Journal of Educational Psychology, 84*(4), 405.

Mayer, R. E. (1996). Learners as information processors: Legacies and limitations of educational psychology's second. *Educational Psychologist, 31*(3–4), 151–161. https://doi.org/10.1080/00461520.1996.9653263

McInerney, D. M. (2005). Educational Psychology – theory, research, and teaching: A 25-year retrospective. *Educational Psychology, 25*(6), 585–599. https://doi.org/10.1080/01443410500344670

Mitchell, M., Wu, S., Zaldivar, A., Barnes, P., Vasserman, L., Hutchinson, B., Spitzer, E., Raji, I. D., & Gebru, T. (2019). Model cards for model reporting. *Proceedings of the Conference on Fairness, Accountability, and Transparency*, 220–229. https://doi.org/10.1145/3287560.3287596

Molenaar, I., Mooij, S. de, Azevedo, R., Bannert, M., Järvelä, S., & Gašević, D. (2023). Measuring self-regulated learning and the role of AI: Five years of research using multimodal multichannel data. *Computers in Human Behavior, 139*, 107540. https://doi.org/10.1016/j.chb.2022.107540

Moreno-Marcos, P. M., Pong, T.-C., Muñoz-Merino, P. J., & Delgado Kloos, C. (2020). Analysis of the factors influencing learners' performance prediction with learning analytics. *IEEE Access, 8*, 5264–5282. https://doi.org/10.1109/ACCESS.2019.2963503

Ngo, D., Nguyen, A., Dang, B., & Ngo, H. (2024). Facial expression recognition for examining emotional regulation in synchronous online collaborative learning. *International Journal of Artificial Intelligence in Education*, 1–20. https://doi.org/10.1007/s40593-023-00378-7

Nguyen, A. (2025). Human-AI shared regulation for hybrid intelligence in learning and teaching: Conceptual domain, ontological foundations, propositions, and implications for research. *Hawaii International Conference on System Sciences (HICSS)*. https://doi.org/10.24251/HICSS.2025.006

Nguyen, A., Gardner, L., & Sheridan, D. (2020). Data analytics in higher education: An integrated view. *Journal of Information Systems Education, 31*(1), 61–71.

Nguyen, A., Gul, F., Dang, B., Huynh, L., & Tuunanen, T. (2025). Designing embodied generative artificial intelligence in mixed reality for active learning in higher education. *Innovations in Education and Teaching International, 62*(5), 1632–1647. https://doi.org/10.1080/14703297.2025.2499177

Nguyen, A., Hong, Y., Dang, B., & Huang, X. (2024). Human-AI collaboration patterns in AI-assisted academic writing. *Studies in Higher Education, 49*(5), 847–864. https://doi.org/10.1080/03075079.2024.2323593

Nguyen, A., Hong, Y., Dang, B., & Nguyen, P. (2022). Emotional regulation in synchronous online collaborative learning: A facial expression recognition study. *ICIS 2022 Proceedings*. https://aisel.aisnet.org/icis2022/learning_iscurricula/learning_iscurricula/12

Nguyen, A., Järvelä, S., Rosé, C., Järvenoja, H., & Malmberg, J. (2023). Examining socially shared regulation and shared physiological arousal events with multimodal learning analytics. *British Journal of Educational Technology, 54*(1), 293–312. https://doi.org/10.1111/bjet.13280

Nguyen, A., Järvelä, S., Wang, Y., & Róse, C. (2022). Exploring socially shared regulation with an AI deep learning approach using multimodal data. *Proceedings of International Conferences of Learning Sciences (ICLS)*. https://2022.isls.org/proceedings/

Nguyen, A., Järvelä, S., Wang, Y., Róse, C., Malmberg, J., & Järvenoja, H. (2021). Multimodal deep learning model for detecting types of interactions for regulation in collaborative learning. *Proceedings of Annual Meeting of the International Society of the Learning Sciences (ISLS)*. https://2021.isls.org/proceedings/

Nguyen, A., Li, Y., Järvelä, S., Liu, Y., & Zhao, G. (2023). Emotional synchrony through regulatory triggers in collaborative learning: A facial expression recognition study. *International Conference of the Learning Sciences (ICLS)*.

Nguyen, A., Ngo, H. N., Hong, Y., Dang, B., & Nguyen, B.-P. T. (2023). Ethical principles for artificial intelligence in education. *Education and Information Technologies, 28*(4), 4221–4241. https://doi.org/10.1007/s10639-022-11316-w

Noroozi, O., Pijeira-Díaz, H. J., Sobocinski, M., Dindar, M., Järvelä, S., & Kirschner, P. A. (2020). Multimodal data indicators for capturing cognitive, motivational, and emotional learning processes: A systematic literature review. *Education and Information Technologies, 25*(6), 5499–5547. https://doi.org/10.1007/s10639-020-10229-w

Ochoa, X., Lang, C., Siemens, G., Wise, A., Gašević, D., & Merceron, A. (2022). Multimodal learning analytics – Rationale, process, examples, and direction. In C. Lang, G. Siemens, A. F. Wise, D. Gašević, & A. Merceron (Eds),*The Handbook of Learning Analytics* (pp. 54–65).

Ochoa, X. & Worsley, M. (2016). Editorial: Augmenting learning analytics with multimodal sensory data. *Journal of Learning Analytics*, *3*(2), Article 2. https://doi.org/10.18608/jla.2016.32.10

OECD (n.d.). AI principles overview. https://oecd.ai/en/principles

OpenAI (2023). *GPT-4 technical report.* arXiv. https://doi.org/10.48550/arXiv.2303.08774

Oviatt, S., Lin, J., & Sriramulu, A. (2021). I know what you know: What hand movements reveal about domain expertise. *ACM Transactions on Interactive Intelligent Systems*, *11*(1), 1–26. https://doi.org/10.1145/3423049

Paas, F., Tuovinen, J. E., Tabbers, H., & Van Gerven, P. W. M. (2003). Cognitive load measurement as a means to advance cognitive load theory. *Educational Psychologist*, *38*(1), 63–71. https://doi.org/10.1207/S15326985EP3801_8

Paas, F., Tuovinen, J. E., van Merriënboer, J. J. G., & Darabi, A. A. (2005). A motivational perspective on the relation between mental effort and performance: Optimizing learner involvement in instruction. *Educational Technology Research and Development*, *53*(3), 25–34. https://doi.org/10.1007/BF02504795

Palincsar, A. S. (1998). social constructivist perspectives on teaching and learning. *Annual Review of Psychology*, *49*(1), 345–375. https://doi.org/10.1146/annurev.psych.49.1.345

Pardo, A., Jovanovic, J., Dawson, S., Gašević, D., & Mirriahi, N. (2019). Using learning analytics to scale the provision of personalised feedback. *British Journal of Educational Technology*, *50*(1), 128–138. https://doi.org/10.1111/bjet.12592

Pardos, Z. A., Rosenbaum, L. F., & Abrahamson, D. (2022). Characterizing learner behavior from touchscreen data. *International Journal of Child-Computer Interaction*, *31*, 100357. https://doi.org/10.1016/j.ijcci.2021.100357

Pastushenko, O., Oliveira, W., Isotani, S., & Hruška, T. (2020). A methodology for multimodal learning analytics and flow experience identification within gamified assignments. *Extended Abstracts of the 2020 CHI Conference on Human Factors in Computing Systems*, 1–9. https://doi.org/10.1145/3334480.3383060

Pekrun, R. (2006). The control-value theory of achievement emotions: Assumptions, corollaries, and implications for educational research and practice. *Educational Psychology Review*, *18*, 315–341. https://doi.org/10.1007/s10648-006-9029-9

Pekrun, R., Frenzel, A. C., Goetz, T., & Perry, R. P. (2007). The control-value theory of achievement emotions: An integrative approach to emotions in education. In P. A. Schutz & R. Pekrun (Eds), *Emotion in Education* (pp. 13–36). Elsevier. https://www.sciencedirect.com/science/article/pii/B9780123725455500034

Pekrun, R. & Perry, R. P. (2014). Control-value theory of achievement emotions. In R. Pekrun & L. Linnenbrink-Garcia (Eds), *International Handbook of Emotions in Education* (pp. 120–141). Routledge. https://www.taylorfrancis.com/chapters/edit/10.4324/9780203148211-8/control-value-theory-achievement-emotions-reinhard-pekrun-raymond-perry

Piaget, J. (1971). Inconscient affectif et inconscient cognitif. *Raison Présente*, *19*(1), 11–20.

Raca, M. & Dillenbourg, P. (2013). System for assessing classroom attention. *Proceedings of the Third International Conference on Learning Analytics and Knowledge*, 265–269. https://doi.org/10.1145/2460296.2460351

Radu, I., Tu, E., & Schneider, B. (2020). Relationships between body postures and collaborative learning states in an augmented reality study. In I. I. Bittencourt, M. Cukurova, K. Muldner, R. Luckin, & E. Millán (Eds), *Artificial Intelligence in Education: AIED 2020* (Lecture Notes in Computer Science, Vol. 12164, pp. 257–262). Springer. https://doi.org/10.1007/978-3-030-52240-7_47

Rajarathinam, R. J., Palaguachi, C., & Kang, J. (2024). Enhancing multimodal learning analytics: A comparative study of facial features captured using traditional vs 360-degree cameras in collaborative learning. *Proceedings of the 17th International Conference on Educational Data Mining*, 551–558. https://educationaldatamining.org/edm2024/proceedings/2024.EDM-short-papers.56/

Ramaswami, G., Susnjak, T., Mathrani, A., & Umer, R. (2023). Use of predictive analytics within learning analytics dashboards: A review of case studies. *Technology, Knowledge and Learning, 28*(3), 959–980. https://doi.org/10.1007/s10758-022-09613-x

Rombach, R., Blattmann, A., Lorenz, D., Esser, P., & Ommer, B. (2022). High-resolution image synthesis with latent diffusion models. In *Proceedings of the IEEE/CVF Conference on Computer Vision and Pattern Recognition (CVPR)* (pp. 10684–10695). IEEE. https://doi.org/10.1109/CVPR52688.2022.01042

Ruiz, J., Li, Y., & Lank, E. (2011). User-defined motion gestures for mobile interaction. *Proceedings of the SIGCHI Conference on Human Factors in Computing Systems*, 197–206. https://doi.org/10.1145/1978942.1978971

Ryan, R. M. & Deci, E. L. (2000). Self-determination theory and the facilitation of intrinsic motivation, social development, and well-being. *American Psychologist, 55*(1), 68. https://doi.org/10.1037//0003-066x.55.1.68

Sanchez, D. R., Langer, M., & Kaur, R. (2020). Gamification in the classroom: Examining the impact of gamified quizzes on student learning. *Computers & Education, 144*, 103666. https://doi.org/10.1016/j.compedu.2019.103666

Schneider, B. & Blikstein, P. (2015). Unraveling students' interaction around a tangible interface using multimodal learning analytics. *Journal of Educational Data Mining, 7*(3), Article 3. https://doi.org/10.5281/zenodo.3554729

Schneider, B., Dich, Y., & Radu, I. (2020). Unpacking the relationship between existing and new measures of physiological synchrony and collaborative learning: A mixed methods study. *International Journal of Computer-Supported Collaborative Learning, 15*(1), 89–113. https://doi.org/10.1007/s11412-020-09318-2

Schneider, S., Beege, M., Nebel, S., Schnaubert, L., & Rey, G. D. (2022). The cognitive-affective-social theory of learning in digital environments (CASTLE). *Educational Psychology Review, 34*(1), 1–38. https://doi.org/10.1007/s10648-021-09626-5

Schönborn, K. J., Bivall, P., & Tibell, L. A. (2011). Exploring relationships between students' interaction and learning with a haptic virtual biomolecular model. *Computers & Education, 57*(3), 2095–2105. https://doi.org/10.1016/j.compedu.2011.05.013

Sharma, K. & Giannakos, M. (2020). Multimodal data capabilities for learning: What can multimodal data tell us about learning? *British Journal of Educational Technology, 51*(5), 1450–1484. https://doi.org/10.1111/bjet.12993

Shukor, N. A., Tasir, Z., Van der Meijden, H., & Harun, J. (2014). Exploring students' knowledge construction strategies in computer-supported collaborative learning discussions using sequential analysis. *Journal of Educational Technology and Society, 17*(4), 216–228.

Siemens, G. & Long, P. (2011). Penetrating the fog: Analytics in learning and education. *EDUCAUSE Review, 46*(5), 30. https://doi.org/10.17471/2499-4324/195

Simonyan, K. & Zisserman, A. (2015). Very deep convolutional networks for large-scale image recognition. In *3rd International Conference on Learning Representations (ICLR 2015)*. Computational and Biological Learning Society. https://arxiv.org/abs/1409.1556

Spikol, D., Ruffaldi, E., Dabisias, G., & Cukurova, M. (2018). Supervised machine learning in multimodal learning analytics for estimating success in project-based learning. *Journal of Computer Assisted Learning*, *34*(4), 366–377. https://doi.org/10.1111/jcal.12263

Sweller, J. (1994). Cognitive load theory, learning difficulty, and instructional design. *Learning and Instruction*, *4*(4), 295–312. https://doi.org/10.1016/0959-4752(94)90003-5

Sweller, J. (2020). Cognitive load theory and educational technology. *Educational Technology Research and Development*, *68*(1), 1–16. https://psycnet.apa.org/doi/10.1007/s11423-019-09701-3

Sweller, J., Van Merrienboer, J. J., & Paas, F. G. (1998). Cognitive architecture and instructional design. *Educational Psychology Review*, *10*, 251–296. https://doi.org/10.1023/a:1022193728205

Tancredi, S., Wang, J., Li, H. T., Yao, C. J., Macfarlan, G., & Ryokai, K. (2022). Balance board math: "Being the graph" through the sense of balance for embodied self-regulation and learning. *Interaction Design and Children*, 137–149. https://doi.org/10.1145/3501712.3529743

Taub, M. & Azevedo, R. (2016). Using eye-tracking to determine the impact of prior knowledge on self-regulated learning with an adaptive hypermedia-learning environment. In A. Micarelli, J. Stamper, & K. Panourgia (Eds), *Intelligent Tutoring Systems* (Vol. 9684, pp. 34–47). Springer International Publishing. https://doi.org/10.1007/978-3-319-39583-8_4

Taub, M. & Azevedo, R. (2019). How does prior knowledge influence eye fixations and sequences of cognitive and metacognitive SRL processes during learning with an intelligent tutoring system? *International Journal of Artificial Intelligence in Education*, *29*(1), 1–28. https://doi.org/10.1007/s40593-018-0165-4

Taub, M., Azevedo, R., Rajendran, R., Cloude, E. B., Biswas, G., & Price, M. J. (2021). How are students' emotions related to the accuracy of cognitive and metacognitive processes during learning with an intelligent tutoring system? *Learning and Instruction*, *72*, 101200. https://doi.org/10.1016/j.learninstruc.2019.04.001

Taub, M., Sawyer, R., Lester, J., & Azevedo, R. (2020). The impact of contextualized emotions on self-regulated learning and scientific reasoning during learning with a game-based learning environment. *International Journal of Artificial Intelligence in Education*, *30*(1), 97–120. https://doi.org/10.1007/s40593-019-00191-1

Tuunanen, T., Winter, R., & vom Brocke, J. (2024). Dealing with complexity in design science research: A methodology using design echelons. *MIS Quarterly*, *48*(2), 427–458. https://doi.org/10.25300/MISQ/2023/16700

UNESCO (2019). Beijing Consensus on Artificial Intelligence and Education. *International Conference on Artificial Intelligence and Education, Planning Education in the AI Era: Lead the Leap, Beijing, 2019*, 1–70. https://unesdoc.unesco.org/ark:/48223/pf0000368303

UNESCO (2021). *Recommendation on the Ethics of Artificial Intelligence*. Paris: United Nations Educational, Scientific and Cultural Organization. https://unesdoc.unesco.org/ark:/48223/pf0000381137

Van den Oord, A., Dieleman, S., Zen, H., Simonyan, K., Vinyals, O., Graves, A., Kalchbrenner, N., Senior, A., & Kavukcuoglu, K. (2016). WaveNet: A generative model for raw audio. In *9th ISCA Workshop on Speech Synthesis (SSW 9)* (p. 125). https://arxiv.org/abs/1609.03499

Van Der Graaf, J., Lim, L., Fan, Y., Kilgour, J., Moore, J., Bannert, M., Gašević, D., & Molenaar, I. (2021). Do instrumentation tools capture self-regulated learning? *LAK21: 11th International Learning Analytics and Knowledge Conference*, 438–448. https://doi.org/10.1145/3448139.3448181

Van Merrienboer, J. J. G., Kirschner, P. A., & Kester, L. (2003). Taking the load off a learner's mind: Instructional design for complex learning. *Educational Psychologist, 38*(1), 5–13. https://doi.org/10.1207/S15326985EP3801_2

Van Merrienboer, J. J. G. & Sweller, J. (2005). Cognitive load theory and complex learning: Recent developments and future directions. *Educational Psychology Review, 17*, 147–177. https://doi.org/10.1007/s10648-005-3951-0

Vanneste, P., Raes, A., Morton, J., Bombeke, K., Van Acker, B. B., Larmuseau, C., Depaepe, F., & Van den Noortgate, W. (2021). Towards measuring cognitive load through multimodal physiological data. *Cognition, Technology & Work, 23*, 567–585. https://psycnet.apa.org/doi/10.1007/s10111-020-00641-0

Walkington, C. A. (2013). Using adaptive learning technologies to personalize instruction to student interests: The impact of relevant contexts on performance and learning outcomes. *Journal of Educational Psychology, 105*(4), 932–945. https://doi.org/10.1037/a0031882

Walkington, C. A., Nathan, M. J., Huang, W., Hunnicutt, J., & Washington, J. (2024). Multimodal analysis of interaction data from embodied education technologies. *Educational Technology Research and Development, 72*(5), 2565–2584. https://doi.org/10.1007/s11423-023-10254-9

Whitehead, R., Nguyen, A., & Järvelä, S. (2024). Exploring the role of gaze behaviour in socially shared regulation of collaborative learning in a group task. *Journal of Computer Assisted Learning, 40*(5), 2226–2247. https://doi.org/10.1111/jcal.13022

Whitehead, R., Nguyen, A., & Järvelä, S. (2025). Utilizing multimodal large language models for video analysis of posture in studying collaborative learning: A case study. *Journal of Learning Analytics, 12*(1), Article 1. https://doi.org/10.18608/jla.2025.8595

Wilson, M. (2002). Six views of embodied cognition. *Psychonomic Bulletin & Review*, 9(4), 625–636. https://doi.org/10.3758/BF03196322

Winne, P. H. (2013). Self-regulated learning viewed from models of information processing. In B. J. Zimmerman & D. H. Schunk (Eds), *Self-Regulated Learning and Academic Achievement: Theoretical Perspectives*, 145–178. Lawrence Erlbaum Associates Publishers.

Winne, P. H. & Hadwin, A. F. (1998). Studying as self-regulated learning. In D. J. Hacker, J. Dunlosky, & A. C. Graesser (Eds), *Metacognition in Educational Theory and Practice* (pp. 277–304). Lawrence Erlbaum Associates Publishers.

Wong, J., Baars, M., De Koning, B. B., Van Der Zee, T., Davis, D., Khalil, M., Houben, G.-J., & Paas, F. (2019). Educational theories and learning analytics: From data to knowledge: The whole is greater than the sum of its parts. In D. Ifenthaler, D.-K. Mah, & J. Y.-K. Yau (Eds), *Utilizing Learning Analytics to Support Study Success* (pp. 3–25). Springer International Publishing. https://doi.org/10.1007/978-3-319-64792-0_1

Worsley, M. (2018). Multimodal learning analytics' past, present, and, potential futures: 2nd Multimodal Learning Analytics Across (Physical and Digital) Spaces, CrossMMLA 2018. *CEUR Workshop Proceedings, 2163*. http://www.scopus.com/inward/record.url?scp=85051982480&partnerID=8YFLogxK

Worsley, M. & Blikstein, P. (2018). A multimodal analysis of making. *International Journal of Artificial Intelligence in Education*, *28*(3), 385–419. https://doi.org/10.1007/s40593-017-0160-1

Worsley, M., Scherer, S., Morency, L.-P., & Blikstein, P. (2015). Exploring behavior representation for learning analytics. *Proceedings of the 2015 ACM on International Conference on Multimodal Interaction*, 251–258. https://doi.org/10.1145/2818346.2820737

Xiao, Z., Yuan, X., Liao, Q. V., Abdelghani, R., & Oudeyer, P.-Y. (2023). Supporting qualitative analysis with large language models: Combining codebook with GPT-3 for deductive coding. In F. Chen, M. Billinghurst, M. Zhou, & S. Berkovsky (Eds), *IUI "3 Companion: Companion proceedings of the 28th International Conference on Intelligent User Interfaces* (pp. 75–78). ACM. https://doi.org/10.1145/3581754.3584136

Yan, L., Martinez-Maldonado, R., & Gašević, D. (2024). Generative Artificial Intelligence in learning analytics: Contextualising opportunities and challenges through the learning analytics cycle. *Proceedings of the 14th Learning Analytics and Knowledge Conference*, 101–111. https://doi.org/10.1145/3636555.3636856

Yan, L., Zhao, L., Gašević, D., Li, X., & Martinez-Maldonado, R. (2023). Socio-spatial learning analytics in co-located collaborative learning spaces: A systematic literature review. *Journal of Learning Analytics*, *10*, 1–19. https://doi.org/10.18608/jla.2023.7991

Zeng, X., Wang, X., Zhang, T., Yu, C., Zhao, S., & Chen, Y. (2024). GestureGPT: Toward zero-shot free-form hand gesture understanding with large language model agents. *Proceedings of the ACM on Human–Computer Interaction*, *8*(ISS), Article 545. https://doi.org/10.1145/3698145

Zimmerman, B. J. (2002). Becoming a self-regulated learner: An overview. *Theory into Practice*, *41*(2), 64–70. https://doi.org/10.1207/s15430421tip4102_2

Zimmerman, B. J. & Schunk, D. H. (2011). *Handbook of Self-regulation of Learning and Performance*. Routledge. https://psycnet.apa.org/record/2011-12365-000

Index

Printed and bound by CPI Group (UK) Ltd, Croydon, CR0 4YY
17/06/2026
14902649-0001